Beyond the First Amendment

Beyond the First Amendment,

The Politics of Free Speech and Pluralism

Samuel P. Nelson

The Johns Hopkins University Press

Baltimore and London

The Johns Hopkins University Press
2715 North Charles Street
Baltimore, Maryland 21218-4363
www.press.jhu.edu

Library of Congress Cataloging-in-Publication Data
Nelson, Samuel Peter.
  Beyond the First Amendment : the politics of free speech and plural-
ism / Samuel P. Nelson.
    p.   cm.
  Includes bibliographical references and index.
  ISBN 0-8018-8173-0 (hardcover: alk. paper)
    1. Freedom of speech—United States. 2. Freedom of speech—Social
aspects. 3. Freedom of speech—Political aspects. I. Title.
KF4772.N45 2005
342.7308'53—dc22   2004026033

A catalog record for this book is available from the British Library.

To Judy Anderson Nelson and Norry Nelson

Contents

Preface   ix

Introduction: Expression, Politics, and Pluralism   1

1 The First Amendment Framework   16
2 Public Debate and the Libertarian Justification   30
3 Self-Realization and the Expressivist Justification   61
4 Equality and the Egalitarian Justification   87
5 A Model of Free Speech Justifications   106
6 Speech Acts   123
7 The Pluralist Framework for Freedom of Speech   139
8 Free Speech Claims under the Pluralist Framework   159

Notes   *183*
Selected Bibliography   209
Index   219

Preface

For most of the twentieth century, state interference was the primary threat to freedom of speech. Advocates of speech rights focused on state censorship and the legal defense of individuals because the state frequently interfered with speakers. Political dissenters such as opponents of the First World War; socialists, communists, and anarchists from the 1920s through the 1950s; and civil rights protestors of the 1960s faced jail time and other penalties for speech acts. The First Amendment decisions of the U.S. Supreme Court in the latter half of the twentieth century, however, extended protection to a wide variety of political and cultural dissenters, substantially reducing the threat of state action to freedom of speech. In turn, Americans have come to believe that the First Amendment and free speech are synonymous and that any significant restrictions on speech can be addressed by appeal to the legal framework of the free speech clause of the First Amendment. Today, however, people face troubling new speech conflicts at home, at work, and at school that test the boundaries of these First Amendment decisions. In the last few years, workers have been fired for posting biblical passages in their work cubicles, foreign courts have ordered companies to desist from advertising Nazi-related materials on American Web sites, and broadcasters have dropped interviews with corporate whistleblowers owing to the threat of civil litigation. There are no easy First Amendment answers to these serious, emerging free speech problems, but the current legal framework for speech undermines our attempts to resolve these and many other problems. In essence, First Amendment law has supplanted the vital politics of free speech necessary to resolve important speech controversies.

Despite the centrality of freedom of speech to liberalism, liberal theorists have essentially ceded this ground to lawyers, thus allowing those primarily concerned with First Amendment claims to set the terms of debate over freedom of speech. In order to make new speech claims visible, we must reconsider important foundational elements of free speech theory apart from the analyses offered by legal academics and First Amendment lawyers. For instance, the First

Amendment legal framework requires that those who make a free speech claim must allege that state action restricted speech. Arguments against private interference in one's freedom to speak do not fit within the structure of legal claims and are therefore excluded from consideration as free speech questions. Claims against private employers or the decisions of foreign courts cannot be addressed by simple reference to the First Amendment. In this book, I develop an alternative, pluralist framework to promote fresh political debate about freedom of speech. Such a framework encompasses the institutional concerns of First Amendment scholars but also goes beyond the First Amendment to recognize the concerns of political theorists, social movements, and individuals working to establish free speech claims that arise outside the jurisdiction of the American legal system. I argue that free speech is a political concept and that the dominance of First Amendment thinking is detrimental to the rich, comprehensive politics of freedom of speech.

This book is a project in political theory that takes the legal theory and practice surrounding the First Amendment seriously. First Amendment debates raise important problems and offer practical solutions to those problems. The most influential First Amendment theorists outline comprehensive justifications of freedom of speech to protect the widest possible range of speech acts—from political dissent to scientific, artistic, and religious expression. At the same time, these theorists generally argue for the protection of diverse kinds of speech in order to promote a single, unitary principle or value. Unfortunately, these attempts are inadequate for many problematic speech situations. I examine three prominent arguments for freedom of speech (libertarian, expressivist, and egalitarian) to demonstrate their boundaries and their failure to provide comprehensive justifications of freedom of speech. Although the First Amendment framework remains the appropriate structure for legal debates over speech within the confines of American judicial institutions, I call for renewed political debates about the meaning and scope of freedom of speech in contexts of private power relations, nonstate institutions, workplaces, the family, and international relations. My project promotes a richer account of freedom of speech by providing a framework that promotes a politics of free speech within which arguments for many types of speech can be made.

Speech emerges from the relationships between speakers, and this book is no different. I owe debts both intellectual and personal to a large number of people who may or may not recognize what I did with their ideas and contributions.

Special thanks go to Marion Smiley, who patiently read many chapter drafts and whose insight helped me discover arguments that I would have missed in the midst of my sometimes convoluted reasoning. Marion sets an example for intellectual rigor and proves time and again that ideas flourish in an environment of dynamic interaction. Don Downs kept me honest on the politics of speech. His commitment to free speech and vigorous debate pushed me to abandon arguments I could not defend. Bernie Yack provided a steady stream of constructive and stylistic feedback, loaned me hard-to-find books, and generally encouraged me throughout. Bert Kritzer contributed at many different points and was especially supportive in the latter stages of this project.

A number of other friends and colleagues have read and commented on parts of this project. Andy Murphy and John Meyer generously read from proposals to final chapters and lent voluminous and perspicacious comment. Early on, Brian Kroeger, Greg Streich, and Joe Soss helped get this project off the ground. Colleagues at Ohio University made a visitor feel welcome: Julie White, John Gilliom, Susan Burgess, and Brett Klopp contributed advice and encouragement and, when that failed, prodded me to complete the project. A summer research award from the University of Toledo provided uninterrupted time to write chapter 4 and complete parts of several others. I am also grateful for the lively interchange of Toledo's Law and Social Thought (LST) working group and in particular to LST codirectors Jerry Van Hoy and Ben Pryor. Tina Fitzgerald lent a shrewd ear for language during the final stages of the project.

A number of friends put up with more than their fair share during various stages of the writing: Marcella Barnhart, Justine Gavagan, Mel Gregory, Stacy Griffith-Kramer, Rebecca Holden, Jarrett Kerbel, Cathy Prendergast, Amy Shenot, Debbie Siegel, Craig Whitehead, Stanley Zupnick, and my sister, Mindy Nelson. This book is dedicated to Judy Anderson Nelson and Norry Nelson, my parents, whose very different contributions were truly indispensable.

Beyond the First Amendment

Expression, Politics, and Pluralism

Every time an American claims "I can say what I want, it's a free country," it is an appeal to freedom of speech as the characteristic freedom of the United States, rather than the right to due process, free markets, or universal suffrage. We think we know what free speech is and believe, to some extent rightly, that we have a lot of it. However, the war on terrorism and legislation such as the Patriot Act highlight the persistent difficulties related to determining the proper balance between speech and other values. With changes to the broader context in which speech takes place, new kinds of speech situations are being created. Emergent technology dramatically expands the number of television channels available in every home and offers individuals access to enormous and complex interactive computer networks. The Internet has solidified its place as a major news medium, but one without firmly established norms or institutional structure. From the concerns of conservatives to regulate pornography on the World Wide Web to the increased awareness after September 11, 2001, that terrorists communicate and organize over the Internet, many people have become worried about the kind of public discourse that now exists in cyberspace and what might be done to regulate it. At the same time, many governments have identified a growing concern with material (racist speech, pornography, libel) that they have historically regulated within their borders but that is now readily accessible by their citizens over the Internet in ways that are difficult for the state to control. At the heart of these new situations are many important questions about power and freedom. For example, this new technology raises questions about access to information and who will be able to produce programming and other speech for these networks, particularly given the desire of those in the telecommunications field to integrate vertically, from production at the source to distribution in the home.

Why, when the battle for freedom of speech seems to many people to have been won, with jail sentences and other visible punishments for acts of speech a thing of the past, does freedom of speech remain a hotly contested political issue and a poorly understood concept in political theory? The root of our problem with free speech is that we have come to expect a great deal more than the mere absence of punishment for our speech, which is what standard free speech arguments focused on the First Amendment have provided. The controversies I explore are important to free speech claims made in speech situations where state action is remote, such as in the workplace, school, or family. People make free speech claims against each other, as well as against the state, every day. Popular culture is saturated with free speech arguments in movies, magazines, and newspapers. The U.S. Supreme Court hears free speech cases every term, even as the number of cases it chooses to hear decreases. All liberal theorists treat freedom of speech as a central liberal value and some as a kind of master process by which all other policy may be justified.[1] Americans argue about speech issues such as arts funding, pornography and hate speech, regulation of commercial speech, the effects of economic inequality on speech, the teaching of Ebonics in public schools, and the influence of the press on world events. Unfortunately, standard free speech arguments, learned by rote like catechisms, substitute ideology for argument and provide little in the way of a real understanding of speech.[2]

In the search for comprehensive justifications for freedom of speech under the First Amendment, many theorists argue that protection for all kinds of speech can be justified by reference to a single value or principle. Stanley Fish criticizes those he refers to as the "(anti)theorists of the First Amendment" for their universalist efforts to come up with a single general principle for free speech and calls for theorists to be more straightforward in acknowledging the politics of their arguments.[3] In the first chapter, I argue that the First Amendment framework for debate over free speech encourages a kind of value monism and that this emphasis on individual values fails to produce a comprehensive justification for free speech. Instead, a new framework for freedom of speech grounded in value pluralism will be more comprehensive than current unitary justifications, make visible previously unrecognized free speech claims, and focus political debates about free speech on the most important differences between opposing views. The pluralist framework I propose encourages a reinvigorated politics of free speech that values political debate and judgment about the boundaries of freedom of speech as opposed to the legal and proceduralist focus of debates about speech under the First Amendment framework. The pluralist framework creates room for new free speech claims, especially those outside the governmental context of the First Amendment. Although the First Amendment framework is necessarily limited to the United States, the pluralist framework is applicable to any democratic polity, to speech disputes that do not involve a state, and to those that cross national borders. It allows for interpersonal moral and normative free speech claims precluded by current unitary justifications of freedom of speech under the First Amendment. The pluralist framework also supports social movements that engage in political activism to address free speech claims that often go unrecognized under the most prominent unitary justifications of freedom of speech and provides a theoretical context in which they can describe currently invisible claims.

There are other free speech problems that can be better addressed by a pluralist framework than by the First Amendment framework. It is nearly impossible to imagine a functioning democratic system that lacked freedom of speech and the political debate that it protects. However, many people choose not to exercise their freedom of speech, while others remain silent because of barriers to participation linked to social hierarchy, lack of opportunity, or the financial costs associated with using mass media. The combination of constant pressure for more free speech and fear of traditional threats to speech results in strong differences of opinion over the meaning of free speech and the proper balance to strike between freedom of speech and competing values, such as racial and gender equality. Free speech absolutism, the view that speech should always take precedence over all other values, is untenable and rarely defended. Free speech and other values must be balanced. Nonetheless, the tenor of debates over balancing is combative and marked by vitriolic rhetoric that prevents the people most concerned with freedom of speech from talking to each other in a way that might lead to greater understanding of free speech as a concept and as a practice. Because the context of the First Amendment provides structure for such debates in the United States, the results are skewed in favor of particular values, whereas others might prevail in a different structure.

There are also problems of adaptation to changing sociological contexts. In the standard marketplace of ideas argument, any government interference with speech limits the range of debate and risks curtailing the progress of truth should true ideas be inadvertently (or purposively) restricted.[4] This same contest of ideas may be seriously flawed under conditions of growing monopolization and reduced competition in the telecommunications industry.[5] With fewer agents involved, those aspects of public debate provided for by mass media may continue to be fully diversified and air a wide range of views, but this diversity is considerably more tenuous than in a decentralized environment of economic and intellectual competition. We need to ask about the role of these large media corporations as gatekeepers and agenda setters in this new public sphere.[6] At the same time, government participation in the marketplace of ideas through funding by the National Endowment for the Arts, the National Endowment for the Humanities, and the National Science Foundation raises many problems concerning the criteria for selection of and conditions placed on recipients. Debates over intellectual property also suggest that the dominant marketplace of ideas metaphor may not respond to changing conditions.[7] This popular metaphor no longer applies when ideas can be traded in actual economic markets. Intellectual property suggests that ideas will be sold to the highest bidder to use as that bidder sees fit rather than becoming part of a generalized debate or marketplace. The problems that this market poses may not have very much to do with the state but instead with deciding who the prominent actors are in that market and who is excluded from participation.

These problems should not be construed as a Chicken Little argument in which an august system of protection for freedom of speech is about to collapse under a falling sky of intolerance or be washed away by a rising tide of indifference toward fundamental civil liberties. There are many free speech problems to address in the United States, yet even in the context of the war on terrorism we do not face the same crises of active governmental suppression of speech as occurred in the seventeenth and eighteenth centuries or the first half of the twentieth. Ear cropping and tongue boring for seditious libel are lost in the hall of historical curiosities, and memories of the McCarthy era blacklist are slowly fading away.[8] Newspapers may publish official secrets (when they can find them out), postal authorities no longer confiscate books and magazines, and obscenity prosecutions are few and far between. Americans experience a broad, formal freedom to speak unimaginable a generation or two ago and not generally shared even by the citizens of other liberal states. Nonetheless, legalistic free speech theory is currently inadequate for the controversies that I examine. There is confusion over the meaning of freedom of speech, yet there is not the free and open debate about it that most free speech advocates promote for other important issues. One reason for this is the rigid, ideological status of standard free speech arguments.[9] As proponents of regulations on pornography have learned, it is difficult even to raise the possibility of such regulations without being branded an enemy of freedom.

The problem is more complicated than unreflective adherence to free speech orthodoxy. Historically, the threat of state action that gave rise to standard arguments outweighed all other threats to speech combined. As long as the state threat remained active, other barriers to free speech failed to divide the ranks of free speech advocates, giving a false sense of consensus on the goals and justifications of free speech. When the threat of state interference in speech recedes into the background, real fissures between different free speech theorists emerge. Many, if not most, have stuck with the standard arguments and attempt to root out the last vestiges of direct state action against speech. Others identify new free speech problems and believe that greater freedom of speech requires different justificatory arguments and even affirmative state action. Too much of free speech debate focuses on the old problems of state interference without recognizing that important differences can and do exist between people who identify themselves as free speech advocates. The libertarian, expressivist, and egalitarian schools of justification leave little room for such differences in their accounts of freedom of speech.

The distinction between law and political theory has become much too stark, and nowhere is that division more clear than regarding freedom of speech. Legal scholars borrow concepts cafeteria style from political theory, while theorists leave aside complex theoretical problems for "practical" solution by lawyers. Political theorists have been remiss in leaving for lawyers and legal scholars many of the problems that I identify in legal debates over free speech and which theorists should address from the perspective of political theory. Liberal theorists routinely rest a great deal on freedom of speech, taking free speech for granted as a universally accepted foundational liberal value.[10] These theorists do not see freedom of speech itself as something that needs to be justified by liberal theory. Instead, they leave it to First Amendment lawyers to define the meaning and content of freedom of speech. This is ironic given that freedom of speech is a relatively recent historical phenomenon and currently contested in even the most liberal states. While freedom of speech is guaranteed by Article 19 of the United Nations Declaration of Human Rights as well as the constitutions of many states, interpretations of its meaning vary so widely that it would be difficult to establish criteria for whether freedom of speech prevailed in any given society. Liberal theorists risk misspecifying a crucial element in their views of the good society if they fail to examine freedom of speech carefully. Political theory needs a rigorously articulated notion of freedom of speech, while First Amendment theorists need the kind of analytically rigorous conceptual definition of freedom of speech that political theory should offer.

Most writers on freedom of speech begin by asserting a right to free speech, that is, with some kind of absolutism and a presumption that all speech should be free. Writers then immediately turn to exceptions from that absolutism consistent with retaining as much free speech as possible. They may offer compelling reasons for a restriction on speech in limited circumstances, such as where there are direct harms to specific individuals. At the same time, most seek to specify the lines between protected and unprotected speech for all speech situations. The language of rights assertiveness is inadequate to draw the required lines without more fully worked out arguments to justify free speech. A few writers, such as Alexander Meiklejohn and Robert Bork, have self-consciously taken up limited defenses of freedom of speech appropriate to particular kinds of speech situations.[11] However, the prevailing contemporary schools of thought on free speech attempt to provide comprehensive justifications. A justification is comprehensive when it protects diverse speakers who perform the same speech acts, protects many different kinds of speech, and allows for a rank ordering of the value of different kinds of speech. For instance, a comprehensive justification of freedom of speech will include an account of how it protects political, religious, artistic, and commercial speech. Comprehensive justifications should also be able to tell us when political speech crosses the line to be a criminal assault or when suggestive advertising is a form of unprotected fraud. Comprehensive justifications establish a kind of equal protection for speakers to protect the political speech of the mainstream and the heterodox. They promote the freedom of the successful and creative artist as well as that of the marginal and obscure.

In addition, prevailing justifications are unitary in the sense that exceptions, line drawing, or the balancing of free speech against other values ultimately depends upon reference back to a single project or principle to be advanced by freedom of speech. From the terms of a comprehensive unitary justification, we will be able to establish a rank ordering of kinds of speech when they come into conflict. For instance, many First Amendment theorists talk about the core and the periphery of First Amendment speech, thus establishing a hierarchy of kinds of speech by reference to the value or principle at the heart of the theory (such as public debate or self-realization). This concentration on unitary value leads theorists in turn to emphasize only one or a few kinds of speech, thereby effectively undermining the comprehensiveness of the justification. These writers may misunderstand the implications of their unitary justifications for kinds of speech other than those they emphasize. If we want to be comprehensive, we need to step back from the search for a unitary justificatory argument. As I argue in the following chapters, libertarians, expressivists, and egalitarians fail to find a justification that is both unitary and comprehensive.

The structure of unitary justifications precludes the very comprehensiveness sought by free speech theorists. In chapter 3, I propose that expressivists emphasize freedom for creative, artistic speech at the expense of political and scientific speech that does not fit within a justification based on the importance of individual self-realization. More controversially, I argue in chapter 2 that free speech libertarians minimize the importance of artistic and emotive speech in favor of the political debate central to their justification of freedom of speech. Libertarians attempt to sweep artistic speech into their justification of freedom of speech, suggesting that since artistic speech often concerns matters such as the ways of life of different social groups, it is political in nature and therefore is protected. Yet not all art has this character. A definition that necessarily links art to political debate clouds the particular nature of artistic speech (as described by expressivists). Egalitarians also exclude certain kinds of speech. In chapter 4, I show that Ronald Dworkin's focus on the equal treatment of speakers by the state excludes from protection all manner of private speech that takes place in forums outside the involvement of state action.

One major problem with unitary justifications is that they lead to the exclusion of kinds of speech that fit poorly with the unitary project or principle, thus undermining the inclusiveness necessary to a comprehensive justification. Free speech theorists rarely begin with an explicit definition of the phenomenon of speech. Instead, what counts as speech emerges from the different emphases in the justification of freedom of speech or in ascriptive lists of what does not count as speech. For example, the Supreme Court held in *Chaplinsky v. New Hampshire* that certain categories of speech, such as obscenity and libel, simply do not count as speech for First Amendment purposes.[12] Another example comes from Mari Matsuda's definition of racist hate speech. She carefully defines a category of hate speech that counts as assault rather than as speech, but she does not define categories that do count as speech, nor does she define speech events more generally. Free speech libertarians similarly avoid definitions of speech, at least ones independent of their arguments. While they sometimes define speech as the communication of messages or ideas, this definition comes directly from their focus on public debate. The relationship between the nature of speech and the justification for making that speech free is murky in each of the schools of thought, and it is difficult to separate out distinct definitions of speech from the arguments for freedom of speech.

What, then, is required for a comprehensive justification in order to allow for better communication about freedom of speech and to push forward the free speech debate to answer the common call for more free speech? I step back from the First Amendment and the associated standard arguments to take a broader perspective on freedom of speech. I do this in order to clarify our understanding of speech and push for a more constructive debate that includes divergent opinions on the meaning of freedom of speech. In chapter 1, I describe the First Amendment framework and criticize the limits it creates by structuring debates about freedom of speech in the way that it does. In the three chapters that follow, I examine the three most influential schools of justification of freedom of speech: free speech libertarianism, expressivism, and egalitarianism. I elucidate the central arguments of each by carefully delimiting the boundaries of their justifications and of their projects (goals, objectives, and values).[13] After describing their core arguments, I recast their arguments in an effort to clarify their positions and make them stronger on their own terms. As I show, however, none of the three schools succeeds in its attempt at a comprehensive justification for freedom of speech. The libertarian justification is self-defeating in that its arguments protect political speech quite well but exclude artistic expression from the core of free speech. Conversely, expressivists provide a strong justification for creative, artistic expression but fail to justify protection for political speech, as it falls outside the expressivist project of individual self-realization. Finally, egalitarians have great difficulty reconciling equal treatment of speakers by the state with the social equality of speakers and audiences.

We need an alternative framework that allows us to debate freedom of speech outside of the ideological rigidity of current debates structured by the First Amendment. My alternative, pluralist framework more accurately describes a wider variety of free speech claims than the First Amendment framework allows. It structures debate over freedom of speech through the application of the definition of speech acts and opens space for political debate and judgment about speech. In contrast to the First Amendment framework, this alternative framework is grounded in value pluralism, recognizes a diversity of speaking subjects, and allows the possibility of multiple justifications of freedom of speech according to the different values associated with speech.

The pluralist framework requires that we stand back from the institutional structure and legal language of the First Amendment framework to consider freedom of speech in the broader context of free speech as a political value. The pluralist framework does not supplant the First Amendment framework, rather it suggests that the legal context of the First Amendment is only one part of the overall free speech picture. Each of the three contemporary schools of justification works within the First Amendment framework for debate, and all three schools borrow elements of the others, sometimes explicitly but usually implicitly. By distancing ourselves from any particular school of justification and the First Amendment framework for debate, we gain a broader perspective on free speech that reveals the dimensions shared by these arguments, and we can examine contemporary accounts of freedom of speech in ways that better allow us to see why such arguments fail in their effort to provide a comprehensive justification of freedom of speech. At the same time, this new framework allows for a vigorous and inclusive politics of free speech.

I articulate a notion of freedom of speech with the pluralist framework that asks hard questions about both speech and freedom. The framework is grounded in a definition of speech act that distinguishes between the concepts of speech and freedom of speech. While mine is not a project in the philosophy of language, it centers on speech first and freedom second. Theorists and legal scholars have had a tendency to focus on the problem of freedom without offering definitions of speech. If we begin with a definition of speech, we can see the ways in which freedom of speech is indissolubly linked to social relations and the context in which speech takes place. I argue throughout that contemporary free speech theories rely upon implicit accounts of the social relationships that allow individuals to engage in speech acts. However, it is not obvious to most students of freedom of speech that this freedom is dependent on the social relationships of speech rather than on freedom. Freedom of speech is seen as a profoundly important individual human right that is violated only by the most oppressive of regimes. In the discourse of human rights, freedom of speech is the property of individuals, not a description of their relations with other individuals. The blustery rhetoric of free speech obscures the social framework and structure of speech. It is important to bring the social relations of speech acts to the forefront of debate over free speech.

The meaning of freedom of speech is always changing. The development of a pluralist framework for free speech questions helps to push this process of change forward by encouraging a broader, more inclusive discussion of freedom of speech than that allowed by libertarian, expressivist, or egalitarian arguments. In addition, the pluralist framework opens up political questions outside the state-centered public sphere by moving beyond the realm of the First Amendment and state regulation of speech. Politics is not a phenomenon limited to the relationship between individuals and the state, nor do all individual political relationships ultimately reflect back upon the context of state action. Individuals exist in webs of political relationships, some of which are moderated by the state, others of which exist outside the framework of state politics. The problem with an account of freedom of speech centered on the First Amendment is that it tends to obscure or even deny the politics of these relationships in civil society. This is especially true when we consider speech that crosses national borders and speech claims that arise in relationships involving citizens of two or more states. The pluralist framework highlights the politics of speech between individuals and groups that takes place on the broader political field outside of the constitutional domain, thus improving that politics. This new framework for free speech questions also provides contextualization of speech situations to allow a richer, more diverse discussion about the content, value, and coverage of freedom of speech.

The alternative framework that I offer is pluralist because it learns from libertarian, expressivist, and egalitarian justifications that there are a variety of compelling values underlying free speech. It also reveals a number of serious threats to freedom of speech that need to be addressed in a vigorous debate over freedom of speech. Just as the pluralist framework explicitly examines the context in which speech acts occur, it explicitly addresses values and threats drawn from libertarian, expressivist, and egalitarian arguments. Theorists begin with a project composed of goals, objectives, and values that they seek to promote through freedom of speech. Different values lead to different emphases within the dimensions of argument over free speech: individualism, social relations, and progressivism. Different values also lead to emphases on different kinds of speech acts. Thus, the seemingly disparate unitary justifications of freedom of speech share a similar structure and many features. The difference between expressivists who emphasize artistic creation by individuals and libertarians who promote the social benefits of public debate stems from the choices between primary values. Possible conflicts between these schools have more to do with the context of these values (along with background values, practical objectives, and perceived threats) than with the ways in which each school justifies freedom of speech. To examine such conflicts constructively, the pluralist framework organizes such debates about free speech around the sources of the differences between the schools of justification and highlights the similarities the schools share. Debate over freedom of speech should not take the form of excluding speech until one justification conquers the others but rather should take each argument seriously and encourage free speech about free speech.

As a political theorist, I stand back from legal debates that are conditioned by legal reasoning, adversarial methods, and constitutional precedents to ask new questions about speech acts. I articulate a pluralist framework for freedom of speech generated from the core of contemporary legal and philosophical accounts of speech. Contemporary debates over freedom of speech are focused by a lens of legal categories and definitions bound together by the First Amendment. Lawyers construct arguments designed to win in courts controlled by a structure of First Amendment doctrine, not to explain the practice of free speech or promote debate over its meaning. While this focus gives legal scholars powerful leverage on certain free speech questions, it blurs important questions outside the concerns of the First Amendment. We should be no more willing to allow debates over free speech to be constrained by the First Amendment framework than we would accept all debates over the meaning of gender or racial equality to be determined by the Fourteenth Amendment's equal protection clause. Legal scholars focus free speech debate on certain issues amenable to description within a legal and constitutional order, with the result that their theories powerfully address a constrained set of free speech problems but transmogrify problems external to the legal order into legal questions and exclude many other issues from consideration at all.

The questions raised by the pluralist framework indicate that "Congress shall make no law . . ." identifies only one context for free speech, a subset of all possible accounts of speech. The pluralist framework I develop forces legal scholars to consider the ways in which they have turned many general free speech problems into legal problems. It asks a series of new questions about the nature and content of freedom of speech that are otherwise difficult to see when speech is viewed through the lens of legal thought and the First Amendment framework. The pluralist framework avoids that legal lens to consider freedom of speech in broad philosophical context and asks not only how to justify freedom of speech most efficiently but what freedom of speech really is. It pushes legal scholars to consider their own assumptions, to address problems in their own justifications of free speech, and to address those free speech problems that exist outside of the field of view of their legal lens. At the same time, legal scholars can benefit from the perspective gained by standing back from the First Amendment when they return to the constitutional arena.

The political objectives, goals, and values of free speech scholars often are submerged in arguments made within legal categories. Political conclusions are then drawn from these arguments without acknowledging the political basis of the arguments. Although rhetorical battles are waged over the theoretical justifications of freedom of speech, many of the real conflicts are political disputes over the underlying values promoted by speech. Unencumbered by the legal lens that focuses contemporary debate, the pluralist framework flushes political differences into the open, which can only help the discussion of free speech. That is, the pluralist framework asks participants in any free speech debate to distinguish their values from their theoretical justifications of freedom of speech. In this way, arguments can proceed over the merits of those justifications independent of the relative weight we may attribute to the political values of various legal and constitutional theorists.

Speech practice must be conditioned by a concern not only for legal or constitutional questions but also by the requirements of citizenship that would allow full participation in speech for all who want to participate. There are a host of free speech concerns that are not covered by the First Amendment. Any person truly motivated by a desire to expand freedom of speech cannot rely solely on the authority of the First Amendment to make that case. The pluralist framework is neither an explanatory model of current First Amendment law nor an account of the legal history of free speech in the United States. A First Amendment lawyer cannot use the pluralist framework to construct a legal case directly, nor can a legal commentator use it to explain why the Supreme Court decided *Brandenburg v. Ohio* or *New York Times Co. v. Sullivan* the way that it did. A legislator will not find much here with which to defend the regulation of speech acts against First Amendment claims. It may seem that the pluralist framework is less amenable to direct application to First Amendment law, and thus to the practice of freedom of speech, than the institutional context demands. However, the practice of freedom of speech should not be limited only to the legal arena. Instead, the pluralist framework details the many ways in which freedom of speech is a social practice, of which legal doctrine is only a part. It provides a structure for arguments about freedom of speech that can be used by social movements and by individuals to engage in political debate about freedom of speech. For instance, those who wish to make a claim that workplace hierarchy constrains their freedom of speech can find little in the First Amendment framework to support their position, but the pluralist framework provides ample room to make such a claim.

Current debates about free speech are often confusing because opponents characterize the speech phenomenon at issue in radically different ways. For example, the central conflict in debates over hate speech as cast by libertarians and egalitarians concerns the proper balance to strike between freedom of speech and political equality. Within the pluralist framework, it is clear that the disagreement over the balance between the freedom to express racial hatred and freedom from racial antagonism is not one between different freedoms but between different evaluations of the meanings of the values of "freedom" and "equality." Each side in this controversy has a different perception of the context in which speech issues arise and the projects to be advanced by freedom of speech. Instead, the hate speech debate now takes the form of recriminations, with each side accusing the other of being a foe of free speech while claiming the free speech high ground for itself. The conflict between the proregulation and antiregulation sides is far more complicated than they realize, as neither may fully understand its own views, let alone the views of its opponents. Pornography is closely related to racist hate speech. A prominent movement to regulate pornography, led by Catharine MacKinnon, identifies sexually explicit material of an acceptable sort as speech and sexually explicit material of the unacceptable sort as pornography, as a form of sex discrimination rather than a form of speech. This approach to pornography creates political controversies and demonstrates conflicts between libertarian and egalitarian understandings of speech. The MacKinnon-backed antipornography ordinance passed by Indianapolis, Indiana, in 1984 was struck down primarily on the basis that all nonobscene pornography is protected speech to be insulated from the kind of viewpoint distinctions made explicit in the ordinance.[14] The pluralist framework shows that both MacKinnon and her opponents misconstrue the pornography problem as one of speech versus nonspeech, when the problem really concerns the context and conditions of speech.

Many new free speech claims are hard to recognize or impossible to resolve under the First Amendment framework. For instance, there are new claims originating from Internet speech that involve speakers in one state and audiences in another. The French government successfully sued Yahoo!, Inc. under a French law that prohibits the advertising or sale of Nazi-era memorabilia, including books, signs, stamps, and pictures.[15] Dow Jones lost a libel suit in Australia over an article published on its servers in New Jersey but accessible in Australia.[16] Yahoo! succeeded in getting an American court to protect it from enforcement of the French order, but Yahoo! has nonetheless desisted from this type of speech, thus demonstrating that the legal protection of the First Amendment does not protect international or cross-border speech acts. In fact, the Yahoo! case was settled by a judgment about the jurisdiction of states, not through an examination of the merits of the speech involved. Similarly, Dow Jones must now worry about the possibility of libel suits not just in the United States but also in Australia, Great Britain, and other countries with stringent libel restrictions. The First Amendment framework provides no argument of any use in British and Australian courts. At best, lawyers working within the First Amendment framework rely on using international law to gain jurisdiction (as in the Yahoo! case) and then apply First Amendment law to the case. In chapter 8, I examine these types of cross-border claims through an analysis based on the pluralist framework. The jurisdictional approach is insufficient because it does not take full account of the speech claim involved but rather focuses on international power relations that have nothing to do with speakers or their speech. The pluralist analysis of speech acts and the values served by speech suggests that cross-border claims are better addressed by regulating audiences in the restrictive state rather than chilling speakers in less restrictive states.

Liberal theory does not rely on constitutional interpretation to define concepts like equality, justice, or toleration, and it should not rely on law for a well-articulated notion of freedom of speech either. Liberal theory depends heavily on speech but allows legal scholars to set the terms of freedom of speech according to the theoretical and institutional structure of the First Amendment. This theoretical gap leads to a variety of problems, including rancorous debates over speech, the omission of free speech problems that lie outside of the First Amendment rubric, and lackluster overreliance on stock justifications of free speech. The best approach to improving communication over the meaning and content of freedom of speech is not to rely on the First Amendment and the framework for debate associated with it and instead to address the problems of freedom of speech with a pluralist framework. My alternative, pluralist framework incorporates many of the core concerns of current justifications of freedom of speech while making each of these concerns more explicit, recognizing divergent free speech projects, and focusing speech debates on the most important differences between opposing sides. Such a framework promises improved communication over the meaning of free speech, focuses debate on the true differences among competing free speech projects, and results in a firmer theoretical foundation for arguments in liberal theory that rest on the value and usefulness of freedom of speech. The pluralist framework also provides a structure for arguments about freedom of speech that can be used by social movements and by individuals to engage in political activism to address their free speech claims. The First Amendment framework and the structure of unitary justifications force judgments about speech to be made by reference to a single underlying value. The pluralist framework provides a means by which to make judgments about speech situations with consideration for the multiplicity of values that give rise to the importance of freedom of speech to legal, political, and social life.

CHAPTER ONE

The First Amendment Framework

The terms "First Amendment" and "freedom of speech" are often used interchangeably, but they do not necessarily refer to the same thing. Any theory of freedom of speech developed in the United States must deal with the large body of law and legal criticism concerned with the First Amendment. The astounding variety of positions taken on the meaning of the First Amendment by the U.S. Supreme Court and by constitutional commentators suggests that we will not find a single principle of First Amendment speech that can be brought to bear on all problems of speech and all kinds of speech. Instead, it is more helpful to think about the First Amendment framework for debate over freedom of speech. As a set of institutional factors, legal history, analytic questions, cultural attitudes, and vocabulary, it structures both First Amendment law and theoretical approaches to problems of free speech in the United States. It is not necessarily a self-conscious construction by those working within it but rather the result of institutional and historical factors in the evolution of speech theory. The First Amendment framework highlights the questions that will be asked of any proposed free speech claim and the kinds of legal, social, and political conflicts raised by that claim. It establishes the criteria by which arguments made by participants (or claimants) will be judged and organizes and simplifies free speech controversy by constraining the scope of debate to a manageable size.

Structuring Debate

Frameworks for debate are a general feature of social and political life. They compose a loose set of parameters to structure debates about a theory and the problems that theory tries to resolve. An individual works within a framework to organize his or her own thoughts on a problem before entering into debate with others. A useful framework allows individuals to get a clear picture of their own ideas and a better sense of the implications of those views. It facilitates debate by forming the description of the problem at hand and the dimensions along which this problem will be discussed. While frameworks for debate aid in the description of problems, they also constrain the possible responses to problems by creating the vocabulary in which they will be discussed. Frameworks set boundaries to arguments, making it easier to support certain positions (those most compatible with the vocabulary) and harder to advocate others (those most alien to the vocabulary). Individuals who argue within the bounds of a framework for debate provide potential solutions to problems. These solutions are then evaluated by other theorists working within the framework. Modern science, for example, describes or orders our understanding of the nature and meaning of physical phenomena in the world around us. It is powerful at this task, and its descriptions have proven to be broadly compelling, predictive, and materially productive. Alternatives to the science framework include creation science, a variety of other theological worldviews, and New Age mysticism. Each of these describes problems of natural phenomena differently and allows for different types of solutions.

Participants in debates would have to start from scratch every time they wanted to make an argument, propose a theory, or offer a potential solution to a problem being debated unless they can rely on some common framework for debate. It is almost impossible to articulate an argument without some shared framework within which that argument will be received. For a proposition or position to be comprehended, the audience must know something about the terms of the argument being made. Frameworks can also act as heuristics to help resolve easy or straightforward cases with minimal debate. They include common patterns of argument and traditional answers to common questions. For instance, relying on precedent in constitutional arguments is a very useful short-cut that facilitates debate over a constitutional issue. For easy cases, we make reference to analogous cases and form conclusions based on how those earlier cases turned out. Many times we can quickly close debate over an issue by making such references, unless the person who proposes a change from preceding cases shows reasons to alter earlier judgments. The framework for debate also helps in these cases by structuring the kinds of criticisms of a precedent (or angles of attack) that are most likely to be effective. A person involved in a flag-burning case, for example, can demonstrate that it is different from earlier cases by linking features of the case to other First Amendment principles regarding hate speech or fighting words.

Constitutional law is not the only area where we rely on frameworks for debate. They improve and simplify everyday political debates that often make reference to historical patterns and precedents as shortcuts to resolution. Politicians in favor of tax cuts maintain that tax cuts have usually been enacted during recessions, so we should have a tax cut during this recession as well. These politicians may not need to make extensive references to economic studies or other evidence because the traditional practice will be convincing to many listeners. Traditional categories and positions also order opposition to that tax cut. The debate over the tax cut does not have to go back to square one, the vocabulary does not have to be defined afresh, and many arguments on each side, because they are familiar, will be more readily understood. Frameworks promote participation in public debate by reducing the barriers and costs of entry to debate. By relying on relatively settled components of the framework, many people who otherwise would have to invest too much of their time or other resources in order to join in a debate that was not structured by a familiar framework can participate in that debate. It is not that "this is how it has traditionally been done" is the best argument in favor of a policy, but it is necessary that often we rely on similar statements to free up limited time and intellectual resources to help us decide the hard cases that require more extended debate.

Frameworks are not solely a feature of political life nor are they limited to adversarial relationships. For instance, speech act theory describes the framework of contextual factors that allow us to make judgments about the meaning of other people's utterances.[1] When I speak to other English speakers, they understand my utterances because we share a framework of vocabulary, sense, and reference that allows the meaning of my utterances to be received. When I speak in English to someone who understands only French, there is no shared framework, and my utterances are not received as speech acts with any definite meaning. Neither I nor the French speakers are wrong; we simply do not share a language framework in which we can solve the problem of what my utterances mean. As this example shows, frameworks do not have to be self-conscious constructions by participants nor will they even be readily apparent to the people who use them everyday. Philosophers or linguists may talk about the framework of speech act theory and the ways in which it illuminates our understanding of everyday verbal interactions, but most of us can speak and listen just fine without ever thinking about the specialized terms of speech act theory.

The existence of multiple frameworks to structure debate in a particular area is not a form of relativism. Frameworks provide the parameters within which participants in debates form judgments about proposed arguments and claims and develop solutions to problems. However, judgments about proposals originating within a framework can be made using criteria that are external to that framework, although such arguments are complicated by the hold that frameworks exert on our debates. Also, not all frameworks are created equal. Some are better than others in addressing certain kinds of problems. We can evaluate these frameworks along many dimensions, such as accuracy of description of the world, effectiveness measured in material terms, and the desirability of their political consequences. These evaluations involve considerations such as the framework's institutional relevancy, its logical consistency, its usefulness to problem solving, and its political implications. Some frameworks are better than others because they simply do a better job of organizing and structuring a debate. Weak or inadequate frameworks fall short when they do not allow the formulation of useful propositions or effective communication between participants. A framework for debate in cosmology that sets as parameters "facts" that Earth is flat and is the center of the universe will be woefully inadequate to help explain the orbits of the planets or the recession of galaxies. Propositions to explain such phenomena will be difficult to formulate according to the parameters set by the framework of this cosmology, and it will be impossible to develop empirically testable theories. For instance, the Copernican theory that the planets, including Earth, orbit the sun is excluded entirely from this hypothetical cosmological framework.

A given framework does not necessarily determine the outcome of a debate or a solution to a specific problem. While some frameworks are incommensurable (such as modern science and creation science) and appear to map onto ideological divisions such as conservative and liberal, many frameworks are used by both conservatives and liberals to argue with each other about various problems.

A framework with a rich vocabulary and a firm foundation of shared assumptions and values can provide the basis for tightly argued and effectively reasoned propositions that can then be carefully scrutinized, even when the participants in the debate disagree strongly about outcomes or the policies that should be enacted. Liberals and conservatives may disagree about whether pornography should be regulated, for example, but they will argue about this issue within the terms of a shared First Amendment framework. Their conclusions may differ, but the language and categories that are the raw material of their arguments will be the same. A conservative might deny the liberal's claim that pornography makes a meaningful contribution to the marketplace of ideas yet still accept the general view, shared by the liberal, that the First Amendment protects the marketplace of ideas.

Frameworks develop and change in many ways. They are not self-conscious constructions but are the product of complex social, political, historical, and institutional phenomena that change over time. Some frameworks change gradually and evolutionarily (modern science), while others change in a rapid or revolutionary way (the political framework in Iraq under U.S. occupation). They can be quite flexible and change in response to crisis, underlying political change, or the effective arguments of the framework's critics. Frameworks have internal resources for change, such as historical experience, general principles, or modes of integrating new events or phenomena into the framework. The First Amendment framework for speech has been around for eighty or more years but has adapted to changing technology, the expansion of political rights for women and racial minorities, and the extension of what counts as speech. Good frameworks are also elastic, capable of adapting to new circumstances and applying to new kinds of problems while still ordering and structuring responses to these changes such that those responses remain consistent with the general contours of the original framework.

The First Amendment framework dominates contemporary American debates, both legal and political, over freedom of speech.[2] To count as valid, a free speech claim must meet criteria set by the First Amendment framework. These criteria are defined either by standing First Amendment doctrine or by the claimant's proposed new interpretation of the First Amendment. Often, a First Amendment ideology that is part of the framework conditions the response to any speech claim or to a proposed regulation of speech.[3] Free speech claims seen as incompatible with the First Amendment criteria go unrecognized or else are dismissed as faulty. The First Amendment framework makes dismissal or denial of these claims seem necessary when in fact it is not. In effect, the constraints of the First Amendment framework channel debates over many kinds of issues in particular directions while they preclude consideration of alternatives.

Even though not all questions of free speech raise obvious First Amendment issues, the First Amendment framework structures legal and philosophical debates over freedom of speech in the United States. Naturally, lawyers focus on the legal issues raised by freedom of speech, and for institutional reasons these must address the meaning and scope of the First Amendment. Institutional factors include the Constitution, court procedures, legislation, and the formal rules of legal dispute resolution. These factors mandate that for many speech issues, the First Amendment framework is most appropriate to structure the ways in which the issue will be decided. However, even the meaning of "free speech" within these institutional constraints changes over time and no longer matches the original intent of the Constitution's framers.[4] Instead, this meaning developed in the twentieth century along a trajectory mapped out by the broader First Amendment framework.

There is no necessary reason that debates over freedom of speech must always be structured by the First Amendment framework any more than debates over equality should always be structured by the framework of the Fourteenth Amendment's equal protection clause. Contemporary political theorists and philosophers frequently work within the First Amendment framework even though there are few institutional reasons to do so. Theorists do not cede responsibility for the meaning of equality to lawyers, why should they do so for speech? Liberal theorists take freedom of speech for granted as a universally accepted liberal value, but they allow its meaning and content to be defined by First Amendment scholars. For example, John Rawls's discussion of freedom of political speech in *Political Liberalism* rests almost entirely upon constitutional precedents, and Joshua Cohen's detailed typology of free speech arguments maps, in contemporary philosophical language, the legal debate over the First Amendment.[5]

The core of the First Amendment framework is the definition of freedom of speech as negative liberty from state interference in individual speech acts.[6] A description of the framework begins with the institutional structure of legal claims.[7] The text of the First Amendment is written in negative terms as a right against state action that interferes in speech. Justiciable First Amendment claims require individual grievances against the state. There must be someone who can show that he or she has been injured by state action. Claims must be made consistent with legal categories and definitions of harm, state action, and interference. State action is construed narrowly and does not include acts of omission.[8] Legal vocabulary is highly specialized and often different from commonsense definitions of the same terms, let alone from the definitions used by philosophers and social scientists. The distinctiveness of this vocabulary also sets parameters for debates about speech.

There are a number of good reasons for the First Amendment framework to structure free speech debates in the United States. The Bill of Rights and judicial review offer remarkable resources with which to pursue freedom of speech that are unavailable in many other societies. In addition, the threat posed by state interference in speech historically outweighs all other threats to speech.[9] As long as the state threat remains active, a general consensus against that threat will continue to dominate thinking about freedom of speech. In the American institutional context, the threat of state action to interfere in speech immediately implicates the First Amendment and a constitutional analysis. The First Amendment provides individuals a powerful basis on which to make a free speech claim and addresses the most serious state threats to freedom of speech.

Legal reasoning, legal categories, adversarial methods, and constitutional precedents condition debates over freedom of speech. Lawyers construct arguments for use in court, but they are not responsible for explaining the meaning or practice of freedom of speech outside the law. This is a great advantage for legal scholars since it allows them to focus on state action and avoid difficult questions external to the First Amendment framework. Unfortunately, when confronted with issues outside the confines of the legal and constitutional order, legal scholars are forced to describe the problems along the lines of legal categories. When extralegal free speech concerns cannot be redrawn as legal issues, they are excluded from consideration. Poor translations into legal vocabulary seriously misconstrue other problems of speech. The First Amendment does not directly address relationships between citizens. While state power comes into play in many interpersonal relationships, First Amendment doctrine requires state involvement in only a few specific cases of interpersonal speech conflict, such as the heckler's veto.[10] Other than such exceptions, debates under the First Amendment framework concern the exercise of state power and its impact on individual speech acts. The structure of making legal claims under the First Amendment involves individuals who find themselves parties in criminal or civil speech-related cases. The history of First Amendment law primarily requires the identification of individual claims against the exercise of state power.[11]

Hate Speech

The familiar yet contentious debate over racist hate speech provides a good example of the way in which the First Amendment framework sets the agenda of which speech claims will be recognized and how that framework privileges particular outcomes. When we consider the conflicting speech claims of diverse individuals in the context of their relations with each other, a balance must be struck between their claims. In practice, the First Amendment framework sets the terms of that debate. For instance, hate speech codes at a public university immediately raise First Amendment issues because the university is part of the state. The balance between the speaker and the target of the hate speech will be drawn within the terms of the First Amendment framework. At a private university, that balance between speaker and target is much less clear, because we could choose to leave the First Amendment framework behind.[12] The proper balance between hate speech and regulation is by no means obvious once outside the institutional context of the public university that invokes the First Amendment framework. It may be that an alternative framework for debate allows for private regulation of speech and encompasses prohibition of harassment based on a broad definition of sexually and racially derogatory expression. On the other hand, arguments favored in an alternative framework might instead highlight the importance of protection of sexual and racial speech as a primary form of expressive behavior, and this could outweigh the arguments for regulation.

Opponents of hate speech rules on campuses and in workplaces often rely on the terms of the First Amendment framework to formulate opposition to those rules, even where the First Amendment is not institutionally relevant. When debates shift from the context of individual-state relations and state regulation of speech to social relations and social sanctions against speech, other frameworks are necessary. For instance, speakers who believe that their speech is threatened by a politically correct climate of social sanction at a private university have no claims within the First Amendment framework because the state is not involved, but they do have free speech claims that should be heard and evaluated. In such cases, an alternative to the First Amendment framework is necessary.

Hate speech raises many compelling speech issues that have yet to be resolved but currently receive a great deal of scholarly and popular attention. This example illustrates the difficulties the First Amendment framework presents for those who make new free speech claims. The First Amendment framework forces critics of hate speech to argue on terms unfavorable to their case while it privileges the arguments made by opponents of regulation. The framework weights debate against regulation of hate speech. Critics of hate speech generally call for some form of state regulation, thus immediately implicating state action and, in turn, a First Amendment analysis of any proposed regulation.[13] Of course, that analysis is called for in situations that involve hate speech rules at public universities or an ordinance or statute that bans hate speech.[14] Such regulations clearly meet the criteria for a First Amendment claim, and that claim must be adjudicated as such in the legal system. Critics of hate speech must show why a proposed regulation passes a First Amendment test or else prove that the First Amendment does not apply. To date, critics of hate speech have not been successful in defending hate speech rules in courts.

Some critics argue that hate speech has negative physical and psychological consequences that justify its exclusion from the protection of the First Amendment. Arguments for an exception carefully delineate the category of hate speech that has these consequences from hate speech that does not. Often this effort at categorization involves attempts to show that hate speech is not speech at all but rather a form of conduct that may be regulated by the state without running afoul of the First Amendment. Those who argue in this vein recommend a specific policy change to include hate speech along with libel, bribery, incitement to illegal action, and other harms-based exceptions to the First Amendment's protection of free speech. Other theorists concentrate attention on more diffuse harms and view hate speech as degrading while also contributing to the subordination of groups. According to this view, hate speech must be regulated in order to promote the equality of status and respect that underlies a liberal theory of freedom of speech.[15]

The First Amendment framework leads critics of hate speech to attempt justifications of regulations that are analogous to current exceptions to freedom of speech. For example, the First Amendment framework drives Mari Matsuda's efforts to define racist speech as regulable conduct within her interpretation of the First Amendment framework.[16] Not even the most extreme First Amendment absolutist believes that all conduct with an expressive component warrants First Amendment protection. Theodore Kaczynski, more commonly known as the Unabomber, could not offer a defense of his bombing campaign grounded in the political message of the murders. In the same way, incitement to illegal action and bribery are excluded from First Amendment speech. If critics can demonstrate that hate speech has direct, concrete harms of a similar sort, they may succeed in defending an exception to the First Amendment.

The harms of hate speech most often cited include the physical effects on a targeted individual. When they occur, hate speech is more akin to physical assault than to insult or calumny. If the effects of hate speech are like those of physical assault, then state action to prevent such harms can be justified by the traditional responsibility of the state to prevent or punish physical attacks. Matsuda lists "difficulty in breathing, nightmares, post-traumatic stress disorder, hypertension, psychosis and suicide" as possible effects of hate speech. Weight loss, sleep problems, and drug abuse have also been linked to being a target of hate speech.[17] The psychological and emotional impact of hate speech on the individual who has been targeted is also related to physical harm in this sense. Some have compared this impact to a verbal "slap in the face," while others highlight the damage to an individual's self-worth in the form of humiliation and self-hatred. Messages of racial hate isolate individuals and inspire fear, particularly in the context of social relations between races often marked by violence that follows hate speech. Other psychological harms suggested to be a result of hate speech include feelings of anger, distraction from work, desire to retaliate, and exhaustion. Psychological harms from hate speech are considered by some to have similar moral status to acts that cause physical pain when the speech is intended to cause such harm.[18]

Much of the response to the critics of hate speech shows the effects of the First Amendment framework even more clearly than do the calls for regulation of hate speech. Henry Louis Gates Jr., for one, concentrates his response on the First Amendment issues raised. Gates highlights flaws in those aspects of the critics' arguments that are intended to exclude hate speech from First Amendment protection. He correctly criticizes proposed hate speech regulations that rest upon discredited traditions in First Amendment discourse, such as group libel or fighting words. Gates also suggests that "like phrases such as 'pro-choice' and 'pro-life', the phrase 'hate speech' is ideology in spansule form."[19] He identifies two prongs of critical race theory's argument against hate speech, each of which operates within the First Amendment framework. One claim is that hate speech is devoid of ideational content and therefore outside the protection of the First Amendment.[20] Another claim rests on concepts of defamation and group libel. Gates acknowledges that regulation of hate speech would probably lead to greater diversity in public discourse (thus furthering the project of a robust public debate) but raises prudential concerns against Matsuda's argument based in the dangers of empowering the state or large organizations to regulate hate speech. Gates points out difficulties with Matsuda's definition of racist insult. He maintains that while Matsuda sees such insults as without ideational content (therefore not protected by First Amendment doctrine), they do in fact have ideational content and thus legitimate protection under the First Amendment.[21] Racist insults are ideas, Gates says, and we will fail if we attempt to place them in a category of excluded speech similar to obscenity and fighting words. Gates argues that if we protect speech because it represents ideas, then we must protect racist insults as ideas.

There are two clear ways for American critics of hate speech to avoid analyses structured by the First Amendment framework. First, an analysis under that framework is not obviously required in situations involving hate speech rules at private universities, private corporations, and other nonstate organizations.[22] Since the First Amendment does not automatically apply in such contexts, Henry Hyde introduced the Collegiate Speech Protection Act of 1991 in an effort to extend to private universities the same First Amendment rule against hate speech codes applied to public universities. Hyde's bill highlights the extent to which the First Amendment framework is considered authoritative even outside its institutional context. Absent legislative efforts to expand First Amendment rights, private universities and corporations appear to be free to act outside the rules of First Amendment analysis. Since many people spend the better part of their day in these private contexts, regulation by private universities and corporations could be an opportunity to make an end run around the First Amendment and address a substantial portion of the harms associated with hate speech. Given the importance of participation in the workplace to economic success and the ensuing social advantages, regulation of hate speech, like regulation of sexual harassment, even if limited only to the workplace, would offer substantial protection to members of historically subordinated groups. The harms of subordination are particularly evident in employment and educational contexts, therefore regulation in private contexts has the potential to reduce substantially the effects of subordination.

Private regulation is not without significant risks for freedom of speech and is not necessarily desirable just because it avoids First Amendment questions. It is only because of the strong hold that the First Amendment has on free speech debates that the option of private regulation appears relatively easy to accept. Inside the First Amendment framework, private regulations appear to be acceptable responses to hate speech because they do not give rise to individual rights claims against the state. Once outside the First Amendment framework, in considering free speech more generally, private regulations on worker and workplace speech are much more problematic for advocates of freedom of speech. For example, Edward J. Blum, a leader of the anti–affirmative action campaign in Houston, Texas, was forced by his employer, Paine Webber, to choose between his political activities and his job as a stockbroker.[23] Paine Webber requires all employees to clear articles and press contacts with its communications department and refused to approve Blum's anti-affirmative action views. Blum was not engaged in hate speech, and his speech activities took place outside the workplace, but Paine Webber, as a private employer, was free to regulate his speech in this way through its employee code of conduct. Serious free speech questions have also been raised about restrictions on sexual expression contained in sexual harassment policies and in private university speech codes.[24] Private regulation is acceptable when evaluated within the terms of the First Amendment framework but may not be acceptable under other frameworks for freedom of speech.

A second alternative acceptable within the First Amendment framework that avoids the problems of private regulation is to answer hate speech with "more speech." It is commonplace for theorists of freedom of speech to prescribe "more speech" rather than state regulation as the proper response to "bad speech." "More speech" is acceptable within the First Amendment framework because it relocates the remedy for "bad speech" from the state sphere of regulation to informal sanctions in civil society. There are a variety of responses that we can consider under the general rubric of "more speech," including demands for apologies; political protests, such as picketing and boycotts; direct responses to hate speakers in the form of argument, debate, or denial; or even silent disregard of hate speakers' words or shunning of the speaker.[25] These responses may be made by individuals, or they may be efforts made by social movements and organized groups. "More speech" is a way to mitigate the harms of hate speech and compensates for the ways in which the subordination reflected in hate speech restricts or reduces the speech of members of subordinated groups. However, the effects that "more speech" might have on the incidence of "bad speech" are not immediately clear. The "more speech" prescription may be useful as a remedy for "bad speech" but also may have the unintended consequence of infringing upon the freedom of speech of some individuals perceived to be engaged in harmful speech.[26] That "more speech" is consistent with the

First Amendment does not mean that freedom of speech is not threatened by overzealous social movements or private employers who overreact to expression in the workplace. A full evaluation of "more speech" may require an alternative to the First Amendment framework.

While the Constitution may be the final authority for some aspects of free speech policy in the United States, it is not the final authority for all normative free speech claims here, let alone in other countries. There are valid free speech claims to be made outside the First Amendment framework. Those claims can be recognized more easily without reference to First Amendment criteria, and improved remedies will be easier to imagine beyond the shadow of the First Amendment framework. Individuals make free speech claims against other individuals every day in the workplace, in the family, and in social gatherings. These claims do not always have a formal structure and may take the form of something as simple as "shut up so I can talk" but represent the perception of a free speech right that goes beyond that contained in the First Amendment.[27] In addition, Congress is not limited to passively observing the negative liberty guaranteed by the First Amendment and can use its power to actively promote speech. Federal support for the National Endowment for the Arts may be controversial, but the provision of this funding is consistent with the Constitution without being required by the Constitution.

The First Amendment framework structures many, if not all, free speech issues in the United States. As in the example of hate speech, debates over campaign finance regulation, sexual harassment rules in corporations, funding for the arts and public television, flag burning, and pornography are defined and organized in the terms of the First Amendment framework. That framework structures general theories or justifications of free speech as well. It dominates discussion, evaluation, and judgment in all of these areas, but such domination ignores the limits of the framework as well as the distinctiveness of many of these problems. The First Amendment framework is uniquely appropriate to the context of individual claims against the state, especially those claims made in courts, but it is notably inappropriate for claims against private power or against the state for inaction. The application of the First Amendment framework to problems outside the institutional, political, and historical context that makes sense of the framework weakens both the arguments about these problems as well as the First Amendment framework. When the framework is used inappropriately or in the wrong context, from the standpoint of the contextual factors that justify its parameters, the framework will be unhelpful at best. At its worst, the framework is an insurmountable obstacle to otherwise legitimate claims. This is not an argument against the First Amendment framework itself. A clearer understanding of the boundaries of the First Amendment framework and the possibility of alternative frameworks for debate about speech would better serve both free speech and the First Amendment.

CHAPTER TWO

Public Debate and the Libertarian Justification

Free speech absolutism is the intuitive starting point for most contemporary arguments about free speech. We believe that all speech should be free—unless there is a compelling argument that some particular kind of speech should not be. Few writers, lawyers, or politicians begin a discussion opposing freedom of speech, although many arguments are later characterized by others as opposing free speech. While hardly anyone claims to be against free speech, on closer examination it turns out that almost everyone is against some kinds of speech and that true absolutists are something of a rare species. Free speech libertarians share absolutists' basic distrust, even fear, of state interference in individual speech activities. Rather than relying upon the intuitive appeal of absolutism, however, free speech libertarians rely upon a complex positive justification of the protection of freedom of speech and an account of the ways in which that freedom may be balanced against other social interests. Free speech libertarians worry about the state, but they still allow for state action regarding speech as long as it is consistent with a robust public debate.

According to Frederick Schauer, "freedom of speech is best characterized as the absence of governmental interference" in communicative activities.[1] This absence produces, in the words of the U.S. Supreme Court in *New York Times Co. v. Sullivan*, "the principle that debate on public issues should be uninhibited, robust, and wide-open."[2] In this chapter, I draw out the primary components of the arguments free speech libertarians use to justify freedom of speech on the basis of this public debate project. These arguments are characterized by their central identification of the threat of state action to the project of public debate and to its objectives of truth and good public policy. The public debate project is favored for its social benefits rather than the intrinsic good of free speech to the individual speaker. Free speech libertarians do not defend speech as an end in itself. Instead, their arguments focus on the unifying importance of public debate to advance broad protection for the individual right, against the state, to speak as a means to rich and diverse public debate. Public discourse, sometimes referred to by the metaphor of the "marketplace of ideas," is an adversarial process whereby social benefits such as truth and good public policy advance through the constant introduction of new ideas to compete with established ideas.

Free speech libertarians differ from libertarians in the general sense because the former do not begin necessarily with assertions of broad principles of general, individual liberty. There is no particular reason that someone who is staunchly antistatist when it comes to free speech will be equally opposed to state involvement in questions involving property rights, workplace safety, or the regulation of fisheries. For example, I refer to Schauer as a free speech libertarian, but he is quite careful to distinguish his own views from those of general libertarians. He wants the free speech principle to be independent of the general liberty principle, so that rejections of general liberty grounded in natural rights or individual autonomy do not automatically lead to rejections of freedom of speech as well.[3] Free speech libertarians focus on public debate threatened by state interference in speech rather than the broader and more general libertarian politics associated with freedom of choice, individual responsibility, and the limited state.[4]

Free speech libertarianism is the orthodox account of freedom of speech under the First Amendment framework in the United States. This dominant position depends on a variety of factors. First, other justifications of freedom of speech, such as expressivism and egalitarianism, exist but are poorly articulated in contemporary debates. Second, debates over freedom of speech take place primarily in the realm of constitutional law. The institutional structure of the First Amendment and the legal process of making First Amendment claims favor free speech theories oriented around the threat of state action. Third, the public debate project and objectives such as the search for truth and good policy are compelling and popular. Fourth, free speech libertarianism developed over a long period of time and has successfully answered many political and legal challenges to the favored position of freedom of speech. However, as will become clear, the same factors responsible for the dominance of free speech libertarianism may also undermine its claim to comprehensiveness. It excludes important kinds of speech from protection and creates conflicts between social projects and individual rights that may be difficult to resolve within the structure of libertarian arguments.

While free speech libertarianism dominates contemporary debates, various objections point out shortcomings that lead it to fall short of an all-purpose, comprehensive justification of freedom of speech (expressivism and egalitarianism also have such problems). One objection suggests that conflicts between the explicit individualism of libertarianism and the social projects at the heart of this justification allow the possibility that individual speech may be excluded or limited by the state to further a social objective such as truth discovery. In a second objection, Owen Fiss points out that the robust public debate necessary to promote truth and good policy may be constrained by economic inequality and private power, as well as by state action, and that the state needs to address such nonstate threats.[5] Third, the consequentialism of libertarian justifications excludes important categories of speech from protection. I consider several possible libertarian responses to these objections but conclude that free speech libertarianism fails to provide a comprehensive justification of freedom of speech while effectively protecting only some kinds of speech.

The Roots of Free Speech Libertarianism

Free speech absolutism is the minority view that all speech, regardless of its content, subject, viewpoint, or style, should be protected from government regulation. In the United States, this view is closely associated with U.S. Supreme Court Justice Hugo Black, who argued time and again, in reference to the language of the First Amendment, that "Congress shall make no law . . . abridging the freedom of speech or of the press" was an absolute prohibition on government regulation of speech—that "no law" meant no law whatsoever.[6] Absolutism, or something very close to it, is also represented by the American Civil Liberties Union (ACLU) and in the editorial pages of the *New York Times*. This was not the prevalent view among Black's peers on the Supreme Court in the 1950s or of any subsequent Court. Absolutism has not been a view popular with the public either. However, absolutism does have the virtue of being simply stated as a bright-line rule and seems to avoid messy disputes over how to balance speech against competing social interests such as security, civility, or truth by excluding the very possibility of such balancing. Absolutism is a comprehensive account of freedom of speech in that it protects all speech and every speaker in all situations. At the same time, it does not require an elaborate justification of its rule. Instead, absolutists assert the existence of a strong right to freedom of speech. Like Black, many absolutists simply point to a literal reading of the words of the Constitution and the authority of that Constitution as evidence for the existence of the asserted right.

Unfortunately for fans of bright-line rules, there are two problems with free speech absolutism as a general account of free speech. First, the version represented by Black relies on the authority of the First Amendment and therefore is inapplicable outside the United States.[7] Second, it ultimately fails to create a bright line around speech because there is no generally shared definition of what counts as "speech." Absolutists hold that speech can never be regulated by the state, even in an effort to balance speech against other values. Instead, absolutists rely a great deal on a speech/conduct distinction to set boundaries on freedom of speech. Black, for instance, did not extend First Amendment protection to commercial speech because it was a part of commercial conduct and not pure speech.[8] Similarly, he argued in dissent to uphold the use of a disturbing the peace statute to arrest protesters who were "trespassing" on public property (a library).[9] Black's brand of absolutism fails because the speech/conduct distinction is woefully ambiguous and lends itself to redefinition to suit almost any end. For instance, an absolutist opposed to flag burning calls it conduct and therefore outside absolutist free speech protection, while an absolutist untroubled by flag burning calls it speech and worthy of protection.[10] The speech/conduct distinction may be a useful description of some elements of legal practice, but it exposes free speech absolutism as an inconsistent and unworkable theoretical justification in any system that has values in addition to free speech. Even intuitive absolutists generally accept that government regulation of libel and blackmail are legitimate, although each represents a significant regulation of words only.

If our absolutist impulse is unsatisfactory, then we need to consider where our more complex modern understanding of free speech comes from and what values it promotes. It is commonplace to begin an intellectual history of freedom of speech with Milton's *Areopagitica* (1644) and its powerful rhetorical attack on licensing of the press. In fact, in addition to Milton, there were also a number of other English Protestant pamphlet writers of the mid-seventeenth century who produced ringing defenses of freedom of the press as a crucial means to advance the English loves of liberty and truth.[11] Writers such as Milton, William Walwyn, and Henry Robinson display strong beliefs about the power of ideas, books, reason, and rational argument to advance truth and help individuals to form true opinions. The argument begins with the assumption that opinions are not chosen, that knowledge is uncertain, and that persuasion can be used to change these judgments while force cannot.[12] The discovery of "religious and civill wisdome" is hindered by licensing and is not subject to force.[13] Truth is the central interest sought through freedom of the press. A free press promotes the search for truth and allows for the reexamination of that which currently is held to be true.[14]

In Milton, we can see the general contours of what later becomes the marketplace of ideas. Milton elevates truth as the primary value to be promoted by freedom of speech and, in a sense, as the primary reason that a person would engage in speech at all. He also relies heavily on an untested hypothesis or belief that forms the centerpiece of any marketplace of ideas argument—the belief that truth is the outcome of an efficient process of competition. Milton puts this in more colorful terms than those who follow, but the belief persists among free speech libertarians today: "And though all the windes of doctrin were let loose to play upon the earth, so Truth be in the field, we do injuriously by licensing and prohibiting to misdoubt her strength. Let her and Falsehood grapple; who ever knew Truth put to the wors, in a free and open encounter."[15]

The central tenet of marketplace arguments is that truth will emerge from competition with falsehood and partial truths. That Milton held this belief can be seen throughout *Areopagitica*. References to truth as the primary value or objective of written speech, in the form of books, pervade the entire essay. "Last, that it [licensing] will be primely to the discouragement of all learning, and the stop of Truth, not only by disexercising and blunting our abilities in what we know already, but by hindering and cropping the discovery that might be yet further made both in religious and civill Wisdome."[16] Milton cites approvingly the works of others who had argued that truth would emerge from a process of competition between ideas.[17] He also employs military images in describing this competitive process: "Assuredly we bring not innocence into the world, we bring impurity much rather: that which purifies us is Triall, and Triall is by what is contrary." He later describes these trials as "Wars of Truth."[18] Truth must be tested or else we can have no real confidence in the validity of those ideas. Restrictions on these trials reduce the status of truth to something similar to the things that schoolchildren learn by rote.[19] Adults must exercise their own independent judgment in discourse to decide what they will believe and thus, by seeing the demonstrations of truth, will be certain in their convictions of truth.

In his familiar defense of freedom of speech in *On Liberty*, John Stuart Mill shares a great deal with Milton. The adversarial logic introduced in Milton's martial language is reproduced in Mill's contest of ideas. Like Milton, Mill does not see speech as a thing to be consumed or as a commodity to be traded but rather as the means to an active, individual consideration of truth and the demonstrations that support it. Mill does not place high value on simply believing the truth or holding the correct ideas. He instead develops a narrower and more demanding standard of knowing or understanding the truth according to personal conviction rather than trust in the authority of church or state.[20] Truth according to custom has little value for Mill. Rather, he understands truth to be valuable when discovered through an active process of contestation where ideas are challenged to weed out falsehood and error while truth is never allowed to go unchallenged.[21]

Mill never invokes the marketplace of ideas metaphor in so many words. Echoing Milton, he holds truth to be the primary value served by freedom of speech. He believes that an adversarial process not only leads to the discovery of truth but also to a kind of individualized conviction about truth. For truth to really have value, individuals must all participate actively in the contest of ideas. Truths learned by rote are little better than falsehoods for Mill.[22] Truth is not a commodity that, once discovered, can be easily transmitted or distributed. It requires a kind of intellectual work and constant, dynamic consideration of one's thoughts and the ideas of others. As he does elsewhere, Mill emphasizes the intellect. Freedom of speech promotes the interests and development of "great thinkers," but it also maximizes the mental development of "average human beings."[23]

The development of free speech libertarianism shifts to the United States in the late nineteenth century. Mark Graber traces the historical, "conservative libertarian" approach prevalent in the United States from the Civil War until the First World War that saw free speech as a component of general liberty that also included freedom of contract and property rights. He cites conservatives such as

John W. Burgess, E. L. Godkin, and Thomas Cooley for their twin support of property rights and speech rights grounded in the principles of individual autonomy and minimal government interference to allow progressive change through increases in human capacity. Even though speech rights were not a primary focus for these proponents of laissez-faire economics and limited government, they include freedom of speech as one of the checks on state power. Conservative libertarians refer back to Mill's arguments in *On Liberty* in an effort to interpret the due process clause of the Fourteenth Amendment to extend the principles of freedom of speech and contract to the states. These writers focus on the harm principle and general liberty rather than on the full consequentialist argument of the contest of ideas.[24]

The idea of a speech marketplace enters contemporary discourse through Justice Oliver Wendell Holmes's brief dissent in *Abrams v. United States* and his famous statement that "the best test of truth is the power of the thought to get itself accepted in the competition of the market."[25] He refers here to a procedural and adversarial view of truth derived from Mill's contest of ideas. Ideas must be presented for judgment in the court of popular opinion; those that are accepted take the title of truth as long as they can withstand the challenges of new ideas. False ideas will be exposed and eliminated. The adversarial system best serves the infinite progress toward objective truths. In this view, government regulation of speech prevents the system from working properly. Accepted truths are not tested but exist as cant and tradition instead. In addition, regulation of the marketplace is bad because, as in Mill's view, it reduces the opportunity for the flowering of human genius and the influence of creative and progressive thought. Government intervention alters the process necessary for progress and prevents the emergence of truth, therefore such intervention should be disallowed. Emphasizing the personal and individualistic quality of the arguments made by Milton and Mill in his famous *Abrams* dissent, Holmes is a twentieth-century adherent of the truth-oriented, adversarial tradition who clearly places truth at the apex of speech values. He stresses the adversarial nature of the "test" of truth. Holmes's skepticism about authority comes through as clearly in this dissent as in Mill's "All silencing of discussion is an assumption of infallibility."[26]

Other early-twentieth-century writers justify free speech not as a component of general liberty but instead as conducive to civic debate and the democratic process. Graber points out that civil libertarians, influenced by the Progressives, were critical of the individualistic conservative libertarian approach to liberty but wanted to retain broad protection of free speech. "In other words, early twentieth-century libertarians were forced to change the premises, rather than the conclusions, of free speech argument."[27] The shift that occurs in First Amendment doctrine with early cases such as *Schenck v. United States*, *Debs v. United States*, *Abrams v. United States*, and *Gitlow v. New York* is not simply a shift in the style of argument from conservative libertarianism but rather a return to the historical objectives of freedom of speech.[28] Late-nineteenth-century conservative libertarians may have favored freedom of speech as part of general liberty, but their arguments represent a departure from projects favored by earlier free speech libertarians while agreeing with the antistatist nature of free speech. Graber may be correct that as a matter of free speech policy, the shift to Progressive-inspired defenses of freedom of speech in the early twentieth century was a step backward for freedom of speech, but conservative libertarian arguments tied to property rights and freedom of contract could not have formed the basis for the broad protection of freedom of speech that characterizes contemporary free speech libertarianism.[29] The earliest cases decided on free speech libertarian grounds, such as *Debs* and *Abrams*, resulted in substantial restrictions on speech, but the constitutional tradition born from such cases has led to much broader protection of speech.

The Justification of Freedom of Speech

Free speech libertarians use consequentialist arguments to justify individual liberty to speak on the basis of social benefits from the ensuing public debate. The central benefits they cite are democratic policy making and the search for truth.[30] "The interest of the speaker is recognized not primarily as an end, but only instrumentally to the public interest in the ideas presented."[31] Free speech libertarians do not treat speech as intrinsically good, even though the centrality of individual speech rights initially suggests otherwise.[32] They do not begin their arguments with definitions of speech or with positive statements to identify their idea of the good or of good speech. Free speech libertarians criticize arguments meant to establish freedom of speech as an end in itself, even though eminent theorists of the First Amendment such as Louis Brandeis, Thomas Emerson, and Martin Redish maintain that speech is, at least in part, a good in itself for the individual speaker.[33] For instance, Schauer argues that freedom of self-expression for its own sake does not belong under his free speech principle because "self-expression is an unworkably amorphous concept" and fails to distinguish between communicative behavior and individual acts. Self-expression, in his view, sweeps too broadly and would have to include protection for any individual behavior as a part of freedom of speech, thus undermining a focused, independent free speech principle. Reliance on the intrinsic value of speech fails to show why speech is any more important than other kinds of conduct.[34] Cass Sunstein also criticizes arguments that treat freedom of speech as an end in itself because they cannot distinguish among different kinds of speech to tell us why some kinds of speech (criticism of government) are protected but not others (obscenity).[35]

Libertarians examine the consequences of a "system of freedom of expression" to justify the protection of individual freedom of speech as instrumental to these consequences. One familiar consequentialist mode of argument applies Mill's harm principle to justify restrictions on individual acts that lead to harm to other individuals. A common, simple, but unsatisfactory justification along these lines for broad protection of freedom of speech suggests that since speech has no bad consequences (costs) for individuals or for society, there is no justifiable reason to regulate it. However, unless one severely limits the class of actions that count as speech, at least some speech we would want to protect has costs. These costs range from offense to or embarrassment of others, to mass disturbances and agitation, to threats to national security. We would have to then examine why costly speech should be protected, thus necessitating a broader justificatory argument.[36] In the end, libertarians justify broad protection of freedom of speech because the benefits of speech outweigh its costs.

Recognizing that speech has potential bad consequences, libertarians protect individual freedom of speech against interference by the state in order to allow vigorous public debate. In turn, debate leads to the realization of several important social objectives seen to be intrinsically good, including truth discovery, effective public policy, democracy, and well-reasoned individual choices about what is best to do and be. Some writers include all of these objectives, while others cite some or only one. There are other possible goods to be realized through public debate that also may be considered. Some suggest that freedom of speech is necessary to secure the progress attained through the practice of "liberal science."[37] Others maintain that freedom of speech protects against state-sponsored "thought control."[38] Nonetheless, each of these libertarian arguments is characterized by the project of public debate as a means to an intrinsic good and by the identification of state interference in speech as the primary threat to that project.

A pure consequentialist would examine each speech case according to the facts of that case and its tangible consequences for truth or good policy. Thus, the consequentialist would look at a specific case of criticism of the government and argue either that to restrict this criticism would be wrong because it would block the discovery of truth or that the restriction would be acceptable because the criticism itself would undermine truth discovery. The clear and present danger test favored in early First Amendment doctrine represents something like this pure consequentialism because it requires scrutiny of each speech act for its probability of successfully achieving its harmful aims.[39] This kind of pure consequentialism proved to be hopelessly unworkable in legal practice since the protection of speech in any specific case turned out to be quite weak. In addition, an ad hoc rule of examining specific consequences falls far short of the predictability that is favored for legal rules. Every act of questionable speech would have to be submitted for judicial scrutiny, in essence creating a system of speech licensing through the courts. Instead, an approach based in more general consequences is necessary. Through a focus on public debate, or what Emerson calls a "system of freedom of expression," libertarians protect speech as instrumental to debate, even if in a specific instance the speech does not contribute directly to truth or other intrinsic goods.[40] Individual speech acts are instrumental to public debate, which is in turn instrumental to intrinsic goods. Thus, for example, libelous speech receives extensive protection, particularly where public officials are libeled, because such speech allows for vigorous public debate even if a false and defamatory statement about someone seems to violate truth by definition.[41] Too much scrutiny of every potentially libelous speech act would have a "chilling effect" on speakers that would act as a disincentive to speak and thus constrain public debate.

Libertarian justifications of freedom of speech ultimately rely upon social values such as truth and democracy rather than on purely individualistic justifications such as those favored by expressivists.[42] The most compelling reason for libertarians to link the individual freedom of speech to broader social objectives is that these objectives offer strong rhetorical support for freedom of speech and suggest that the importance of speech exceeds whatever importance we might place on any one speaker or that speaker's rights. To baldly assert an individualistic freedom of speech might suggest support for licentiousness rather than the ordered liberty favored by most liberals. The real strength of the argument rests on the weight attached to intrinsic goods, such as truth and good policy, that make public debate important. Truth finding has proven to be a strong objective to motivate arguments for freedom of speech because the idea that truth is valuable is widely shared.

Since most libertarian writers concerned with free speech work within the context of American constitutional law and constitutional constraints, the language and history of the First Amendment have a powerful formative effect on the kinds of justifications that these writers consider persuasive. Individual speaker's rights were curtailed in early First Amendment cases such as *Schenck* and *Debs* due to the Supreme Court's concern with security and the smooth functioning of the state.[43] When weighing the health of the state against the desire of an individual to speak out, courts ruled against the individual. Given that it is difficult to justify freedom on strictly individualistic grounds when that freedom is seen to threaten social welfare, libertarians develop justifications that suggest that individual freedom, while good for the individual, is even better for the community and supports the long-term health of the state.

The ultimate ends of public debate in the "absence of governmental interference" are more complicated than this simply stated negative principle would at first seem to indicate. Libertarians justify the absence of governmental interference as a practical instrument to promote public debate. The aggregate of many individuals' freedom of speech is some sort of public discourse. Public debate itself is only an intermediary means to the ultimate social objectives.[44] Roscoe Pound, for one, argues that even though freedom of expression is often "guaranteed as an individual natural right," it is the social interest in the moral and social life of the individual that establishes this right.[45] Some, like Mill, see the search for ultimate truths as an end, while others see open processes as the only way to deal with the uncertainty created by our lack of faith in ultimate truths. Both understandings of truth, either as objective or as socially determined, are compatible with the public debate argument. Virtually all libertarian theorists include robust public debate as a component in their free speech arguments, although they differ in their justifications of that debate. A few theorists see the contest of ideas as an end in itself and do not proceed to another level of justification.[46] Most libertarians, however, justify public debate as an intermediary goal that serves as a means to other ends. The adversarial process of public debate provides the greatest hope that the truth will be discovered through the contributions of geniuses and the defeat of falsehood, all to great social benefit.[47]

Even absolutists eventually admit that freedom of speech must involve the balancing of interests, and free speech libertarians find that to hold up free speech as an intrinsic good offers little if any guidance as to how to perform this balancing.[48] Instead, libertarians look for compelling interests that are served by freedom of speech, particularly for interests that are of such central importance that libertarians almost always favor freedom of speech over competing methods to realize those interests. Free speech libertarians are not absolutists and recognize exceptions to freedom of speech. These exceptions usually are the result of balancing freedom of speech against the objectives identified in the libertarian project of public debate. Some of the most commonly accepted exceptions are restrictions on libel, bribery, incitement to illegal action, and fighting words.[49] Each of the exceptions can be defended on the basis that the speech in question does not further truth and good policy. For instance, libelous falsehoods undermine the search for truth in addition to harming the individual who is libeled. Legal arguments made by supporters of broad First Amendment rights often take the form of establishing exclusions from the categories of protected speech by demonstrating that certain speech lacks value, that it does not promote the objectives of free speech arguments.[50] Free speech libertarians set boundaries on freedom of speech based on harms to the goals enshrined in their consequentialist defense of free speech. When an entire category of speech such as libel or obscenity violates the objectives of public debate, a strong case can be made to exclude that category from protection to prevent damage to public debate itself.

Good policy is the outcome of a process of political deliberation that establishes political truth. That is, good policy equals political truth. Of course, we will need further criteria of what constitutes "good" in policy outcomes. In fact, there are as many kinds of truth as there are types of speech. If good policy is the truth of political speech, there will be appropriate measures for the truth of scientific speech (technological progress, accuracy of prediction), religious speech (salvation, unity in the religious community) or artistic speech (mimesis).[51] Clearly, the libertarian project of truth discovery is complicated by the lack of consensus as to what constitutes truth, but perhaps skepticism about the very possibility of truth also motivates the project. Free speech libertarians seek truth but fail to indicate criteria to judge it. They pursue open processes of discussion that do not predetermine outcomes. They are specific that their pursuit of political truth is the search for good policy because political speech is a question of particular importance in the history of thought on freedom of speech in the legal-constitutional domain. They are less specific about how the objective of truth relates to artistic and other speech that is not necessarily political.

As should be clear by now, "truth" is a capacious term that subsumes a variety of related values or objectives. Truth as an objective has the significant advantage of being acceptable both to those who believe in objective truth (Mill and Milton) and those who see truth as socially determined or relative (Brandeis). It is a particularly strong argument for the latter group, as only an open process makes an end result take on the quality of truth. Any market failure or procedural imperfection would bias a final result toward the interests of some but not all, thus limiting the desirability of the result. As long as all ideas are out there, what we agree on in the end can be called truth with a certain degree of confidence, because all ideas will have been represented and the choice will be made between all options for social policy. One value of truth as an objective is intrinsic—many people believe that truth finding is a worthwhile activity. For others, the value of truth is that it represents good social policy. Yet another value of truth as an objective is that it allows individuals to do what is best as individuals and to understand the reasons why what they do is the best course of action.[52]

This procedural argument from truth is present in one form or another in many free speech theories. It is a part of the democratic self-governance argument or contest of ideas to determine the political truth as represented in the collective will. C. Edwin Baker subsumes self-government arguments under the marketplace of ideas for this reason.[53] Self-government theories are concerned not only with realizing beneficial social policy but also with diversity and acts of participation by individuals. Ultimately, these arguments seek political truth through public debate. While Brandeis favored the language of deliberation over Holmes's marketplace of ideas metaphor, he paved much of the way for libertarian free speech theory by translating the intellectual currents of pragmatism into constitutional argument.[54] Brandeis's concurring opinion in *Whitney v. California* suggests that the original intent of the First Amendment was to guarantee the kind of political process pragmatism sought, one where discussion was an indispensable part of a process to truth.[55] Brandeis claims in the *Whitney* opinion that "public discussion is a public duty" and fundamental to American government. Brandeis values dissent, and the attendant diversity of views, not as an end in itself but for its role in attaining social consensus and participation.[56] Graber argues that Brandeis represents a kind of transitional figure between an older, conservative libertarian tradition that had defended free speech as a part of general liberty associated with freedom of contract and the emerging civil libertarian tradition that supports audience theories. Brandeis, he says, accepts the conservative libertarian protection of free speech as an individual liberty and bases his concurrence in *Whitney* on those arguments, even though he opposed the general individualism of that approach and favored social justifications.[57]

Thomas Scanlon attempts to draw out a single principle of freedom of speech, one that guarantees the right of "having a good environment for the formation of one's beliefs and desires."[58] An individual right to free speech instrumentally guarantees this environment of consumer choice by providing an array of ideas from which an audience can choose. Scanlon weighs the interests of three groups relevant to any free speech situation—speakers, audiences, and bystanders—but focuses primarily on audiences.[59] He disavows his own earlier argument to protect the autonomy of individuals participating in the speech marketplace but retains the core of the autonomy view in the form of individual choice in the matters of opinion, belief, and course of action.[60] Scanlon defends a social process of public debate that considers the central individual right within this debate to be the right to choose as a member of the audience. Again, public debate provides the mechanism for the realization of truth as individuals consider their own choices.

Democracy is another end realized through the means of public debate. However, democracy in the view of free speech libertarians does not involve universal political participation or strict majoritarian practices. Democracy cannot be purely majoritarian because libertarians justify a right to freedom of speech that represents a check on state power, hence, a limit on the reach of majoritarian decision making. They disallow censorship regardless of any majoritarian pressure to engage in limits on speech. Instead, the democracy envisioned by libertarians is procedural and closely related to Mill's truth argument.[61] Democracy, in this view, is the search for political truths and effective public policy.[62] Democratic self-rule requires that citizens set the political agenda according to their ideas, not the authorities'. The more ideas that enter political debate, the greater the chance to arrive at the best political outcomes with the greatest social benefits. The democracy objective is closely related to the objective of truth because the former is driven by uncertainty as to what the best policy should be, just as the argument from truth is grounded in uncertainty as to what the truth is.[63]

The primary obstacle to the realization of free speech libertarian objectives is state action that curtails robust public debate. The common libertarian language of "threats" to free speech refers to threats from the state or state actors. Related to this focus on state action is a minimal concern with private interference with speech. Libertarians share deep skepticism about any state action, but, unlike absolutists, most recognize certain areas of speech in which state action is justified, such as the regulation of libel or blackmail. While the heckler's veto doctrine recognizes some state responsibility to protect speakers from hostile audiences, private corporations, private schools and institutions, and families are left to regulate speech as those in charge see fit. Schauer, for example, excludes private exercise of power entirely from his free speech principle by definition and suggests that there may be a parallel liberty principle to deal with such problems but that private power should not be addressed by law.[64]

The libertarians' focus on state threats to their project of public debate stems from a combination of historical, institutional, and prudential factors. As a simple matter of power, the state has enormous capacity to restrict speech through direct application of criminal law and the use of police force. Historically, free speech arguments develop in response to state action, such as licensing of the press and repression of antiwar protesters. Institutionally, the lion's share of writing on free speech is about the First Amendment, which is clearly oriented against the threat of state power. In addition, the legal system of the United States is particularly well suited to the protection of freedom of speech, thus further emphasizing the role of state action in public debate.[65]

Of course, definitions of state action vary significantly, and much of the debate within libertarianism concerns how this term is to be defined. Most thought on state action and speech uses a circumscribed notion of what constitutes state action.[66] A direct act of censorship by a government body in the form of a prior restraint on publication clearly qualifies as state action. The state interferes in the availability of political information with a law that caps expenditures on political campaigns by individuals.[67] State action, in this view, is limited to those cases where the government acts to affect the status quo, but often such a view ignores the government's role in establishing that state of affairs. Cass Sunstein argues for an expanded notion of state action that accounts for the role the state plays in the current distribution of opportunities and venues for speech. For Sunstein, state action involves both changes in the status quo and the acts that establish or contribute to it through the law of trespass or contract, for instance, leading him to accept an activist state in the speech realm while remaining consistent with the libertarian project.[68]

Free speech libertarians promote a project of vigorous public debate that will lead to one or more socially valuable, intrinsic goods such as truth discovery, good public policy, and progress through liberal science. The key threat to the realization of this project is state action that eliminates, restricts, regulates, or biases public debate in some fashion. The guarantee of freedom of speech for individuals is the means by which free speech libertarians produce vigorous public debate and the ensuing intrinsic goods. Absent restriction by the state, individuals will speak, engage in public discourse, argue, and debate questions of public importance. They will criticize each other, the state, and actions taken by state officials. Many will espouse orthodox views, but these views will be challenged by heterodox individuals in a progressive process of continuous, adversarial contest of ideas, resulting in truth discovery and good public policy.

Definitions of state action and politics come into play when we consider the exercise of private power and free speech. Free speech libertarians usually use a fairly narrow definition of state action limited to questions of state policy or the direct exercise of state power, while minimizing the role the state plays in maintaining private power. The distinction is one between the state acting to restrict speech through censorship and the state allowing the exclusion of some speech as a consequence of state inaction. Schauer, for one, excludes private restrictions on speech from his definition of the free speech principle. Instead, he argues that any private act that limits the speech of another individual is a speech act by the actor and does not involve the state directly. In his example, a newspaper editor who refuses to publish an unsolicited article hardly can be said to censor that speech, the editor simply makes a decision in line with his or her authority to determine the newspaper's contents.[69] These kinds of private choices are inevitable, Schauer says, and the legal system generally acknowledges them as legitimate. Indeed, a law mandating that a newspaper publish replies to its articles by interested parties would constitute an infringement on the publisher's freedom of speech.[70] This analysis obscures, however, both that many people do speak of acts of private "censorship" and that power can be exercised in ways that restrict the speech of individuals, even when those restrictions are not speech acts by the authority in question. The analysis also obscures the ways in which the legal system is involved in such restrictions on speech through the law of trespass or through the licensing of television and radio stations.[71]

Moreover, the private exercise of power is not always a conflict between the speech rights of two individuals. Sometimes the conflict is between the power of one and the speech of another. For example, an employer who forbids employees from speaking to the press at the risk of their jobs exercises a power to control the speech of other persons, but it is difficult to see this as a simple case of private choice.[72] Newspapers that forbid their employees to participate in political protests and other activities to avoid the appearance of the journalistic impropriety of nonneutrality exercise power beyond the publisher's choice to speak. Secrecy and nondisclosure agreements signed by employees of some state agencies and private corporations are justified as part of the property rights of these institutions in information but sweep broadly to restrict speech irrelevant to those property interests. Shopping malls have replaced town squares and other traditional public forums yet are closed by their owners, exercising property rights, to the speech of citizens wishing to canvas or leaflet inside the mall. Rules prohibiting federal employees from receiving speaker's honorariums, even for subjects unrelated to their employment, may sweep too broadly as well. Parents who control the speech of their children are exercising power beyond their own private choice to speak. In all of these examples, libertarians, to be consistent with their social ends, would need to recognize a positive right to freedom of speech. This even might require state action to "level the playing field" or provide an opportunity to individuals to speak. Absent some such action, the public debate will suffer from a lack of the diversity of ideas and information necessary to effective public policy.

Objections to Free Speech Libertarianism

It will be helpful to examine in detail three objections to the free speech libertarians' justification of freedom of speech. The first two are internal criticisms that emerge from the staunch antistatism of the argument. The third is an external criticism concerned with speech that may be excluded from protection. One internal objection is that the priority placed on the project of public debate leaves open the possibility that individual speech may be regulated to advance that project. A second objection states that public debate is threatened by economic inequality and private power in ways that undermine the diversity and representativeness of participation necessary to achieve the objectives of debate. The third objection is that while political speech is well protected by a public discourse–centered consequentialist argument, nonpolitical speech may be excluded from protection.

Objection No. 1: Some Speech Undermines Public Debate

The consequentialist libertarian arguments rely upon the high value people generally place on truth, good policy, and good reasons. The strong appeal of these social objectives supports individual freedom of speech even when there are substantial costs of that speech and tangible benefits such as increased security and stability might be promoted through a regime of limited freedom of speech. The structure of the consequentialist argument suggests that the stronger our attachment to truth as an objective, the greater our support for individual freedom of speech as a means to attain it should be. However, if social objectives truly justify the public debate project of libertarian theory, libertarians should be willing to accept restrictions on individual freedom of speech to secure social benefits such as truth or good policy. This argument takes its most common form when it is maintained that we should not tolerate those who advocate the overthrow of the institutions of freedom of speech. Thus, the investigations and restrictions of the McCarthy era could be legitimated with arguments consistent with the social justifications of freedom of speech. Prosecutions of Communist conspiracies under the Smith Act were approved by the Supreme Court in *Dennis v. United States* on the logic that Congress has the power to protect the government against armed rebellion and that this power extends to the prohibition of the advocacy of doctrines meant to lead to such rebellion, if such advocacy shows any signs of possibly being effective.[73] That is, the Smith Act is legitimate, in this view, because the idea that the current form of government is illegitimate and should be overthrown violates the very Constitution that protects freedom of speech. Such subversive views cannot be entertained as a part of public debate focused by the search for truth and good policy unless the discussion is far removed from any intent to take action on those ideas. Carl Auerbach defended the ban on the Communist Party under the Communist Control Act of 1954 along these lines. For Auerbach, a legislative finding that the Communist Party represented a threat to security and freedom justified a blanket proscription of the party. He argued that the Communist Party cannot be allowed to exist because it represents totalitarianism and opposes the First Amendment's assumption of freedom grounded in skepticism about political orthodoxy and absolute truths.[74]

Freedom of speech represents the one political orthodoxy that cannot be challenged, because it allows all other orthodoxies to be challenged.[75] The statement is a paradox, but the argument is simple from the standpoint of practice as long as one accepts the view commonplace in 1954 that communism cannot possibly be true and could only prevail in the marketplace of ideas through trickery and conspiracy. We cannot allow communism to flourish because, if it does, freedom of speech is lost, thus preventing any further process of truth discovery (or rejection of communism). Ultimately, then, Auerbach rests the case for proscription of the Communist Party on an empirical argument that "successive waves of events since the Bolshevik revolution should have removed all reasonable doubts about the true significance and intentions of the world communist movement," in spite of the public affirmation of civil liberties made by the American Communist Party.[76] For Auerbach, it is clear that allowing the speech of the Communist Party would undermine the objectives of truth and good policy both because the party's ideas are plainly wrong and because they would damage or eliminate the freedom of speech necessary to further libertarian projects. In this view, freedom of speech is not absolute; it may be curtailed to maximize truth and good policy.

Thomas Emerson sees arguments like Auerbach's as a "minority view" also associated with Karl Popper and Walter Lippmann.[77] Mark Graber calls this type of argument "old wine" and suggests that in every generation "the leading proponents of various bans on certain ideas have insisted that the First Amendment does not fully protect the right to deny or criticize what their generation regards to be fundamental constitutional values."[78] Such arguments proliferate in times of perceived threat but recede as threats become less salient. Thus, the Supreme Court backed away from its support of the Smith Act as the McCarthy era faded (*Yates v. United States*; *Brandenburg v. Ohio*), but the existence of the Smith Act and the Communist Control Act, as well as *Dennis*, indicate that the "minority view" is a plausible one within free speech libertarian justifications of freedom of speech.[79] The implications of post-9/11 antiterrorism efforts for speech policy are still not clear, and one suspects that this argument for restriction of speech will return in some guise. However, Graber suggests that calls for hate speech regulations rest on arguments parallel to Auerbach's notion that racism is universally rejected and that equality is so fundamental to the Constitution that speech in support of inequality opposes the Constitution itself in a way that removes such speech from First Amendment protection.[80]

If social objectives have priority, then it seems likely that we would be willing to trade off even more of the instrumental good, individual free speech to realize the primary objectives of truth and good public policy. This is already accepted in cases such as bribery and libel. Lines must be drawn and boundaries set between the intrinsic goods and allowable restrictions on instrumental goods. Constitutional doctrine draws these lines between acceptable infringements on individual freedom of speech (such as in these cases) and unacceptable limits (such as prior restraints on the press to promote national security) in the legal practice of hearing First Amendment rights claims. Just because these lines can be drawn in legal practice does not mean that they are theoretical necessities. The Supreme Court must constantly wrestle with the proper balance between social objectives and individual speech rights. Free speech absolutists such as the ACLU may not agree with the idea of such boundaries and instead favor total deregulation of speech, but most others argue for some form of balancing of social objectives and individual freedom. The bulk of the speech cases before the courts involve identifying the relationship between the facts of the case, social objectives, and the individual speech infringed upon by the regulations in question. The basic constitutional theory of the First Amendment is relatively stable; the practice of that doctrine continues to be controversial. We may have come to politically acceptable accommodations of individual freedom of speech and social objectives, but the fact that the Supreme Court hears a number of free speech cases every term suggests that these accommodations are contested and that conflicts between individualistic justifications and social projects persist both in practice and in theory.

There are three primary libertarian responses to the objection that consequentialist, social justifications of freedom of speech leave the door open to restrictions. These arguments develop in the context of actual restrictions on speech that rely on this purported contradiction. First, skepticism about the capacity of government to make determinations of what furthers truth and good policy is at the heart of free speech libertarianism; thus the state may not justify any restrictions on speech on the grounds that it is obviously false or leads to bad truth or policy outcomes. Second, it is a free speech catechism that freedom of speech is the most efficient means to realize the projects of truth and good policy regardless of whatever claims to expertise the state may offer.[81] Third, it can be argued that while such restrictions were allowed in past legal practice, current legal practice is much more protective of even advocacy of illegal action; thus the issue of this objection is more or less settled, and there is little danger of backsliding.

Libertarians respond to the anticonsequentialist objection with a mix of skepticism about state action and confidence that freedom of speech will prevail in the process of public debate about free speech. Emerson and Schauer have both suggested that freedom of speech itself must remain open for debate or else it becomes "dead dogma."[82] Schauer argues that freedom of speech needs to apply the Millian process of public debate to itself if arguments to support freedom of speech are to be stronger. According to Schauer, there is little "free speech about free speech" and an overreliance on rhetorical phrases such as "chilling effect" and "slippery slope" rather than on careful analysis of arguments.[83] State action similar to the Communist Control Act that restricts debate over freedom of speech or the institutions that protect it is ultimately counterproductive because it undermines arguments about the freedom it is meant to protect. State policy grounded in the careful and logically compelling arguments of this first objection to free speech libertarianism will do more to harm freedom of speech, the public debate that it protects, and its attendant objectives than it will do to promote these ends. The objection collapses of its own weight because free speech about free speech ultimately serves the ends of public debate better than would limited speech about free speech, as this first objection suggests. There is some risk that free speech about speech could lead to restrictions on freedom. Arguments to limit speech could win in public debate if, for instance, anti–free speech candidates won a majority in Congress or came to dominate in the judiciary, but libertarians are confident that this will not happen, the same confidence that they require for all participants in public debate whatever position they might defend. Libertarians assume that citizens participating in public debate will ultimately favor the process of public debate itself and that the process benefits from political attacks on freedom of speech.[84]

Once it is established that freedom of speech is one means to truth and good policy, two questions still have to be asked. First, is freedom of speech the only means we have to realize truth? Second, if not, is speech the most efficient means? Since societies with little commitment to freedom of speech have made great progress toward scientific, artistic, and political truths, the answer to the first question must be no. The second question, of efficiency, is at least partially an empirical question that has not been answered and may not be open to investigation. Instead, the efficiency of free speech as a means to other ends is a matter of free speech orthodoxy.[85] For instance, First Amendment cases that rely upon the marketplace of ideas use that metaphor to import the efficiency ascribed to economic markets but do not independently establish that efficiency. The Supreme Court does not base these decisions on a finding of fact by a lower court or rest its decisions on social-scientific evidence to establish the instrumental efficiency of free speech. Freedom of speech may be the best means to truth and good policy, but there is at least some doubt, which leaves the door open to regulation of speech in order to advance the priorities indicated by libertarian justifications for freedom of speech.

Libertarians can make a strong argument against the claim that their consequentialist justifications subordinate individual freedom by pointing to Supreme

Court decisions that extend freedom of speech to individuals and not to social groups or the community as a whole. They might argue that if free speech is protected in practice, then it should not matter that free speech is only instrumental to other ends. The empirical state of American constitutional doctrine of freedom of speech does broadly defend individual freedoms and refrains from trading off individual freedom in the interests of maximizing the social goals of good policy and truth seeking. However, that the Supreme Court protects free speech in practice today does not mean that speech will always be protected to the same extent in other circumstances or political contexts. Rehnquist Court rollbacks in the protection of criminal defendants' rights under the Fourth, Fifth, and Eighth Amendments suggests that the progressive expansion of constitutional liberties can turn into a contraction in changing political contexts, especially in times of security threats such as an undeclared war on terrorism. Broad First Amendment protection of freedom of speech is a relatively recent development, not a "timeless verity" etched in stone.

Objection No. 2: Owen Fiss, Economic Inequality, and Market Failure

A second objection raised against libertarian justifications also examines the ways in which the consequentialist argument may fall short of the realization of its own project of public debate. A number of recent arguments attempt to preserve the marketplace approach to speech by extending the economic metaphor to discuss failures in free speech markets. Foremost among these is the work of Owen Fiss. Fiss agrees with the social project of public debate and with the value placed on truth discovery and good public policy. However, he criticizes free speech libertarianism for its exclusive focus on state interference in speech activities and argues that this does not in itself guarantee the proper functioning of the procedure of public debate. Inequalities in wealth, access to media, and government funding all contribute to market failures in speech. Fiss is concerned that individual freedom of speech understood only as a procedural safeguard is not sufficient and maintains that the effects of state action, other than censorship, on public debate must also be examined by policy makers and the courts.[86] The state, he argues, must act to extend public debate, to increase the quantity of ideas available for consideration and protect the messages at the fringes of the market that otherwise might be silenced by social conditions. Fiss begins with the same social project adopted by libertarians but argues for an expanded process governed by an activist state to promote the process further. A straightforward laissez-faire marketplace of ideas fails to advance its own objective of the search for truth, but Fiss maintains that a modified process can realize those goals more efficiently. He recognizes the dangers inherent in both progressive censorship and in state action to reduce the influence of certain ideas, so his proposal is for a somewhat more restricted positive state action, namely, state funding of marginal speech through agencies like the National Endowment for the Arts (NEA) and the Corporation for Public Broadcasting.

Fiss considers the problem of economic inequality and departs significantly from free speech libertarianism without abandoning its basic public debate project. If state regulation is called for in the economy, he suggests that state intervention may also be required in the speech marketplace. The dominant understanding of free speech as a limit on state interference, Fiss argues, allows public debate over policy to be structured by the same forces that dominate the social structure (that is, wealth). Fiss suggests that we take public debate as the direct goal of freedom of speech (rather than autonomy or truth). If public debate is the goal, then state action to promote such debate is warranted, even required, by the First Amendment. "The state is to act as a corrective for the market." He proposes that the state involve itself in the public debate through a combination of subsidies (increased funding for the Public Broadcasting System), regulation of the media (the fairness doctrine), and court scrutiny of the actions of state agencies as they participate in public debate.[87]

Fiss calls for reform based on a social reality of government participation in speech markets.[88] Sunstein echoes this with an argument for a "New Deal for Speech" meant to reform the already extensive system of government interference in speech activities enforced by property rights and telecommunications law.[89] The government already does far more than merely protect negative liberties, they each argue, so this is not a major stretch from our current understandings of the First Amendment. *Rust v. Sullivan*, a case concerning federally funded speech, illustrates this problem well.[90] The Supreme Court upheld the so-called gag rule, which prevented doctors in federally subsidized clinics from discussing abortion with their patients and prescribed specific responses to abortion-related questions if asked. The government executed this decision through restrictions on Title X family-planning aid. In earlier cases, the Court had ruled that the government could not use subsidy powers to suppress dangerous ideas through viewpoint discrimination.[91] In *Rust*, the court ruled that the government could use subsidy powers to restrict truthful speech (that is, speech referring to the legal activities of abortion and abortion counseling). This interferes with truthful speech as well as belittles the doctor-patient relationship, in spite of a traditional understanding that such a relationship falls within the private sphere. Were the federal government to apply similar content regulations to other subsidy recipients, such as universities, NEA-funded artists, the unemployed, student loan recipients, or tobacco farmers, free speech as we know it would be eliminated entirely. Fiss and Sunstein argue that something like this has already happened, just not so overtly as the requirements of the "gag rule."

The libertarian focus on state action leads to neglect of the problems that private power creates for consequentialist justifications of freedom of speech. However, the state is not the only actor that may interfere in a social process of public debate and truth discovery. While the state may have the largest concentration of power and individual agents of the state may have the necessary motives, other organizations and individuals have the necessary power and motivation to disrupt the processes created by freedom of speech. If the objective actually is truth or the best political decisions, the community probably needs more than the negative guarantee against state interference. Private restrictions on liberty will have many deleterious effects on the smooth functioning of the procedures suggested by libertarian theories and result in a failure to realize the central objectives of a wide-open public debate. To be consistent, libertarians would have to recognize that private power threatens their ultimate objectives of truth and good policy while at the same time preventing many individual speakers from participating in public deliberations.

Libertarians can argue that reliance on the state for market correction or to alleviate inequalities in private power is problematic for several reasons. It seems unlikely that the state is in a position to know or to understand which points of view need support or belong in the public debate. That is, for institutional and epistemological reasons, even a state making a good faith effort to improve and enrich public debate is not capable of determining what belongs in the debate. The most significant reason supporting public debate in the first place is skepticism about the state's ability to deal with a full range of issues. Libertarians such as Mill favored public debate because of the incapacity of states to do so. State support for speech along the lines suggested by Fiss simply replicates the problem that public debate was meant to solve.

Another problem involves the "good faith" of the state. It is not at all clear that the state would be likely to exercise the subsidy power for the ends to which it was granted this power. Many free speech writers are frightened by the prospect of more government involvement in speech, even for benevolent purposes. In addition, a hornets' nest is opened up in the subsidy context, as each decision to subsidize one speaker is a decision not to subsidize another, with dramatic effects on the content of public debate. Highly detailed scrutiny of such decisions would be required to ensure fair and neutral government action. Of course, if government action here is neutral, the beneficial effects on public debate of the subsidy will be canceled out by increased funding to already prominent works. In addition, it seems unlikely that groups that have enough political power to enact subsidies for themselves or to limit the speech of others would find themselves subject to exclusion from public debate. In other words, groups subject to being silenced in the marketplace of ideas through their subordinate economic or social status probably do not have the political power to alleviate that situation through subsidies and restrictions anyway.[92]

In addition, libertarians can claim that no process is perfect. They can acknowledge that private power creates problems for public debate, perhaps even limits it in significant ways, yet argue that we will eventually get to the truth, just more slowly than in an ideal market. The costs and risks involved in use of state power for market correction are too great when, at best, they might only expedite a process that will eventually lead to truth discovery and good policy anyway. Any marginal improvement, due to affirmative state action, in the efficiency of public debate as a means to an objective like truth discovery would come at a high risk to the process itself.

Objection No. 3: Private Power and Excluded Speech

A third possible objection to free speech libertarianism is not with the consequentialist structure of the argument but rather with the necessary exclusion of certain types of speech to make the consequentialist argument self-consistent. The libertarian focus on communication of messages within debate over matters of public importance suggests that speech that does not take the form of communication of messages lies outside of libertarian protection of freedom of speech. Nonrational speech such as a howl of rage, for instance, appears to have no place in public debate intended to produce truth or good public policy. Some libertarians go so far as to argue that "casual chit-chat among two or a few people is not protected by the First Amendment because it is not sufficiently related to the free marketplace of ideas."[93] Chief Justice William Rehnquist does not even see voting as political speech protected as a part of public debate.[94]

Public debate is a cognitive conception with no room for noncognitive speech. If speech does not represent an idea, then it cannot be considered, evaluated, or judged by listeners and hence can be no part of their own cognitive processes. For example, the distinction between cognitive and noncognitive speech plays a significant role in discussions of pornography and obscenity. A frequent argument against protection for sexually explicit materials from both the right and left is that pornography is not an idea but rather "masturbation material" or sex itself.[95] Videos, pictures, or stories designed to elicit sexual arousal do not ask the viewer or reader to engage in discussion or to consider cognitively the materials as contributions to a public debate, therefore these materials are not speech and can be excluded from free speech protection.[96] Of course, current practice protects sexually explicit material other than that which meets the three-part test for obscenity from *Miller v. California.* Under this test, words or pictures that are patently offensive, appeal to the prurient interest, and lack serious artistic, political, or scientific value are considered obscene. This is consistent with the unitary libertarian justification in two senses. First, as application of the *Miller* test demonstrates, it is hard to find speech that is without some ideational content that would grant it protection. Second, even hard-core violent pornography can be seen as an idea or part of public debate if it sparks opposition.[97]

Much artistic expression also appears to be excluded from libertarian arguments since it may have little connection to objectives such as good policy or the search for truth. Artistic expression takes place for many reasons that have nothing to do with public debate. Much of it may be completely self-indulgent or directed at resolution of private impulses disconnected from rational public deliberation. Art can be produced for the purpose of persuasion or even the introduction of "ideas" into public debate, but this is not always its purpose. The creation of a religious icon for the purposes of veneration of a saint is far removed from the kind of vigorous, robust public debate favored by free speech libertarians.

Comprehensiveness requires that highly valued kinds of speech such as artistic expression be brought within the structure of the libertarian justification of freedom of speech. The only way to do this is to bring artistic expression under the umbrella of the good consequences of public debate. Art has a critical function that casts doubt upon established, orthodox ways of seeing the world as well as a cultural value of opening up possibilities from which individuals can choose. These two political capacities of art bring artistic speech within the public debate, thus securing free speech protection under the unitary, libertarian justification. However, not all artistic speech is directed at these political capacities;

some is solely personal expression performed for individual reasons independent of broader social significance. In addition, many artists never produce any work of significance and lack any audience that would establish the artistic production as a communication.[98] The speech of the less talented lacks broad social value and is protected by the libertarian approach only as an afterthought, as an assertion of a shared value or in recognition of doubt as to the value of the work in question. The artistic speech of ordinary people is not likely to advance the social objectives of public debate, therefore it is not necessary to the smooth functioning of the procedure of public debate. The public debate rationale protects good artists and political artists but gives little comfort to the nonpolitical and mediocre.

Many types of self-expression that are important to individuals, their emotional or artistic expression, for instance, end up outside of the libertarian justification of individual free speech rights. These highly valued forms of expression may not have much instrumental value within public debate for the advancement of good policy or the social search for truth. It is true that the artistic genius who reveals a new understanding of a way of life or exposes submerged elements of our culture may play a social role that supports the premises of public debate favored by libertarians in that these individuals generate new ideas and options from which the community can choose. Nonetheless, many of these ideas, as original, creative, and important as they may be, have little impact on the debate over good policy or truth. At best, much art has only a tangential relationship to the kinds of debate that libertarians consider in their justifications for freedom of speech. The same can be said for a great deal of academic writing and teaching, pornography, many kinds of advertising, and direct emotive statements.

The best way for libertarians to bring artistic expression and other speech under the umbrella of good consequences is to expand the definition of political speech to include a broad array of speech acts. Definitions of political speech range from the very narrow (Robert Bork) to the very broad (Cass Sunstein), providing a corresponding range of protection to various kinds of speech. Bork defines political speech in "Neutral Principles and Some First Amendment Problems":

> The category of protected speech should consist of speech concerned with governmental behavior, policy or personnel, whether the governmental unit involved is executive, legislative, judicial or administrative. Explicitly political

speech is speech about how we are governed, and the category therefore includes a wide range of evaluation, criticism, electioneering and propaganda. It does not cover scientific, educational, commercial or literary expressions as such.[99]

Bork goes further to exclude advocacy of revolution and violation of existing law from this definition of political speech, as these violate the constitutional structure of government.[100] For Bork, political speech is a part of political procedures set forth in the Constitution and is protected in order to provide for those procedures. On the other hand, Sunstein bases his definition of political speech in constitutional procedure, and yet it is substantially more inclusive than Bork's. "For present purposes I mean to treat speech as political *when it is both intended and received as a contribution to public deliberation about some issue.* This is a broad standard. It categorizes all speech that bears on potentially public issues as falling within the free speech core."[101] Sunstein explicitly states that his definition does not limit political speech to the discussion of government action or policy. Instead, it encompasses much contained within the categories of speech that are most often seen as nonpolitical: artistic, scientific, and emotive speech.

No categorization of speech is perfect, and categories overlap to some extent. Along with emotive, expressive, artistic, and scientific speech, political speech is one of the important categories of speech. These are not wholly distinct categories; a good deal of artistic speech is political, as is some scientific and emotive speech. Political speech clearly includes all of that speech encompassed by Bork's statist definition—speech of or relating to government officials and policies. As Sunstein highlights in his definition, contributions to public deliberation are political as well. It is confusing, however, to treat all or most speech as political. Libertarians deny the special character of emotive, scientific, and artistic speech when they include them within the category of political speech, while at the same time they dilute the conceptual definition of political speech. It is not that emotive and artistic speech are unimportant to politics, far from it. They often have political consequences and are conditioned by political environments, but the involvement with politics is secondary rather than characteristic of these categories of speech. The categories are not absolute. Some art is clearly political both in intent and in the audience's understanding of it; politics is often expressive or emotive.

Sunstein's definition identifies political speech as the "free speech core" while simultaneously defining political speech broadly. It is not clear how all speech that we might value for any reason would not fall under his definition of political speech and hence within the free speech core. If all speech is political in this way, Sunstein's argument would make him a free speech absolutist, but he explicitly denies being an absolutist. Thus, we must assume that there are some speech acts that are not political and have value. Yet if there are such categories, they seem to receive little protection within Sunstein's focus on political speech. His definition is so inclusive as to undermine the special and distinct character of artistic, emotive, and scientific speech acts commonly seen as nonpolitical.

Let me illustrate with an example. Artistic speech is often included as part of the category of political speech. Within Sunstein's definition, it is easy to see how virtually all artistic speech would be considered political, as most of it would be "about some issue," broadly construed. Artistic speech, however, has conventions of its own. Specific, albeit pliable, conventions apply to what counts as painting, printmaking, or performance art. In the case of the prosecution of Dennis Barrie, director of the Cincinnati Arts Center, over the Robert Mapplethorpe show, part of the defense was that the photographs in question had political value, consistent with Sunstein's definition, since they depicted certain aspects of homoerotic lifestyles. While the photographs do have this political quality, the categorization of them as political speech is controversial, in large part because they do not follow widely held beliefs about the conventions that define a political speech act. For many, they do not even follow the conventions of artistic speech but rather of pornography. To categorize the photographs as political speech simply because to do so is an effective legal argument does a disservice to the context and conventions that better categorizes them as art (or pornography). Defenders of these photographs who relied on arguments specific to artistic expression were more consistent and clear.[102]

Alexander Meiklejohn maintains that all political ideas must be heard but not all people.[103] Viewpoints can be represented without necessarily granting all individuals time or opportunity to speak. The logic of libertarian justifications requires a representative sample of people's opinions rather than the expression of each individual opinion.[104] The public debate only needs to reflect the diversity of ideas and interests in the society. Since the marketplace of ideas or public debate is justified primarily on the grounds of providing audiences with many ideas to choose from rather than providing a forum for individual ideas, an individual may be closed out of participation as long as his or her general viewpoint is already represented. Advocates for competing positions are heard, and this is sufficient to guarantee the consumer choice that libertarians protect. For example, although a few representative senior citizens express their views on Medicare reform in town meetings called by their representatives in Congress, in interviews with the media, and through political advocacy groups such as the American Association of Retired Persons (AARP), the vast majority of senior citizens do not speak out on this important matter of democratic public policy choice. They have a full range of ideas to hear in order to help formulate their views and voting choices, but the expression of their views in public is not important to democratic policy making once similar views have already entered the marketplace.

This is not to say that superfluous expression would be censored or even that the state would be likely to attempt to regulate repetitive speech. Nonetheless, it is clear that the expression of every individual is not necessary as a means to libertarian ends, and therefore no effort need be made by the state to promote such speech, even if it is good for the individuals in question. Not all individual speech is necessary or valuable to the libertarian consequentialist justification of freedom of speech. At best, this represents a surprising coldness to individual speech as an end in itself. At worst, it supports ideas like James Fishkin's deliberative opinion polls transformed into a policy-making apparatus.[105]

Important objections to the libertarian argument include challenges to the efficiency of an unregulated public debate, such as those raised by proponents of the Communist Control Act and by Owen Fiss. Objections can also be raised concerning the kinds of speech only tangentially related to public debate that may be excluded from free speech protection. Free speech libertarians can respond to these objections with strong arguments to defend their consequentialist justification of freedom of speech, but even considering these responses, libertarianism falls short of a comprehensive justification of freedom of speech. Libertarian extensions of their public debate project to include kinds of speech that many people are passionately defensive about, such as artistic expression and nonrational speech, are ultimately incomplete. Vigorous debate over matters of public importance provides a compelling project to justify individual freedom of rational and political speech but pulls nonrational and nonpolitical speech in under the umbrella of the good consequences of speech in only a secondary or weak way. It is unclear that individual freedom of speech, guaranteed against state interference, as a means to public debate and to truth and good policy is sufficient to cover all of our preferences and judgments about free speech or to explain why people make free speech claims in some situations that seem quite distant from state action.

The free speech libertarian justification of freedom of speech is a consequentialist argument that erects strong barriers to state interference in the speech acts of individuals in order to produce a vigorous public debate, which in turn is an instrument for attaining objectives such as truth discovery and good public policy. The argument rests on the key assumption that public debate is an efficient means to realize libertarian objectives and skepticism about state capacities to promote these objectives either through regulation of public debate or replacement of debate with some other means to libertarian objectives. The libertarian, consequentialist account of political speech is compelling and tightly links free speech and political benefits, but it fails the test of comprehensiveness.

CHAPTER THREE

Self-Realization and the Expressivist Justification

Americans are passionate about freedom of speech even as they become less and less interested in political life. If the robust political debate favored by libertarians really motivates this passion, then it is surprising that interest in free speech does not decline along with political participation. There must be other reasons for popular attachment to freedom of speech as an individual right and an important value. It seems unlikely that attacks on the reduction of federal arts funding or regulation of pornography on the Internet (the Communications Decency Act) will hamper vibrant and participatory political debates. The defense of arts funding and the attack on copyright law center on individual expressive freedom as a good in itself rather than an instrument for political debate. Instead, the centrality of individual expressive activity found in these kinds of arguments represents a distinct, expressivist justification for free speech independent of the libertarian account centered on political debate.

At the very least, the ideas of expressivists appear to capture the motivation behind many public defenses of free speech. However, individuals with expressivist concerns have been forced by the inherent difficulties of expressivist arguments to take up consequentialist "public reasons" that obscure their commitments and their desire to protect the space in which to engage in expressive activity. Expressivism emphasizes freedom of speech as an independent value rather than as a means to an externally realized good. Arguments based on expressivism are more appropriate to certain kinds of speech acts, such as art, than are libertarian arguments grounded in the social interests to be advanced by public debate. Furthermore, expressivism brings the focus in speech debates back to individual speakers and away from an overreliance on metaphors like the marketplace of ideas. This focus on speakers has additional implications for the boundaries of freedom of speech, for instance, the trend toward treating corporations as First Amendment speakers. Expressivists attempt to provide a comprehensive argument for free speech through a compelling account of the relationship between speech and the self that encompasses artistic and religious speech in ways frequently excluded from contemporary political defenses of speech. Despite this effort, expressivist justifications of freedom of speech, in their current form, are too limited to do this work. Expressivism needs to be reformulated to offer a richer account of the independence of free speech as a value. The relationship between the self and self-expression also should be tighter. Self-realization is frequently cited as an objective to be secured by policies that protect freedom of speech. Unfortunately, as it stands today, the argument for it is theoretically impoverished and suffers from several debilitating weaknesses.

Expressivism can be reconstituted to increase the attention paid to the concept of the self, the scope of the value of self-realization, and the link between self-realization and freedom of speech. I draw on romantic sources of the modern understanding of the self and prominent contemporary interpretations of those sources to fill out the relationship between self-realization and freedom of speech. Through developing that relationship, expressivism can better address those critics who argue that social interests such as security, progress, or social harmony trump any potential individual interest in expression.

Contemporary Expressivism in Law

All expressivists share a set of general commitments that differentiate them from free speech libertarians. Expressivists such as C. Edwin Baker and Martin Redish promote self-realization (sometimes referred to as self-fulfillment) through acts of creative expression.[1] Alexander Meiklejohn, Cass Sunstein, and Rodney Smolla pursue goals such as truth discovery or good public policy and see free speech as an efficient means to these ends.[2] Early popularizers of a similar consequentialist argument include Roscoe Pound and Zechariah Chafee.[3] Expressivists focus on individual speakers, whereas these free speech libertarians focus on audiences.[4] Expressivists treat free speech as a good in itself rather than as a means to other goods.[5] They tend to use a language of dissent or defiance of societal norms by individuals, whereas libertarians value dissent for its effect of broadening the scope of public debates.[6]

There is an important expressivist tradition in the history of free speech debates, although the dominance of libertarian arguments under the First Amendment framework obscures that tradition. Early expressivists include American romantics such as Ralph Waldo Emerson and Walt Whitman and Germans such as Johann Gottfried von Herder, Friedrich von Schlegel, and Wilhelm von Humboldt.[7] Expressivism appears in legal decisions as well, albeit less prominently. Self-realization, or self-fulfillment, as a value to be served by free speech emerges as a part of the First Amendment tradition when Justice Brandeis asserts in his tantalizing concurrence in *Whitney v. California* that the Constitution's framers "valued liberty both as an end and as a means."[8] It is fair to say that Brandeis posed a challenge both to free speech theorists and to interpreters of the First Amendment to reconcile individual expressive freedom and social interests, a challenge that many have avoided.

However extensive this tradition of expressivism, older expressivist arguments fall short of a comprehensive defense of freedom of speech. A variety of efforts have been made to renew the expressivist justification of freedom of speech. These contemporary arguments share a number of features. Expressivist arguments that focus on individual creative acts are attractive initially for reasons independent of any social benefits that might result from such freedom. First, speech provides psychic and emotional benefits to individual speakers that other kinds of activities, such as reading, riding a bicycle, or smoking cigarettes, do not. Speaking offers a unique experience of freedom highly valued by individuals under many different kinds of political regimes. Regulation of speech can result in a number of emotional or psychic harms to the individual, such as feelings of repression or of being "bottled up." Second, freedom of speech may be a fundamental liberty to be considered independent of its consequences, good or bad, for the individual or society. The specific enumeration of freedom of speech in the Constitution might be recognized as evidence of the fundamental nature of free speech. Some expressivists passionately defend free speech absolutism grounded in the authority of the First Amendment.

Thomas Emerson's extended categorization of values served by freedom of expression begins with a description of self-fulfillment that neatly summarizes the contemporary expressivist argument: "First, freedom of expression is essential as a means of assuring individual self-fulfillment. The proper end of man is the realization of his character and potentialities as a human being. For the achievement of this self-realization the mind must be free. Hence suppression of belief, opinion, or other expression is an affront to the dignity of man, a negation of man's essential nature."[9] Emerson's description actually conflates two tightly woven strands in contemporary expressivism. The first strand emphasizes the direct, individual experience of performing expressive acts, that is, the experience of speaking, writing, or creating works of art. The second emphasizes a rich environment of expressive acts within which individuals create their individual acts of expression. A vibrant and diverse cultural context stimulates individual speakers and writers to spur their expressive efforts. This environment provides necessary support for goals described in the first strand of expressivism.

The two strands can be distinguished by the two different roles played by individual speech acts in a system of freedom of expression that values self-realization. In the first strand, the experience of performing expressive acts is directly relevant to the individual's efforts to realize his or her full potential. The realization of individual talents and abilities depends directly on creative acts such as speaking, writing, or painting that help locate and develop an as yet unrealized core self. In this first sense of self-realization, speech acts are intrinsically valuable to the individual speaker, and the right to free speech exists to protect and promote the individual interest in self-realization. Thus, writing is important because it is necessary for the writer's self-fulfillment, not because it contributes arguments or ideas to public debate. Similarly, sculpture, painting, and performance art are important activities for individuals, not crypto-political contributions to democratic deliberation.

In the second sense, individual expressive acts have a role in self-realization in that they contribute to a rich social environment of beliefs, opinions, and ideas from which other people may draw in their pursuit of self-realization. Such an environment promotes what Joshua Cohen has called the informational interest in freedom of speech.[10] At first the informational interest looks something like the consequentialist metaphor of the marketplace of ideas. Unlike the social consequences of the marketplace of ideas, however, exposure to this creative environment improves individuals who derive important benefits from the ideas found there. No single individual in isolation can spontaneously create every idea, piece of information, or potential life plan. But individuals exposed to the creative work of others can draw on the collected expression of their community while developing their own themes and ideas.[11] In solitary efforts to realize one's self, the isolated individual may never strike upon the ideas crucial to his or her potential. Individuals can, and often do, experience certain moments of inspiration or clarity upon reading a book, seeing a movie, or hearing a political speech that crystallize thoughts they have been unable to articulate. Memoirs and biographies are filled with these types of defining moments in people's lives.[12] Even the greatest creative genius relies upon the thought and expression of others in the realization of his or her potential. At the same time, the boy raised by wolves is surely unlikely to have realized his potential self (absent the possibility that he has a wolf-self).

The work of three contemporary First Amendment scholars—C. Edwin Baker, Martin Redish, and Steven Shiffrin—best represents these two strands of expressivism. Each scholar emphasizes different aspects of the general expressivist justification of freedom of speech but remains consistent with its key commitments. These contemporary expressivists, however, fail to overcome key challenges to their arguments.

C. Edwin Baker grounds his justification of freedom of speech (the "liberty theory") in a unitary "ethical postulate" of respect for ethically autonomous individuals that mandates self-fulfillment or self-realization as the key First Amendment value. Baker treats liberty as fundamental and argues that it implies democracy as a political system. At the same time, respect for liberty requires limits on democratic choice, such as those provided by constitutionalism (free speech, for instance). Constitutional rights claims provide a possible basis for the assertion of autonomy. Baker argues that "the practice of addressing claims to others arguably implies respect for the other as an equal or nondominated autonomous agent." While collective democratic decision making is crucial, constraints on democracy consistent with autonomy take precedence. From autonomy, Baker draws the implication that self-realization is a fundamental purpose of the First Amendment but admits that his independent justification for self-fulfillment is meager. "Nevertheless, without trying to develop further this justification for the centrality of these two values, . . . I will merely rely on the widely accepted conclusion that *individual self-fulfillment and participation in change are fundamental purposes of the First Amendment.*" Baker regards self-realization as a "commonsense notion" of the importance of speech.[13]

Baker's liberty theory emphasizes speakers' acts as the phenomenon of most concern to free speech theory.[14] A speaker's autonomy requires not only the free choice to speak but also autonomy in the choice of what to say. When the speaker does not choose the content of speech, the speaker is not autonomous, and free speech issues are irrelevant.

> Nevertheless, to the extent that speech is involuntary, is not chosen by the speaker, the speech act does not involve the *self*-realization or *self*-fulfillment of the speaker. Focusing on the self-expressive uses of speech directs the inquiry toward the responsible source, not the content, of the speech. For example, once a person is employed to say what she does, the speech usually represents not her own self-expression but, at best, the expression of the employer.[15]

Baker favors the creative potential of speech and language. "In each case either the speaker or the listener or both possess something new—new images, new capabilities, new opportunities, new amusements—that did not exist before and that were [*sic*] created by people's speech."[16] He offers a distinction between coercive and noncoercive speech to be used in determining what types of speech might be regulated. The creative potential of language allows speech to foster self-realization and culture building. This same potential suggests that some speech may be coercive, that it might restrict or disrespect the individual autonomy of listeners. Even though some coercive speech may contribute to the speaker's self-fulfillment, if that individual speaks without respect for the autonomy of the listeners by attempting to change the listeners' options (through fraud, perjury, or blackmail, for instance), then such speech may be regulated by the state.[17]

Unlike Baker, Martin Redish deals with both of the two strands in expressivist argument. Redish grants priority to self-realization over all other free speech values. "The institutional guarantee of free speech ultimately serves only one true value, which I have labeled 'individual self-realization.'" He adds that "to the extent that one accepts the value of free speech at all, one must necessarily accept the self-realization value, for there is no other." Redish inverts typical libertarian arguments that see free speech as a means to democracy to argue instead that democracy is valuable because it promotes self-realization. "The moral norms inherent in the choice of our specific form of democracy logically imply the broader value self-realization." Democracy is a form of collective self-rule, thus autonomy or individual self-rule is its ultimate purpose. Redish treats both strands in the contemporary expressivist position as aspects of self-realization.

He argues that other values generally at the heart of libertarian justifications of freedom of speech, such as a well-functioning political process, can be subsumed under self-realization and described only by reference to self-realization as the primary value.[18] Redish deals first with the sense of self-realization that concerns the self-development of an individual's talents and abilities to realize the individual's full potential. The focus of this strand is on the act of expression itself and how it leads to individual self-realization. The individual pursues his or her potential through performing expressive acts. Self-realization requires self-expression. Redish also explicitly addresses the second sense of self-realization, describing it as concerned with individual control over life-affecting decisions. In this sense, a free mind reflecting upon the wide spectrum of beliefs and opinions expressed by other individuals facilitates the realization of one's life goals. This second strand of self-realization rests on freedom of choice from a menu of ideas rather than on individual acts of expression.

Steven Shiffrin articulates an alternative argument that attempts to give content to self-realization and explain current First Amendment law within a romantic, expressivist framework. Shiffrin grounds his argument in the individual dissent and nonconformity that he believes characterize romanticism. He suggests that dissent is an American value, a key component of the American understanding of democracy, and that the protection of dissent is a neglected aspect of the meaning of the First Amendment. Shiffrin believes that dissent is a metaphor that encompasses many of the values that First Amendment doctrine relies upon, in addition to capturing the commonsense meaning of free speech to ordinary Americans. He bases his definition of dissent, and the values that it represents, on romanticism understood as a broad, coherent, historical movement including German, English, and American sources.[19] His specific analysis, however, rests almost completely upon the romanticism of Ralph Waldo Emerson and Walt Whitman.

Drawing on Emerson, Shiffrin constructs an argument for freedom of speech that focuses on the value of dissent understood as opposition to tradition, custom, existing institutions, and authority. He defines romantics as "those who would break out of the classical forms: the dissenters, the unorthodox, the outcasts." Furthermore, "The first amendment's [*sic*] purpose and function in the American polity is [*sic*] not merely to protect individual liberty, but also affirmatively to sponsor the individualism, the rebelliousness, the anti-authoritarianism, the spirit of nonconformity within us all."[20] His argument is extremely useful in highlighting some of the romantic quality and expressivist rhetoric of contemporary free speech debates. He is quite right to criticize the dominant marketplace metaphor and to suggest that there are many metaphors we could use in deciding free speech cases. Specifically, his argument that the U.S. Supreme Court might have to reconsider its precedents in cases involving access to the means of expression, freedom of speech in the workplace, and decency regulations promulgated by the Federal Communications Commission (FCC) are supported by expressivism.

The Case against Expressivism

Contemporary attempts to articulate expressivist justifications for freedom of speech are theoretically underdeveloped. For instance, Rodney Smolla describes one popular view of freedom of speech as "a right defiantly, robustly, and irreverently to speak one's mind *just because it is one's mind* . . . freedom to speak without restraint provides the speaker with an inner satisfaction and realization of self-identity essential to individual fulfillment." Smolla characterizes the argument for speech as an end in itself, as an individual right linked to satisfaction and individual fulfillment. This primarily rhetorical argument continues by suggesting that pleasure seeking through speech warrants more protection than other types of pleasure seeking because speech is linked to the human capacity to "think, imagine and create."[21] It sounds good, and most Americans would probably see something here with which to identify, but this simple expressivist formulation of freedom of speech is wide open to attacks that it is self-involved and incapable of dealing with the tension between an individual's freedom to speak and the social consequences of that speech.[22] Smolla does not make a strong case as to why a right to speak one's mind should outweigh the negative consequences such speech might have for other individuals or society in general. If one's mind is to express racial hatred in the form of racist epithets, it is not at all self-evident that the speaker's inner satisfaction and self-identity should be more important than the damage likely to be done to the satisfaction and identity of the person targeted. If expressivism is simply a defense of self-assertion, then it will be difficult for expressivists to answer criticisms based on the bad consequences of some kinds of speech. If all theories of freedom of speech must provide an account of how to balance individual liberty and the social consequences of speech, expressivism in the simple formulation above must fail, for it offers no such guidance.

While the libertarian justification of freedom of speech is consequentialist, linking protection of freedom of speech to social interests in truth, democracy, or a well-functioning political process, expressivism sees creative expression as a good in itself for the individual speaker. The problem with a personal good, whether a good in itself or a consequentially derived good, is that it suffers when situations demand that it be balanced against the social harm for which the individual is responsible. For instance, whatever the benefit to the individual of a treasonous speech act such as the publication of secret troop deployments during wartime, the harm of such speech to a society engaged in war probably outweighs the benefits to the traitor. Treason is a relatively easy case. Hate speech is more difficult. The conflict between the expressive benefits of hate speech to the individual speaker and the harm done to its targets and society is difficult to unpack.[23] Free speech libertarians ask not who should win or lose so much as which option, regulation or permissiveness, contributes more to the social interests in truth, good policy, or wide open public debate. Under expressivism, someone must lose out in the decision between regulation and nonregulation of hate speech. Either the self-fulfillment of the racist speaker is prevented by a prohibition of hate speech or the targeted listener, or society more generally, loses where such speech is allowed. Of course, any such balance also rests on the respective importance the speakers and listeners place on the injuries and benefits. If listeners have very thick skins and are never harmed by racist speech, there may be no conflict.

There are significant problems with contemporary formulations of expressivism. For instance, Baker takes the unitary value of self-realization in Emerson's constitutional history of the First Amendment as common sense instead of providing his own independent historical or analytical investigation of freedom of speech or its objectives.[24] Baker does not answer questions about the nature or meaning of the self raised by his account of autonomy (what is autonomous, for instance) or self-realization (what it is that will experience realization). Self-realization warrants substantial elucidation before a justification of freedom of speech can be built upon it. Ultimately, Baker leaves self-fulfillment or self-realization ambiguously defined by reference to a putative tradition and "common sense," does not take up the question of what sort of self is involved in free speech, and leaves policy makers with extremely difficult problems in distinguishing coercive from noncoercive speech.

Redish also fails to provide a very convincing account of the source or nature of self-realization as a value. He is purposely vague as to the definition of self-realization yet draws his theory from implications of that definition.[25] These implications remain as ambiguous as the definition itself. Furthermore, he posits self-realization as the ultimate political value but tells us nothing about what self-realization is while begging the question of what benefits self-realization might produce. Starting with American political practice, he argues that "the moral norms inherent in the choice of our specific form of democracy logically imply the broader value, self-realization." He then reduces the status of democracy to a secondary value that merely serves as a means to self-realization.[26] Redish investigates the possible reasons that the framers selected a democratic system and concludes that they must have done so to promote self-realization, although he recognizes that they did not mention, define, or articulate this value explicitly.

Because democracy is only one among several means to advance self-realization, Redish argues democracy must be considered a "subvalue" of self-realization.[27] He understands democracy as a kind of collective self-rule that implies self-realization as its ultimate goal. While collective self-rule may or may not imply individual self-realization, it does suggest the importance of exposure to a wide variety of ideas. Redish criticizes the exclusion from freedom of speech, especially by Meiklejohn and Bork, of all but political speech and believes that by subsuming democracy as a value under the broader concept of self-realization, his theory can account for an accordingly broader range of speech. However, the weight Redish attaches to the second strand of expressivism, the cultural context, brings his argument much closer to the libertarian justification he disputes so strongly and reduces the extent to which his account of self-realization maintains a genuine focus on individual expressive activity.[28]

Like Redish, Shiffrin focuses on the elements of romanticism that support an interpretation of the First Amendment similar to the second strand of expressivism, choice from a menu of beliefs and opinions. Shiffrin places dissent at the center of his argument but in a way that looks more like the libertarian justification than a new justification of freedom of speech based on the importance of self-realization. After introducing dissent as an alternative guiding light to First Amendment adjudication, he shifts ground and begins to discuss it as one of many ways to consider First Amendment cases. He is careful to link the value of dissent back to the social interests characteristic of libertarian arguments about free speech. While he distinguishes the dissent metaphor from the marketplace metaphor introduced by Justice Holmes, Shiffrin accepts the basic goals and methods of the arguments associated with the marketplace of ideas. He argues that "dissent is predominately a form of social engagement whether groups or individuals are leading the charge."[29] At first, the dissent metaphor was supposed to emphasize opposition to all traditions, institutions, and authority. But now dissent begins to look like a synonym for overt political activity that fits easily within the standard libertarian defense of free speech. While suggesting that his dissent view is distrustful of any statements about truth, Shiffrin invokes Mill's arguments about the search for truth and suggests that protection of dissent supports the diversity that Mill called for in the contest of ideas that leads to the truth.[30] Shiffrin does not address distinct questions about self-realization and speech as an end in itself that create tensions between individual rights and social interests. Shiffrin's dissent metaphor, while a useful legal argument, ties free speech to ends external to the individual self and ultimately does not move far from contemporary justifications grounded in social interests. In the end, Shiffrin resolves the tension between individual and social interests by emphasizing the ways in which individual speech fosters public discussion rather than the personal interest in self-realization.

There are several compelling arguments against expressivism that contribute to its relatively low status in contemporary thought on free speech. For one, Frederick Schauer maintains that reliance on the intrinsic value of speech is insufficient to protect speech as any more important than other kinds of conduct. "The argument for self-fulfillment suffers from a failure to distinguish intellectual self-fulfillment from other wants and needs, and thus fails to support a distinct principle of free speech."[31] According to Schauer, self-expression is an ambiguous concept that cannot be differentiated from other kinds of behavior. At best, self-development might help justify general liberty but cannot be distinguished from it. "But the most striking feature of all of these self-development theories is that they identify as the value underlying the principle of freedom of speech a value that is not peculiar to speech." Freedom of speech can promote self-realization or self-fulfillment, but so could other kinds of activities.

> I can also express myself in my attire, my occupation, my sexual activity and preferences, my residence, my hobbies and other recreations and so on. The list is virtually endless, and that is exactly the point. Communicating is obviously a form of self-expression, but it is by no means the form of self-expression that is most important to everyone. Thus, the argument from self-expression leads to the conclusion that all forms of self-expression are worthy of equivalent protection. As a result, it is impossible to distinguish an argument from self-expression as an argument for freedom of speech from an argument from self-expression as an argument for liberty in general.[32]

Schauer's free speech principle focuses on communicative activity in order to establish the distinctiveness and priority of speech over other rights. He holds that while self-fulfillment may be a good argument for freedom more generally, it offers little additional leverage as a justification of freedom of speech.[33] If we were to defend self-fulfillment as the important principle, we would have no way to argue for special protection of speech as compared to any other kind of activity that might lead to self-fulfillment. Schauer's chief concern appears to be that unless we regard speech as distinct from, and prior to, other kinds of conduct, we cannot escape the problem of balancing the value of speech to the individual speaker against harm caused by that speech.[34] "Thus we want to protect speech not because it causes no harm, but *despite* the harm it may cause. Our search for a justification, therefore, is a search for a reason to distinguish speech from the entire range of intentional actions."[35] The possibility then would exist that free speech would only be favored in situations in which it exacts few costs.

Sunstein takes up a criticism similar to Schauer's and maintains that while the argument from personal autonomy or self-fulfillment protects speech, it does a poor job because it cannot distinguish among different kinds of speech or explain current First Amendment law. While Sunstein hopes that judges will be sensitive to self-development interests in speech cases, he believes that ultimately only a political justification of free speech will work. History, our fear of government interference, and the particular weight of the threat to political speech support the need for protection of political speech, with a secondary concern for speech related to self-development.[36] Both Schauer and Sunstein point up the key tension between the individual right to speak as an end in itself favored by expressivists and the social interests in truth and robust public debate favored by libertarians. This tension exists because it is difficult to justify protection of individual speech without reference to broader social interests, particularly when this speech does not regard matters of public controversy. An individual's speech act announcing his or her state of mind, a judgment that something is aesthetically pleasing, or a basic desire does not immediately, in itself, warrant special protection any more than riding a bicycle or smoking. It is not that human self-fulfillment is unimportant in the eyes of critics of expressivist arguments, it is simply that self-fulfillment does not strike them as a good enough reason to protect speech when compared to the strong social interests that could conceivably be served by placing limits on fulfillment. Society may benefit from a prohibition on expressing one's state of mind loudly with a bullhorn or quietly by chain-smoking a pack of cigarettes.

Conflation of the two strands of expressivism also can be a problem, as can be seen in Redish's overly capacious definition of self-realization. His notion of self-realization is hopelessly broad and includes every conceivable speech act, with the possible exception of a string of obscenities. Standard arguments resting on the importance of speech to political decision making are too easily subsumed, along with every other kind of speech, under self-realization, since it is uncontroversial to suggest that the availability of political speech might be related to "life-affecting decisions." Redish knows that self-realization is the one true value served by free speech because "the moral norms inherent in the choice of our specific form of democracy logically imply the broader value, self-realization."[37] Unfortunately, he begs the question by leaning on the cultural context in a way that turns his argument into a defense of robust public debate rather than a defense of individual expressive activity. Also, Redish's loose definition of self-realization gives no explanatory leverage on the types of speech acts that we commonly and uncontroversially exclude from free speech protection.[38] He must fall back on a straightforward balancing argument, but his version of a self-realization principle offers no special guidance on how to establish a balance between self-realization and other, competing interests. It is not clear what role self-realization has in expressivism as long as it includes so much while little attention is given to fleshing out the importance of expressive activity beyond its role in fostering a rich menu of ideas.

In sum, expressivism in its current formulation lacks an account of why self-realization is a value to be distinguished from other important individual values. Even if expressivism did include such an account, it still lacks a clear explanation of why freedom of speech promotes self-realization in any special way. In light of these difficulties, it is hard to justify freedom of speech, and the possible harm associated with that speech, by reference to individualistic values such as self-realization. So far, expressivism faces several hurdles before it can succeed as a comprehensive justification of freedom of speech.

Reinvigorating Expressivism

Schauer's concern that expressivism insufficiently distinguishes free speech from other types of freedom is a serious one as long as self-expression is an ambiguous concept and the importance of self-realization to the individual is poorly defined. If self-realization is simply a question of one's saying or doing what one wants when one wants to, then it seems likely that costly speech will lack protection. If we were to investigate these concepts more carefully and come up with an account of the value of self-realization that was less ambiguous, Schauer's criticism that speech be distinguished from other forms of conduct can be overcome. Rather than a fundamental flaw of all arguments grounded in self-fulfillment, a weakness in the current state of thinking about self-fulfillment or self-realization creates the problem Schauer raises. Further investigation into what self-realization means might result in a different calculation of the individual benefits and social costs. On the other hand, renewed attention to the meaning and content of self-realization might suggest that the balancing of interests is the wrong way to approach the problem altogether.

What is the right way to balance individual benefits against the social harms of speech? We cannot determine the answer unless we first adequately describe those benefits and harms. Social harms such as wartime casualties resulting from treasonous speech, injuries sustained in riots, or general social unrest have relatively clear meanings in contemporary usage. Individual benefits such as self-realization do not. Second, the full consequences for individuals, and for society, of ignoring self-realization cannot be known or considered unless we investigate what self-realization is. It is not at all clear what, if anything, society gives up when it declines to grant priority to self-realization as a value in free speech arguments. Third, even if we grant priority to self-realization without an account of what it is (as Baker and Redish do) and believe that (without necessarily understanding why) individual self-realization trumps social interests, we will have no way to know if a regime of freedom of speech would advance self-realization as a value. Expressivists need to answer two questions: What is self-realization? Does speech promote self-realization? In other words, what is the relationship between self-realization and freedom of speech?

To be convincing, an individualistic, expressivist justification of freedom of speech must address the problem of establishing the link between speech and self-realization. We need a richer account of self-realization as a value than that prevalent in current expressivist works. To differentiate self-realization from other individualistic values, we must work from a compelling notion of self-realization. To a certain extent, a conception of self is implicit but underdeveloped in contemporary expressivist arguments. In the first strand of expressivism, the self is active, possesses a creative faculty of some kind, and strives to develop certain potentials. Corresponding to the second strand, the cultural context, the self is open to change based on exposure to the expression of others. These implicit features of the expressivist understanding of self are a good place to begin, but richer accounts can be given.

The self can be viewed as a source of truth, in contrast to the understanding of many free speech theorists that social processes lead to truth discovery.[39] In *Sources of the Self*, Charles Taylor argues that the inward turn in search of self-knowledge is characteristic of the self and the primary means by which the self can access natural truth. This philosophy of nature as source is, according to Taylor, a constituent part of modern culture. Another important feature of the self is the sense of the difference and originality of individuals.[40] To approach an understanding of the natural order, the individual seeks out his or her "inner voice." The self is not, then, engaged in a dynamic act of self-creation, as with Henry David Thoreau's heroic individual, but rather seeks knowledge through examination of the natural drives or impulses of the self. The external manifestation of this inward turn is in the form of the expression of sentiments. The individual who wants to know the truth strives to access the self, the inner voice known by sentiment.[41] Truth is found in individual feelings that are manifestations of the truth of nature located in the self.

The second important characteristic of the self to consider is its capacity for, or power of, creative imagination. The capacity for creative imagination combines with natural impulses to give a rich picture of an individual, original self that not only can but must engage in expressive activity.[42] The understanding of the self as a source of truth leads directly to important implications for understanding the idea of self-realization and the role that expression plays in it. Individuals do not simply access the inner voice and then make decisions accordingly. Self-knowledge comes instead from active engagement with the self. Expression is necessary, according to Taylor's account of expressivism, to make these inner truths manifest. "If our access to nature is through an inner voice or impulse, then we can only fully know this nature through articulating what we find within us."[43] In a modern sense, the act of expression gives shape to partially formed ideas and the vague notions of the inner voice. Expression is part and parcel of the inward turn because the natural impulses and drives that constitute the self cannot be fully known unless articulated in the more formal act of expression. Self-realization, the process of coming to know the inner truth of the self, requires expressive activity. For instance, the vague sentiments of the poet's self are not fully accessible to the poet absent the act of writing, or speaking, the poetry. As Taylor notes, "Fulfilling my nature means espousing the inner élan, the voice or impulse. And this makes what was hidden manifest for both myself and others." The act of formulation of one's inner voice defines the shape of one's life.[44] Taylor's sense of self-realization is as an activity that brings the self, the inner voice, to light, while also being a creative activity. The self is the source of expression, but expression further develops the vague impulses of the inner self.

Nancy Rosenblum investigates the romantic self and its implications for liberalism in *Another Liberalism*. From the diversity of literary romanticisms—American, English, and German—she offers an account of a sovereign self ruled by the "law of the heart."[45] To some extent, she derives the nature of the romantic self from the form of political organization favored by romantics to accommodate individual selves. Romantics favored anarchy to make room for heroic individuals who would express their unique individuality in the form of feelings usually left unexpressed. Romantic anarchy is built on a guarantee of privacy and the individual detachment necessary for the romantic to pursue individual emotional needs. Social and political engagement are ruled out by the extent to which the romantic individual is self-involved and unable to consider others.[46]

The characteristic feature of this self is dynamism unleashed by the individual's withdrawal from social life.[47] In contrast, the dynamic impulse of free speech libertarianism is found in social interaction in the marketplace of ideas or in political life. In Rosenblum's view, liberalism retains elements of romantic detachment in the form of protection of individual liberty against the state. However, modern liberals do not take this detachment to the anticivic and antisocial extremes of earlier romantic figures. Liberals value privacy as a means to protect rational activity, while for romantics, privacy represents withdrawal or detachment. Romantic detachment does not lead to stoic self-abnegation but rather to a different kind of engagement in the form of self-expression.[48] For romantics, the individual finds the source of innovation and development through turning inward toward the dynamic self. The creative impulse exists as a part of the individual self rather than as the product of social interactions or political processes. The self is neither an atomistic and static bundle of prepolitical preferences nor a passive consumer of the creative products of others.

Heroic self-assertion provides an important link between the dynamic nature of the self and freedom of speech. Society benefits from the creative efforts of the individual's inward turn that leads to heroic self-assertion (in the form of self-expression).[49] If the inward turn is solely a personal act with no outward expression, there may be no political reason to care about the creative efforts of the individual. At the same time, if we grant priority to individual creativity but it has no social or political consequences, then privacy is called for, not necessarily freedom of expression. Personal privacy would be sufficient to protect the inward turn if heroic self-assertion were separable from the creative processes of the self. For example, if the only aspect of the self we cared about was the dynamic, creative impulse, a general social policy protecting personal privacy would be sufficient to promote the individual interest, even if there was also a general social policy of strict censorship of expression. Privacy would protect the efforts of the poet to compose poetry in the inward domain of his or her own thoughts or even in writing if the paper copies were kept locked away. If we only care about the poet's creative life of the mind and not expression, we could certainly prohibit the poet from making his or her poems public, but something about a regime of strong privacy and strong censorship strikes a very sour note. There must be more than internal dynamism to this romantic self for freedom of expression to matter. There must be a way in which expression itself is a constituent part of the romantic self. Thoreau's heroic self-assertion must be intrinsic to the creative self and not just a social value.

While contemporary accounts of English and American romantics do not provide sufficient reason to believe that the self relies on expression to the extent that we can build a justification of freedom of speech on it, German romantics do provide that connection. Friedrich von Schlegel and Wilhelm von Humboldt offer especially rich sources for conceptions of the self and the relationship between self, self-realization, and expression.[50] While the romantic movement of the late eighteenth and early nineteenth centuries is far removed from the American constitutional and legal context, the movement's philosophical innovations are an excellent source for the articulation of a definition of the self that can be used to strengthen and improve the contemporary expressivist justification of freedom of speech. The characteristic feature of German romantic thought is its reliance on individual creative activity to realize human freedom. While Charles Taylor focuses his analysis of romanticism on nature as the source of truth, German romantics were very much concerned with the realization of freedom and individual potential as the complete development of the individual's creative and moral faculties.[51] Consider Humboldt: "The true end of man, or that which is prescribed by the eternal and immutable dictates of reason, and not suggested by vague and transient desires, is the highest and most harmonious development of his powers to a complete and consistent whole."[52]

According to Humboldt and Schlegel, the self is original and capable of freedom understood as self-determination.[53] Each argues, however, that the self is not usually free.[54] Instead, most individuals fail to live a fully human life; they are not free, and their decisions are determined by factors external to their own will. In this sense, the individual's decision to rescue a drowning child may be a matter of free will, or the Samaritan's true nature, or awareness of moral codes of right behavior, or a simple desire not to be seen as a bad person.[55] For romantics, freedom lies in acting from free will. The key intellectual problem that they faced was how to become free, how to become autonomous and independent of external causality. Autonomy is not a birthright for the romantics, nor is it assumed on the basis of a social contract or a constitution of enumerated rights.[56] It is a goal to be pursued by an active process of self-realization. Self-realization, in this view, means that the individual avoids determination by external causes, that the individual acts on the basis of free will.[57] Social interaction and the exercise of power by the state partially determine the development of the self and therefore undermine freedom.[58] Unfortunately, autonomy is an elusive goal, which leads to infinite striving, in the form of creative activity, after self-realization.

Humboldt is the most individualistic of the romantics, but there is a communitarian theme running through romantic thought as well. This socially oriented strand concerns the idea of cultivation or self-development (*Bildung*).[59] Without limiting the importance of spontaneous creative imagination, self-development also involves interaction with others. At the most extreme is Herder's understanding of belonging to the group or culture, that the individual self manifests through creative expression playing on the beliefs and traditions of the culture.[60] Goethe, for example, expresses his own individuality through developing themes of German mythology and his attachment to the German culture. While the self is particular, it thrives on the shared imagination and culture of the group.

Schlegel also develops the theme of *Bildung*, while emphasizing the primary importance of the creative faculty of the individual author striving after freedom.[61] For Schlegel, self-development is necessary for the ultimate realization of freedom and the fully human life.[62] In addition, the link between self and expression is most clear in Schlegel's romantic thought. Creative, expressive acts constitute a process of direct and individual realization of self-determination or freedom. Poetry, for Schlegel, expresses "the entire spirit of an author," and romantic poetry "alone is infinite, just as it alone is free; and it recognizes as its first commandment that the will of the poet can tolerate no law above itself."[63] Creative thought has the power to bring about a harmony of nature (the self) and freedom from external determination, that is, the power to promote self-realization.[64]

The Self, Self-Realization, and Freedom of Speech

The romantic understanding of self-realization shows that freedom of speech is important not because people are free, or ought to be free, but because they pursue freedom. C. Edwin Baker grounds freedom of speech in an ethical postulate of equal respect for the inborn autonomy of persons.[65] Schauer criticizes this type of autonomy because it justifies many different kinds of freedom of action and fails to distinguish speech from other activities.[66] Romantic self-realization, however, can distinguish speech from other types of activities and support a justification of freedom of speech when the meaning of self-realization is clarified and its relationship to speech more clearly articulated. Expression is the practical activity that allows individuals to pursue the freedom that they are not born with. In contrast, the freedom to ride a bicycle or smoke cigarettes is not related to the pursuit of freedom itself.[67] These are possible freedoms, but the performance of these actions does not lead to more freedom or to a new kind of freedom. One can exercise the freedom to smoke, but smoking is as far as that goes in most circumstances.[68] If we have the freedom to smoke, then we may choose to smoke or not, but smoking is all we get from the exercise of the freedom to smoke. Expressive activity is different in that expression actually leads to more freedom, it is not simply the exercise of a guaranteed freedom. Speech has a special claim on protection when we understand it as the pursuit of freedom, while it lacks a special claim on protection when it is no more than the exercise of an existing freedom.

Expressivists value the full development of individual powers toward their full potential. Self-realization, in this view, is an active process rather than the exercise of a guaranteed right. The active sense of self-realization helps to distinguish speech from other activities. It is very important that speech have special, even fundamental status compared to other activities. But it is also important that that status be supported by more than mere assertion or the strength of "common sense." When we look at the right to smoke or the right to own handguns, we must make policy judgments that balance those rights against their negative social consequences. Smoking has negative secondary effects on nonsmokers, therefore smoking may be restricted. Smokers have no more claim to a right than nonsmokers. Handguns also have negative social consequences for victims of gun crimes and accidents. Gun owners have stronger rights claims than smokers because of the Second Amendment, but the regulation of gun ownership and use is still compelling because of the seriousness of the harms that occur under a regime of nonregulation. Gun ownership is different from speech. It is an exercise of an externally guaranteed right, and it is a kind of action (possession); but it is not like speech because it does not promote individual self-development or the further development of new freedom.

Self-realization also distinguishes speech from commercial activity. While the freedom to engage in commerce, to practice a trade, or to pursue business activities is very important, in a market society such freedom is not as important to the individual as speech. While the Constitution and American political practice grant high status to commercial practices and locate this freedom near the core of protected liberty, we also accept vast regulation of business activities. We balance the benefits of free commerce with its social harms, such as pollution, fraud, risk of injury, and bad aesthetics. Commercial speech plays no role in individual self-realization or self-development, therefore expressivism is consistent with regulation of commercial speech. Regulation of commercial speech may be called for in those instances where it interferes in individual expressive activity, as when a tidal wave of commercial speech drowns out individual expressive speech acts.

Expressivism differentiates speech from substantially regulated activities such as smoking, gun ownership, and commerce. It shows that speech is special, that speech should not be open to regulation in the same way that other common forms of conduct can be regulated. Speech is different because it is more than just the exercise of a constitutionally protected freedom. Expressivism demonstrates that there is an intimate link between self-realization and speech that does not exist for other activities. Neither selling cigarettes nor trading pork bellies exhibits the special relationship to self-realization that distinguishes speech from other activities.

Expressivism grounded in the romantic understanding of self-realization distinguishes freedom of speech as intrinsically good because it represents individual striving after autonomy. In this sense, a modified expressivism still values the cultural context for creative expression favored by contemporary expressivist accounts such as Shiffrin's or Redish's. However, in the modified version, both strands of expressivism are more closely related than under the contemporary version. In the second strand of contemporary expressivism, protection of freedom of speech is a means to provide individual freedom of choice from a menu of ideas. This rich environment of expressed ideas and beliefs is important in a modified expressivist argument. The significance of the availability of ideas is that cultural and historical context partially determines the self, and the individual draws on shared imagination for his or her own process of individual expression. Public expression of one's own ideas is a part of this cultural context, although it is the activity of expression in public, as well as in private, more than the content of the ideas that is important.[69] Expression forms social bonds, but expression also draws on those bonds for support. Thus, freedom of speech generates more speech and at the same time is the activity of seeking freedom. Freedom of speech is a self-supporting cultural process as much as it is an individual pursuit.

Exposure to culture and the expression of others has a developmental effect on the individual, according to the romantic sources.[70] Art exposes people to new ideas important to their individual life choices and decisions in the same way that freedom of political speech exposes individuals to options in their political choices. The contemporary expressivist account of self-realization is similar to the cultural aspects of *Bildung*. By emphasizing the cultural context strand of expressivism, however, Shiffrin and others protect the individual more as a member of an audience than as an expressive agent. Their view protects freedom of choice from a menu of ideas, but the romantic sense of cultivation should tie this choice directly to the activity of expression. Culture, in the romantic view, produces effects in listeners that are manifested in their expressive activities. The option to choose from a diverse array of aesthetic material does matter, but unless individuals express their own ideas, the freedom to choose from the production of others does little to help them gain their freedom. Passive choices are externally determined, and individuals have had a minimal role in developing themselves or determining the choice. Freedom of choice is not sufficient to secure self-realization. The choices made must also translate into further expressive activity. Freedom of speech is not a right to consume, it is a liberty of action.

The activity of expression allows the individual to tap emotional and sensual resources that indicate an inner source of truth. Charles Taylor argues that this view of inner truth is a constituent part of the modern self, but this view is missing from current free speech theory.[71] Cultivation is meant to promote and develop inner truth. Inner truth is not a preformed, essential fact about an individual that simply emerges through a process. Instead, it is a combination of the core of the individual's personality and the experiences and context of that person's life. Such combinations are described by many of the romantics. Schlegel, for instance, wants to pursue the infinity of actual human life, its variety and endless possibilities, but he also realizes that individuals pursue this infinity, in part, through the experience of poetry and art. Humboldt demands a minimal state that guarantees negative liberty in order to allow the strictly individual elements of the personality to make choices unfettered by the state, but he also understands social experiences and cultural context to be important to those individual choices.

Limits on freedom of speech are restrictions on the practical activity of expression, thus such restrictions are obstacles to self-realization. Expressivism identifies a variety of possible threats to freedom of speech. Obviously, state censorship poses serious problems. Direct censorship of the arts is a common enough occurrence, even in the United States, to warrant special attention. Censorship prevents the outward, public expressive activity necessary for self-realization. In addition, when the state prohibits specific speech acts or whole forms of expression, it limits the diversity and range of material from which individuals may draw in their own expressive activities. When the state removes art works from public display, as in the censorship of the Cincinnati Arts Center's Robert Mapplethorpe show, it blocks the expressive activity of the individual artist and removes specific points of view from the menu of cultural choices.[72] Also, a general law that, for instance, prohibits mimes from performing in public places, popular as such a law might be, is an obstacle both to the expressive pursuit of freedom by affected mimes and to those who might learn from the mimes or be drawn into mime performance themselves. The problem with state censorship, in expressivist arguments, is that it directly blocks expression by artists and preempts the expression that audience members may produce in the future as a result of having been exposed to the artwork in question.

One problem with the libertarian justification of free speech is that the focus on audiences and a "robust public debate" privileges the most famous speakers while providing little in the way of encouragement for ordinary speakers. Participation cannot be limited to a few articulate opinion leaders or commercial producers of ideas. Expressivism shows that participation through speech must be widespread and common. Unfortunately, the current norm regards speech as a liberty only a few choose to exercise, protected more for the *New York Times* or recognized artists than for citizens more generally. Expressivism renews the democratic notion of a participatory population, not by reinterpreting all speech to have political importance but by showing that expression matters to everyone independent of the worth of their speech or the significance of the social contribution that their speech might make. Instead of asking which speech is socially valuable (or potentially valuable), expressivists consider the value of the speech to the individualist project of self-realization.

The expressivist justification is more appropriate to certain kinds of speech acts than are free speech libertarian arguments. While some artistic speech can accurately and legitimately be described as political speech, thus falling within the core of libertarian arguments, much artistic speech does not. Art constitutes its own category of speech act, one that can only be treated appropriately by a justification of freedom of speech that recognizes why artistic expression matters. Meiklejohn, Sunstein, and others recognize our intuition that artistic speech must be protected in any meaningful system of freedom of speech, but the impulse to place all kinds of speech under the umbrella of a monistic account of free speech leads them to redefine art as a kind of politics so that it will fit their consequentialist argument. This does a disservice both to artistic and political speech. It is disturbing that all controversial art must be justified as a political statement when in fact it may represent a manifestation of diverse ways of life or even the idiosyncratic pursuit of self-realization by a unique artist.[73] Many individuals engaged in artistic expression have no interest in politics; their work should be protected speech whether or not an outside evaluator (art experts, judges, juries) ascribes the status of political speech to it.

Expressivism is useful for debates about the boundaries of free speech. Libertarian arguments, through the capacious definitions of political speech necessary to bring art within the purview of their justification, expand the boundaries of speech even farther than they intend. For example, free speech libertarians protect commercial speech and advertising on the same basis as individual political and artistic speech. They treat corporations as First Amendment speakers. While corporations are rights-bearing entities in many contexts and subject to criminal penalties in others, this move constitutes a major shift in the way that we think about speech rights. The shift would make sense if we focus only on audiences, on the supply of information to consumers rather than on the speech acts of speakers. If advertising is considered to be just more speech about matters of public importance, there is no more justification for restriction of commercial speech than there is for restriction of political or artistic speech. In the United States, commercial speech has never been protected in this way.[74]

Meiklejohn, for instance, originally thought that radio warranted no First Amendment protection because programming was motivated by profit.[75] Baker criticizes all profit-oriented speech as coercive and therefore undeserving of protection.[76] Mark Graber also suggests that profit-oriented speech may not qualify for protection under a theory of free speech grounded in political membership.[77] Aside from a full-blown critique of capitalism that would be far outside the scope of speech debates, it is difficult to understand why profit-oriented speech should be singled out for such strong criticism. Expressivism can help explain why corporate or commercial speech lies outside the boundaries of freedom of speech. Corporations do not have expressivist interests; they have no self to realize or to develop. Advertisements are just as relevant to political life as many artworks, but historically courts and First Amendment scholars have treated art and advertising in very different ways.[78] Expressivism can separate art from advertising and other commercial speech through the focus on the speaker and on individual self-realization.

Finally, expressivism contributes a kind of intellectual honesty to debates over the meaning and boundaries of freedom of speech. There are many romantics writing about free speech but few expressivists. Many academic free speech theorists and many First Amendment advocates show, in one form or another, romantic expressivist commitments. Their public statements would be more convincing if they would acknowledge that expressivism motivates their interest in freedom of speech. Expressivist arguments are a lot harder to make and produce more gray areas than arguments expressed in the consequentialist public reasons of shared social benefits. It is easier to justify the costs of speech (offensiveness, hate speech, damage to national security) by reference to social benefits such as democracy or good public policy. But there is strong, visceral opposition to censorship that does not stem from a love of democracy or a commitment to efficient social policy. The expressivist self is a part of the modern liberal self, and it demands the freedom to pursue self-realization.

The expressivist justification of freedom of speech as it relates to self-realization protects a wide range of artistic, religious, moral, and emotional speech, but it fails as a comprehensive justification. It protects other kinds of speech as secondary concerns. Political speech, for instance, is not a central concern of expressivism unless political speech has a role to play in individual self-realization. Everyday political speech motivated by self-interest or advocacy for certain distributive arrangements may not contribute to self-realization in the expressivist sense and would have minimal support in expressivist justifications of freedom of speech. For example, typical lobbying and campaigning activities or writing to a senator in support of a particular bill likely would not fit the expressivist justification of freedom of speech. On the other hand, political expression is important to the self-realization of those for whom politics takes the form of active engagement in public life. This active sense of politics, while compatible with expressivism, is by no means the standard definition of political speech. Libertarians protect political speech in order to preserve a kind of political procedure that expressivism does not encompass. Distinguishing between the two kinds of politics is difficult in practice; thus expressivism is not particularly protective of political speech.

Expressivism is not an absolutist defense of free speech. All justifications for freedom of speech must eventually provide for some balance between speech and competing goods. For free speech libertarians, this is fairly straightforward, as the same social interests that typically have the strongest claim against speech are the ones that support the justification of freedom of speech. Expressivist justifications, as Schauer and others point out, offer little guidance as to how to balance individual self-realization against security, progress, social harmony, and other social interests. The absolute primacy of expressive activity as a means to self-realization is problematic. Restrictions on speech constitute an obstacle to self-realization and the pursuit of freedom, but expression has many consequences for other members of society and for social relations themselves. To deny the expression of an individual's "inner truth" or the pursuit of his or her full potential is a serious burden to place on that individual. Thus, competing interests must be very compelling before we can accept regulation of speech. Nonetheless, such interests will predominate in certain contexts, and in at least some cases, speech will have to be regulated. Expressivism has lacked a clear account of how to balance self-realization with other values. It has limited resources to explain which social interests may be more important than individual self-realization. A key objection to expressivism is that in its breadth, it offers no clear account of the exclusion of certain undesirable kinds of speech, such as racist hate speech or libel. Baker's version of expressivism, for instance, would exclude hate speech, pornography, commercial speech, and profit-motivated speech of any kind from protection. He argues that expression that is, or attempts to be, coercive should be excluded from protection.[79] Such a narrow theory protects too little and cannot be explained without appeal to values external to expressivism. If we take Baker's argument at face value, he would have to exclude freedom of the press because most news organizations are for-profit corporations. He also would have to exclude most art and literature because, ultimately, artists make their living by selling their work for profit.

The expressivism I propose improves this justification of freedom of speech in two ways. First, expressivism provides a tight link between self-realization and speech that shows that speech is distinct from other activities and cannot be balanced easily against other values. Because balancing will always be necessary, expressivism must give some guidance on how to balance speech against other values in those cases where expressivism is the most appropriate justification for freedom of speech. Thus, for instance, expressivism will not tell us much about the balance between political speech and political stability because that balance is best covered under contemporary libertarian arguments. In the context of art, an improved expressivism provides much better grounds for balancing speech against social costs such as offensiveness or immorality. Free speech libertarians, when faced with the balance between art and offensiveness, must fall back on identification of art as a kind of politics.[80] Expressivists are more likely to protect art as art because offensiveness is a question of little importance to self-realization.

An expressivism that carefully considers the concept of the self, the value of self-realization, and the relationship between free speech and self-realization has many strengths to contribute. The objections to expressivism raised by Schauer, Sunstein, and others can be better addressed by increased attention to individual expressive activity rather than by attempts to use the socially oriented cultural context to make expressivism compatible with standard libertarian justifications of freedom of speech. The first strand of expressivism posits that speech is an activity that is important in and of itself. Expressivists understand the self to be potentially active. Libertarians accept that individuals speak infrequently and more commonly participate merely as passive consumers in the marketplace of ideas. It is expressive activity itself that provides the possibility of freedom, not the externally determined range of possible opinions and matters for debate offered by libertarian free speech theory.

Increased attention to definitions of the value of self-realization and an increased focus on individual creative activity promise a richer, more compelling expressivist justification of freedom of speech. At the same time, expressivism by itself would be inadequate to deal comprehensively with the full range of questions and problems raised by speech.

CHAPTER FOUR

Equality and the Egalitarian Justification

When the subject of the relationship between free speech and equality is raised, criticism of hate speech and pornography often first comes to mind.[1] If equality and freedom of speech are necessarily at odds, as some have cast it, then there could be no distinct egalitarian justification of free speech. While some egalitarians argue for new limits on certain kinds of speech, others present what can be considered to be an egalitarian justification of free speech. This misunderstands the situation, however, because these are not the only issues relevant to an egalitarian idea of free speech. Unfortunately, since debate over speech and equality focuses on hate speech and the critics of hate speech have not done well in the courts, the case for egalitarianism seems to many people to be weak.[2] Even if arguments against hate speech fall short, not all egalitarians are primarily concerned with hate speech or want the state to regulate speech that reflects or exacerbates subordination. In fact, Ronald Dworkin claims that equality requires protection of the speech of pornographers and racists. This chapter examines a more general egalitarian justification of freedom of speech that is not limited to the issues of hate speech and pornography. Egalitarianism, particularly the Dworkinian version, parallels both libertarianism and expressivism in that it attempts, but ultimately fails, to provide a comprehensive justification for freedom of speech.

The vitriolic rhetoric of hate speech debates is matched only by the ambiguity of the justifications for freedom of speech underlying these arguments. The call for regulation emerges in the form of egalitarian criticism of current legal protection of hate speech and pornography under the First Amendment.[3] Those who support this position seek to create a new exception to free speech along the lines of other exceptions commonly accepted within the First Amendment framework. However, the most prominent critics of hate speech do not provide an independent, positive justification for free speech. This makes it very difficult to see the many and complex ways in which equality and speech are intertwined and the effects restriction of hate speech might have on that complex relationship. The debate is often seen as one between egalitarians and libertarians with clearly differentiated views, one side favoring equality as the primary value, the other elevating liberty. It is not as simple as that. Some consequentialists may allow the regulation of pornography, while some egalitarians insist on protecting racist hate speech.[4]

A comprehensive egalitarian justification should protect political speech, artistic expression, and other kinds of speech, as well as widely protect the opportunity to speak. It is not a justification, comprehensive or otherwise, simply to take for granted extensive protection of freedom of speech and then carve out exceptions to that general rule. We need to be able to see the relationship between the reasons that justify free speech and where it may not be justifiable at all. Ronald Dworkin presents a positive egalitarian justification of free speech that proves to protect speakers against state interference but fails as a comprehensive justification because it does not account for the effects of private power on the real opportunity for speech.

Equality of Status

In debates over speech policy, there are two distinct senses of the term "equality." Each identifies a useful, valid conception of equality, but the two do not lead to the same conclusions when applied to speech. This exacerbates confusion over what is at stake in egalitarian speech arguments and makes it much harder to see that there is a positive egalitarian justification for free speech. For clarity, I will refer to one sense of equality as equality of status and to the other as equality of respect. Ronald Dworkin is the most prominent advocate of equality of status, which primarily pertains to equal treatment of all by the state. Equality of respect focuses on the substantive quality of race and gender relations in the context of private power. In the United States, this view is favored by, among others, Catharine MacKinnon and many critical race theorists.[5] The dispute between these competing kinds of equality cannot be resolved by simple reference to the Constitution, nor does the Constitution provide for a balance between them. It is equally futile to turn to philosophy for a clear determination. These are distinct conceptions with very different implications for free speech.

American constitutional theorists generally look for the meaning of equality in the Fourteenth Amendment's equal protection clause, but this clause, in and of itself, is remarkably unhelpful in directing us toward an unequivocal definition.[6] Extensive case law has developed around this clause, and the clause has grown in importance over time as the U.S. Supreme Court has applied it to issues ranging from school segregation to contraception and abortion.[7] Even with this extensive constitutional history, it is difficult to ascertain the meaning of equality for purposes of egalitarian speech claims. Defenders of status equality and advocates of substantive equality of respect each claim constitutional authority for their definitions of equality. Since the Constitution fails to resolve this problem even for purposes of First Amendment theory, it is unlikely to resolve the problem for broader theoretical debates about the meaning of free speech.

In *Taking Rights Seriously*, Dworkin defines equality of status as the "right of each man to be treated equally without regard to his person or character or tastes." Equality is guaranteed to all "human beings with the capacity to make plans and give justice."[8] Initially, Dworkin derives this view of equality as a necessary step to make sense of the systematic arguments for liberty in John Rawls's *Theory of Justice* rather than locating equality in the constitutional structure. In recent work, Dworkin derives the right to equality from the Constitution and from legal practice rather than as constituent of Rawlsian liberty.[9] Like critics Matsuda and MacKinnon, Dworkin now looks to the central guarantee of equality in the Fourteenth Amendment's equal protection clause as well as the historical context of the framing of the Civil War amendments (the Thirteenth, Fourteenth, and Fifteenth) for guidance. As in his earlier work, equality continues to mean equality of status. In his recent work, Dworkin argues that this is the clear meaning to be found in the Constitution as well as in analytic liberal theory. What Dworkin now calls "citizen equality" requires the government to protect equal participation of citizens as individuals but does not require that these citizens have equal influence over outcomes.[10]

Equality of status is an abstract concept when compared to more tangible ideas of material equality of outcomes or the majoritarian political principle of one person, one vote. Dworkin rejects simple majoritarianism as a description of constitutional democracy in favor of moral membership in the political community, membership marked by full participation in the decisions of the community. The Bill of Rights and the Fourteenth Amendment require that "government must treat everyone as of equal status and with equal concern."[11] Dworkin's understanding of equal status focuses clearly on the way that the state treats individuals rather than on the relations between individuals or on actual outcomes of the political processes that meet his conditions for equal treatment under the law. As long as the state treats individuals as having equal status in their participation in political procedures, the "egalitarian command of the Constitution" is met.[12] The idea is not to guarantee equal material outcomes for individuals, or to guarantee any specific sorts of relationships between citizens or the groups to which they belong, but rather to guarantee a certain kind of relationship between the state and the individual. Dworkin seeks to avoid state action whereby the state systematically excludes anyone from participation in the decision-making process, but he does not rule out the possibility that private speech, absent some state action, may have the same undesirable effect. He argues that limits on hate speech, for instance, violate citizen equality because they clearly limit the speech of some racist speakers while convincing empirical evidence that these limits will mitigate the silencing effect of hate speech is lacking.[13] That is, as long as those who maintain that hate speech violates citizen equality cannot prove that claim, any state action that certainly does violate the equal treatment of some speakers must be prohibited.[14]

Kenneth Karst presents a similar analysis of equality. In his view, the Fourteenth Amendment clearly guarantees equal citizenship based on the capacity of citizens for responsibility and respect.[15] The constitutional guarantee of equality is expressed in Supreme Court decisions such as *Brown v. Board of Education* and the civil rights jurisprudence that followed. Karst also identifies this same concern with equality in American civic culture and history.[16] He goes on to find a concern with stigma and stereotype enshrined in these constitutional decisions that suggests that full citizenship involves freedom from stigmatization under the law.[17] The consequences of stigmatization manifest themselves in unequal social relations. Like Dworkin, Karst places responsibility for unequal status on the state acting through legislation to create or express stigmatizing associations on group membership. Thus, Jim Crow laws were the expression, through law, that African Americans were not full participants in American political life, that they were not to have equal status or equal respect. A decision like *Brown* expresses the opposite position in that it invalidates the stigmatizing law and promotes inclusion within the community of citizens.

Through their state-centered view of equality, Dworkin and Karst attempt to offer a comprehensive justification of freedom of speech. They arrive at different policy conclusions but work in a similar egalitarian vein. Rather than starting with an empirical assessment that inequality is a feature of American political and social life and a normative commitment that must be addressed and overcome, Dworkin and Karst see egalitarianism as a defining characteristic of American civic culture and constitutional law. Their project is not to promote equality by invoking the regulatory state to create an exception to free speech. Instead, they derive a complete speech policy from the principle of equality that they see as a central point of constitutional agreement. Dworkin and Karst identify different obstacles to the realization of free speech created by state action, while they treat private harms to respect as secondary concerns.

In his version of egalitarianism, Dworkin emphasizes political participation and argues that restrictions on state power, rather than legal restrictions on speech acts with bad consequences, are necessary to advance citizen equality. Restrictions on individual speech deny the equal status due to citizens by suggesting that their views are beneath respect or that these individuals are not morally responsible for their speech. To restrict speech is to deny the censored individual full participation. "Equality demands that everyone, no matter how eccentric or despicable, have [*sic*] a chance to influence policies as well as elections."[18] For Dworkin, this means that restrictions on pornography, like those suggested by MacKinnon, deny the equality of pornographers and curtail their citizenship. Dworkin is not oblivious to the kinds of harms detailed by MacKinnon in her criticism of pornography, but for Dworkin, they are secondary to the harms of unequal treatment of citizens by the state. Freedom of speech is important "because it is an essential and 'constitutive' feature of a just political society that government treat all its adult members, except those who are incompetent, as responsible moral agents."[19] Dworkin's priority is equal status before the power of the law, rather than equal social status in private relations between individuals or groups. Thus, he favored the outcome in *R.A.V. v. St.*

Paul, in which the Supreme Court ruled, in an opinion written by Justice Antonin Scalia, that cities may not proscribe certain kinds of fighting words (racist ones in this ordinance) if they do not proscribe the entire category of fighting words altogether.[20] An ordinance against cross burning and swastikas persecutes some ideas, hence some individuals who express these ideas, while protecting others. For Dworkin, equal status means that the state acts in such a way that it does not deny each individual an equal chance to participate in collective decisions. Laws that violate this idea of equality would include poll taxes and Jim Crow laws, selective bans on entry into professions, and censorship.[21]

An obvious question to ask of Dworkin's position is a version of the old tolerance of the intolerant paradox. If freedom of speech is justified by a view of equality grounded in the premise of moral responsibility, we might ask if the racist hate speaker or Holocaust revisionist has abdicated that responsibility by taking up a position intolerant of others. If the racist's position is that others should not have equal status or respect due to their race, then the racist has excluded himself or herself from the community by not sharing its commitment to equality. Again, Dworkin focuses on the relationship between the individual and the state and argues that the state loses its legitimacy in its relationship with the racist if it denies his or her moral responsibility and equality while also treating other citizens (the audience of the racist speech) as less than morally responsible for their own reactions to the speech.[22] The state must respect the rights of the racist speaker to make a contribution to the "moral climate" as well as respect the capacity of the audience to reject those racist views in favor of views more compatible with a community of equal status.

Karst also opposes laws such as these because they are expressions by the state that those subject to such laws are not full members of the community. Not only will these people be subject to illegitimate laws that restrict their freedom, the state will send a message of stigma that other people should also treat those subject to the restrictive laws as outsiders. Karst draws conclusions similar to Dworkin's from the egalitarian premise but builds on these to include some of Matsuda's and MacKinnon's concerns. Where Dworkin sees any infringement by the state on the content of speech as denying the equality of citizens, Karst argues that state power and law are implicated in social inequality in ways that restrict the freedom of speech of minority group members. For Dworkin, membership in the community is a function of treatment by the state, but for Karst, membership is also a function of treatment by other people. Karst's principle of equal citizenship "presumptively insists that every individual is entitled to be treated by the organized society as a respected and responsible participant. Stated negatively, the principle presumptively forbids the organized society to stigmatize an individual as a member of an inferior or dependent caste, or as a nonparticipant."[23] Direct state action to deny individuals equal citizenship is central to the problem, but the concern with stigma is only partly a problem of state action. The state contributes to stigmatization through laws that exclude groups, but stigma is acted upon by citizens. That is, the costs to stigmatized groups are only partly exacted by state action. Stigmatized groups may be discriminated against in employment, education, and use of public facilities by citizens acting from beliefs that result from those stigmas. Karst offers as an example Colorado's constitutional amendment prohibiting local communities from passing gay rights ordinances. This amendment has the effect of inhibiting expression (coming out is more dangerous), creating a stigma that excludes gay Coloradoans from full participation, and fostering privately inflicted harms.[24]

Karst's remedy for inequality goes far beyond the arguments made by Dworkin or even the critics of hate speech, for he proposes "the reacculturation of scores of millions of people" through "symbolic speech" (state policies) such as the integration of public spaces to create "a more inclusive conversation."[25] Rather than restrictions on private hate speech and pornography, Karst advocates civil rights legislation and decisions in the courts that promote integration and thereby foster equality, because these are speech by the state that minority groups previously excluded by law are now included. Obviously, this goes far beyond the requirements of even a broadly construed First Amendment or other theory of freedom of speech.[26] Where Matsuda would restrict a certain class of speech (racist hate speech) to promote substantive equality, Karst favors promotion of substantive equality to "create a more inclusive conversation" and "encourage listening across our cultural boundaries."[27] In the end, Karst leaves behind the egalitarian justification of freedom of speech to promote the project of substantive equality directly. He calls for "a generous definition of first amendment freedoms" for women and minorities to allow for liberating expression to promote the equality of these groups.[28] Increased access to public spaces leads to liberating expression, which leads to greater substantive equality. Karst's definition of First Amendment freedoms leaves the Constitution behind as he describes an egalitarian program that, desirable or not, is no longer a program of freedom of speech. Many of the policies he calls for, such as civil rights laws and affirmative action, are already in place, so his proposal is not for radi-

cal social change in that sense; but it is a radical conclusion to draw from constitutional commitments to freedom of speech.

Dworkin offers a theory that might be able to replace the prevailing libertarian justification for freedom of speech with one grounded in an egalitarian project that remains broadly consistent with the practical (constitutional) results of
libertarianism. State neutrality is the primary policy prescription of both libertarianism and egalitarianism. Dworkin's approach alleviates two problems common to many contemporary egalitarian arguments. First, it attempts to justify
freedom of speech comprehensively and to derive specific policy from that justification for a wide range of speech situations. Second, any regulations on
speech that may remain will be intrinsic to the justification itself, as opposed to
exceptions to a general but unarticulated freedom of speech, as in the case of
laws that would prohibit hate speech. To the extent that Dworkin's egalitarianism countenances restrictions on speech, these restrictions should be consistent
with the egalitarian project of equal status under law rather than exceptions
based on harms described by criticism external to his argument.

Status egalitarianism provides a comprehensive justification of freedom of
speech as far as the range of kinds of speech is concerned. Equal status before
the law, or citizen equality, protects political speakers, artists, religious believers, and scientific investigators on a level playing field. No one kind of speech is
at the core of this theory, nor is any kind of speech relegated to a periphery of
limited protection. Since the speaker's status, rather than the content of the
speech, justifies protection of speech, there is no requirement to develop a hierarchy of categories of speech. At the same time, "equality in the processes
through which the moral as well as the political environment is formed" prohibits imposing a hierarchy of protection on speakers.[29] Egalitarianism is also
comprehensive in that it should provide coverage to explain why speakers will
not be protected in certain kinds of situations. Equality of status justifies protection of speakers unless their speech can be proven harmful to the "security
and interests of others."[30] For Dworkin, this means an expansion in the amount
of speech currently protected by First Amendment law. He would, for instance,
restrict the reach of libel law through application of a more demanding legal test
that plaintiffs would have to meet in order to win and thus increase the protection of defendants (the press).[31] Plaintiffs who believe that they have been libeled would need to prove something more (malice) than merely being offended
or insulted by false and defamatory statements. Libel actions would still be
possible but only in cases where there are provable harms to the interests or

security of victims. Speech that constitutes intimidation or harassment may be restricted based on the direct harms to the security or interests of those targeted. Neither citizen equality nor citizen interests can be advanced by restrictions on others that would serve to mitigate indirect harms. For instance, even if the contributions of wealthy campaign donors dilute the speech of some citizens (thus undermining their political status), Dworkin would not allow direct restrictions on wealthy spenders because doing so would deny them equal treatment by the state. He would, however, accept something like a ceiling on campaign expenditures if it added to democracy without damaging citizen equality.[32]

Equality of Respect

While Dworkin and Karst define equality as equal status before state power, other theorists define it in terms of substantive equality of respect by fellow citizens.[33] Critical race theorists such as Mari Matsuda and antipornography feminists led by Catharine MacKinnon see inequality in the relations between groups in American society and develop egalitarian arguments aimed at alleviating that inequality. Where Dworkin's project is to seek guarantees against state action, Matsuda and MacKinnon take up a project to secure social progress toward substantive equality. Their understanding of equality of respect is very different from Dworkin's or Karst's equality of status in that it is critical of the exercise of private power and concerned with private speech rather than state restrictions on speech. Matsuda and MacKinnon advocate the use of state power against private speech that creates inequality. State power used in this way clearly contradicts the strict limits on state action favored by Dworkin and suggests that these two different understandings of equality are incompatible.

Matsuda calls for an examination of hate speech in the context of a history of racial subordination in the United States and of contemporary racism. The racial insult helps to maintain this atmosphere of subordination by conditioning the self-image of minority children and reinforcing feelings of superiority in some whites.[34] Expression such as labeling of out-group members is an important part of the subordination of blacks by whites.[35] Both the state and private individuals are involved in this subordination. For instance, Jim Crow laws, as Karst argues, were symbolic speech by the state that involved messages about group status and personal identity that served to enforce the subordination of blacks.[36] Similar messages of exclusion expressed by individuals, rather than the state, have the same kinds of effects. Expression forms the images that members of groups have of other groups, and these images play a major role in the social relations that condition speech acts.[37] Richard Delgado sums up the phenomenon succinctly: "It is no surprise, then, that racial stigmatization injures its victims' relationships with others. Racial tags deny minority individuals the possibility of neutral behavior in cross-racial contacts, thereby impairing the victims' capacity to form close interracial relationships. Moreover, the psychological responses of self-hatred and self-doubt unquestionably affect even the victims' relationships with members of their own group."[38]

Matsuda's argument against hate speech consists primarily of an account of the bad consequences of hate speech. She allies herself with civil libertarians, worries about state interference in speech, is an individualist, and argues within her interpretation of the First Amendment tradition.[39] Matsuda attempts to create an exception to free speech libertarianism that allows for regulation of hate speech. Her argument boils down to an effort to carefully define racist speech in such a way that it is not speech but rather a form of racist conduct punishable through an analogy to criminal assault. Racist speech is a sui generis category outside protected discourse because of its ties to violence and degradation.[40] The effort to redefine undesirable speech as regulable conduct is pervasive in First Amendment law, but the line between speech and conduct can never be firmly established. Matsuda argues that tolerance of hate speech is a tax on those least able to pay to support free speech. Members of racial minority groups give up some of their free speech because environments where hate speech is tolerated rather than condemned curtail participation. Racist hate speech is exclusionary: "target group members must either identify with a community that promotes racist speech or admit that the community does not include them."[41]

Charles Lawrence also focuses on the inequality created and maintained by hate speech. He specifically identifies equality as a part of civil liberty along with freedom of speech and argues that equality as a constitutional value must be taken into account when considering free speech.[42] A racist insult is a "dignitary affront [that] consists of the expression of a judgment that the victim of the racial slur is entitled to less than that to which all other citizens are entitled."[43] Matsuda narrows this definition and sets up specific conditions to identify a racist insult that rest on more than offensiveness or other instant harm. The racist speech that she would exclude from free speech protection must meet a three-part test:

"1. The message is of racial inferiority
2. The message is directed against a historically oppressed group
3. The message is persecutory, hateful and degrading."[44]

The message of most concern to Matsuda is that which "proclaims racial inferiority and denies the personhood of target group members" while working as a "mechanism of subordination, reinforcing a historical vertical relationship."[45] Her three-part definition brings together the distinct aspects of inequality by considering both historical and current inequality. It is not the expression of dominance and subordination by itself that constitutes a racist speech act but the combination of the speech, historical context, and social background that makes such speech especially harmful in a way that undermines substantive equality in the political community.

Arguments for the regulation of pornography are similar to those against hate speech. Subordination is the organizing theme of a recent anthology on hate speech and pornography by Laura Lederer and Richard Delgado that treats each issue as an instance of the same social problem. Lederer and Delgado consider pornography under the rubric of hate speech, as do many of the contributors to their volume. While there are some important political distinctions between these arguments, each views subordination similarly.[46] The antisubordination argument against pornography is most commonly associated with and most clearly articulated by Catharine MacKinnon in a number of essays and in *Only Words*.[47] MacKinnon's key concern is with the ways in which pornography constructs gender and reproduces the subordinate status of women in society. "What pornography does goes beyond its content: it eroticizes hierarchy, it sexualizes inequality." She sees pornography as the practice of subordination of women rather than as a set of ideas being communicated in public debate. "Pornography dispossesses women of the power which, in the same act, it possesses men: the power of sexual, hence gender, definition."[48] Thus, pornography dehumanizes and excludes women.

MacKinnon argues that pornography is an institution of gender inequality, that pornography not only constructs gendered hierarchy but relies upon that inequality for sexual arousal. "Pornography sexualizes rape, battery, sexual harassment, prostitution, and child sexual abuse: it thereby celebrates, promotes, authorizes and legitimizes them. More generally, it eroticizes the dominance and submission that is the dynamic common to them all."[49] Pornography is about power and powerlessness in much the same way that racist hate speech is about power. The racist epithet relies upon background social relations of the subordination of racial minorities in much the same way that, MacKinnon argues, pornography relies upon subordination of women. Pornography could target men, but it would fail to have the same subordinating consequences that it has for women because men are dominant in social-sexual relations. Absent a history of subordination, pornography and hate speech would not have the effects that they do because of that history. Hate speech directed at whites can be racist and deeply offensive, but its effect will not be to exclude whites from the political community in the way that racial minorities are excluded by hate speech and women are excluded by pornography.

The regulation of subordinating speech is a special-purpose argument, a negative argument for an exception to the First Amendment framework, which these theorists, and many others, take more or less for granted. Matsuda, Lawrence, and others all begin by stating commitments to civil liberties and to freedom of speech.[50] While their arguments eventually lead to conflicts with free speech libertarianism, I do not doubt their overall commitment to freedom of speech. Theorists of equal respect can be said to promote individual liberty even though the language used by these egalitarians involves the subordination of groups, restrictions on individuals according to group identity, and political action against subordinating portrayals of groups. Each aspect of group subordination, however, threatens the liberty of individuals as members of certain subordinate groups. Equal respect concerns the equality of individuals as it is threatened by subordination on the basis of external ascription of group identity. Individual liberty is threatened by racism, sexism, and other forms of discrimination based on group status; thus egalitarians promote individual liberty by questioning the group relations that restrict freedom in practice. That said, there is no obvious way to extrapolate their argument against hate speech or pornography to a full justification of freedom of speech. While the strength of Matsuda's definition of racist messages lies in its tight focus, this precludes any application to regulation outside of the context of hate speech. The explicit narrowness of her argument heads off an approach to hate speech that would sweep too broadly and curtail other kinds of speech. Critical race theorists intend the regulation of hate speech to be an exception to the current constitutional treatment of speech under the First Amendment. The exclusion of hate speech does not explain other categories regulated under the First Amendment, such as libel or false commercial speech.[51] It does not explain protected categories such as political debate or symbolic speech like flag burning. The antisubordination version of egalitarianism centered on equality of respect lacks an independent justification for freedom of speech.

These objections suggest that if critical race theorists and antipornography advocates accept a consequentialist defense of freedom of speech, then their arguments for an exception that allows regulation of subordinating speech are inconsistent. This and the fact that antisubordination egalitarians have no independent justification of freedom of speech suggest that they need a new argument to promote their project of equality of respect and outcomes. A new egalitarian justification of freedom of speech that leaves consequentialist arguments behind may be better suited to answering these kinds of problems and promoting the project of equality of respect. Rather than attempting to reformulate the antisubordination argument, a new egalitarian justification firmly grounded in an egalitarian project may be more self-consistent.

Equal Dignity

Given the significance of the criticisms of private power relations raised by theorists of equal respect and the weight of the equal status argument against state power, one wonders if some synthesis of equal respect and equal status is possible. A brief look at the international concern with equal dignity may help. Arguments about dignity represent a point of contact between the projects of equal status and equal respect. This category of harm is most often cited in U.N. covenants and treaties as well as legislation enacted in Germany, Canada, and the United Kingdom to control racist expression. Whereas psychological and physiological harms are described in clinical and scientific language, harms to personal dignity are necessarily less rigidly defined. Basic documents such as the U.N.'s Universal Declaration of Human Rights specify personal dignity as the basis for fundamental human rights. Article 1 of the Declaration states that all human beings are free and equal in dignity and rights by birth. Personal dignity is a quality that all persons share (like autonomy or rationality), by virtue of which they are guaranteed certain basic rights. German basic law defines hate speech as, in part, an attack on human dignity and the individual's right to live as an equal member of society.[52] German law also proscribes criminal insult as an offense against personal honor, an individualized form of dignity.

While the direct harms of targeted racist expression such as the racist insults on which Matsuda or Lawrence focus are substantial, it is the equality of social groups that carries the most weight in Canadian arguments for the regulation of hate speech. Canada uses the criminal law to protect equality rights enshrined in the Canadian Charter of Rights and Freedoms and to enforce obligations entered into by the signing and ratification of all U.N. conventions on human rights. Hate speech, in these various legal views, can represent a direct harm to the dignity of an individual, thus denying that person respect as an equal member of the community. Canadian egalitarians see hate speech as harmful not only to its individual targets or victims but also to society as a whole because it undermines group relations and often results in the permanent subordination of some groups. While the U.S. Constitution has been interpreted to require neutral treatment of racist and nonracist ideas, the Canadian Charter has been interpreted to allow nonneutral state action to address hate propaganda.[53] These interpretations rely upon significant structural differences between the Bill of Rights and the Charter. American lawyers and writers are forced to deal with a conflict between two constitutional values, since the U.S. Constitution gives no specific guidance as to whether speech under the First Amendment or equality under the Fourteenth Amendment should have priority. On the other hand, Section 1 of the Canadian Charter can be read, as it was in *Keegstra*, to grant priority to equality over certain kinds of expression protected by Section 2(b).

There are two questions that must be answered when deciding if a statute violates the Charter. The first is whether a specific Charter right, such as freedom of expression, has been violated by the state.[54] At this stage, the speaker who challenges the application of a statute attempts to prove that the statute violates the value of freedom of expression. These arguments appear similar to the kinds of arguments of principle made in American courts under First Amendment analysis and might look at the values promoted by free expression such as the search for truth, democratic self-governance, or individual self-realization.[55] So far, it appears that, under Section 2(b), the presumption will be in favor of a broad understanding of free speech, short of direct acts of expressive violence. Broad exceptions to free speech similar to the exclusion from First Amendment protection of fighting words and obscenity are less likely in the two-part Charter analysis.

The *Keegstra* case provides the clearest contrast between U.S. and Canadian doctrine on hate speech. Keegstra was convicted under Section 319 of the Canadian Criminal Code for willful promotion of hatred against an identifiable group. Specifically, over a period of more than a decade as a public school teacher in Alberta, Keegstra had included a variety of anti-Semitic content in his lessons, including ascriptions of negative character traits and tales of Jewish conspiracies to control media, politics, universities, and churches. Students were required to accept these statements as part of the content of the class and include these as answers on exams. While his speech was false and damaging, Keegstra appealed to the cognitive faculties of his students (backed by his substantial power as teacher, of course). The *Keegstra* court easily found that his speech was protected under Section 2(b) as it was speech and not a direct act of violence.[56] Other considerations of harm do not enter in during this first stage of analysis. If we imagine for a moment that Keegstra had been teaching in the United States, an American court would find itself largely in agreement that Keegstra's lessons were protected speech. As hateful as Keegstra's speech was, it does not meet the definitions of targeted racist insults offered by writers like Matsuda or Lawrence, nor does it meet the definition of fighting words in *Chaplinsky* and *R.A.V.* In the United States, a statute used to punish someone like Keegstra for this speech would be unconstitutional, even if the Supreme Court accepted an exception for racist fighting words or targeted insults. Under the neutrality doctrine of *R.A.V.*, a state could no more punish Keegstra than it could punish a cultural group for a visit to a school to promote awareness of Jewish history and culture.

There the analysis would stop in the United States. Keegstra might not get his job back, but he would face no further trouble with the criminal justice system. The Canadian approach goes one step further to consider whether Keegstra's protected speech violates other Charter provisions, specifically Section 1. The Charter opens with the guarantee that "freedoms set out in it [are] subject to such reasonable limits prescribed by law as can be demonstrably justified in a free and democratic society."[57] While some might read the Fourteenth Amendment's equal protection clause to say much the same thing, such an analysis does not command a majority on the Supreme Court. Under Section 1 analysis, if the state can prove that its regulation is a reasonable limit on a protected freedom, the regulation will stand. The Canadian court must balance speech against the interest in a free and democratic society.[58] This balance reflects a concern with equal dignity or status and requires a theory of the relationship between dignity, which may be harmed by speech such as Keegstra's, and democratic participation or membership in the community.

The Canadian Human Rights Act prohibits discrimination and is grounded in the idea of equal dignity. "The purpose of this Act is to extend the laws in Canada to give effect, within the purview of matters coming within the legislative authority of Parliament, to the principle that all individuals should have an opportunity equal with other individuals to make for themselves the lives they are able and wish to have."[59] Nonetheless, there is an empirical leap from this statutory concern with equal dignity to the kind of limit on a "free and democratic society" required by Section 1 of the Charter. The Human Rights Act suggests that Parliament has the responsibility to foster both equality of status and equality of respect, and the prohibition of willful promotion of hatred in the Criminal Code seems to do so. It is not obvious, however, that Keegstra's anti-Semitic speech undermines democracy to the extent required by the Charter to justify a restriction on such speech. For instance, such a link is not commonly accepted in the United States. The *Keegstra* court does accept the link between the harms to the dignity of Jews as a group and membership in the political community.[60] As long as this link exists and harms to dignity also undermine full membership in the democratic community, state regulation of hate propaganda is reasonable under the two-part Charter analysis. Willful promotion of hatred against an identifiable group can be punished because of the indirect harm to constitutionally protected membership rights for groups rather than the direct harms to identifiable individuals targeted by the expression.

Section 1 analysis acts to limit the sense of equal status favored by Dworkin. It is, in a case like *Keegstra*, an indication that under the Canadian Charter, equality of respect takes priority over equality of legal status in certain contexts such as hate propaganda. There is no clear indication in the U.S. Constitution of how to prioritize equality of status and equality of respect. Given the generally libertarian state of First Amendment law, it is not surprising that the Supreme Court would favor equality of status with its limits on state action over equality of respect, which would require state intervention. We can understand Dworkin's view as broadly consistent with, although distinct from, the Supreme Court's conservative majority's view of speech. The question that separates Dworkin's proposal from the Canadian approach to equal dignity is whether to treat each individual speaker as having equal status before the law (hence, before state power) or to treat all people, whether or not they speak, with equal respect before private power. The two-step Charter analysis in Canada seeks to balance equal status with equal respect, which may expand opportunities for speech and political participation but at a cost to some current speakers.

The Canadian approach does not represent a full justification of freedom of speech either. It is an institutional accommodation of competing equality claims, but by separating the analysis of speech from the arguments in favor of restricting certain kinds of speech, it brings us no closer to a comprehensive egalitarian justification. In effect, the Canadian approach allows for free speech absolutism under Section 2(b) tempered by nonspeech-related arguments about harm under Section 1.

The egalitarian justification of freedom of speech, particularly in Dworkin's work, suffers from several problems. For one, it appears to be indeterminate in relation to the problem of exceptions to free speech. Dworkin would protect a number of libelous speakers who currently are subject to libel suits. If hate speakers and pornographers are to be protected in order to observe the equal status due to each member of the community, why not also protect speakers who blackmail, offer bribes, or engage in false commercial speech? A justification of freedom of speech cannot be considered comprehensive if it cannot explain excluded speech in a way that is consistent with the structure and purposes of the justification. If malicious libel, for instance, is to be excluded because it is harmful to the interests of its targets, why not exclude harmful racist speech? For Dworkin, the issue turns on the empirical proof of harm, proof that is lacking for the silencing effects claimed by critics of hate speech.[61] Dworkin's evaluation of this evidence may be correct, but it raises the important question of whether other speech traditionally restricted on the basis of its harms has been empirically proven to be harmful. It would be helpful if Dworkin offered a few more examples of properly restricted speech so that we could see how this part of the argument would work in practice. He suggests that the state properly restricts speech that intimidates individuals in a way that effectively excludes them from political participation.[62] However, an empirical distinction between the cases where restrictions are legitimate and where they are not is bound to be controversial and difficult to prove. In many areas, it may not even be possible to formulate the question in a way that allows empirical proof one way or the other.

The protection Dworkin extends to racist speakers and pornographers conflicts with a commitment to equality as many people understand it. Dworkin's focus on equality of status under law leaves aside the inequality found in real-world, face-to-face speech situations. He excludes the harms to equal respect identified by antisubordination writers in order to avoid any situation where the state must make a judgment of value about some speech acts. By limiting equal status to a condition on state action, Dworkin leaves an enormous amount of nonegalitarian speech in place. In order to solve this problem, Karst would vastly exceed the scope of the First Amendment and of freedom of speech more generally. Because Karst recognizes that private speech is a substantial part of social inequality but also sees state restrictions on speech as problematic, he proposes even more dramatic state interventions supported by arguments that must be external to the justification of freedom of speech. While affirmative action and other civil rights policies that he discusses may very well have good consequences for the inclusion of currently excluded groups in public discussions, those policies cannot be justified solely on the basis of those consequences. In the end, the two most prominent American efforts to develop a comprehensive egalitarian justification of freedom of speech end up either not addressing existing social inequality (Dworkin) or else going far beyond freedom of speech into the realm of extensive civil rights legislation (Karst).

Dworkin's egalitarianism falls short of a comprehensive justification because it fails to account adequately for the effects of private power on the opportunities individuals have to speak. It is a strength of Dworkin's approach that he focuses on the protection of speakers rather than limiting his argument to one or only a few categories of speech. This justification does not require definitions of high-value versus low-value speech or attach primacy to one kind of speech over others. It succeeds in being comprehensive across a wide variety of speech. It is also comprehensive across many kinds of speech situations, as long as the state is an actor in those situations. Of course, the state may have no role in many important speech situations. The justification is not comprehensive in its protection of speakers. While equal status is a statement of comprehensive protection from the state, it neglects the role private power plays in restricting speech. The primary criticism by antisubordination writers of a position like Dworkin's is this exclusion. Beyond those criticisms lies the problem of real-world obstacles to speech, such as material inequality that precludes access to the means of communication. Equal status before the law may be necessary for a speaker to speak, but it is not sufficient. This insufficiency results in not all potential speakers having an opportunity to perform speech acts. While Karst hopes to promote equality of outcomes, his call for state speech to affirm the position of groups actually does little to counter the effects of material inequality on the opportunity to speak.

In the end, Dworkin's justification of freedom of speech replicates the kind of state neutrality favored by libertarians who worry about the effects of state action on public debate. Equality means equal opportunity to offend or to contribute to public life free from interfering judgments of quality or legitimacy by the state. Equality of status for racist speakers requires that the state make no judgment about the desirability of their speech, its consequences for other people, and its role in undermining constitutional equality. Equality of status means state neutrality in speech. State neutrality is precisely what critical race theorists and antipornography activists argue against. The critical race theory argument against hate speech asks the state to declare that racist hate speech is illegitimate and that it violates constitutional requirements when considering evidence of inequality in American society. A neutral state, in this view, allows inequality to flourish in spite of the fact that equality is a central objective of the American Constitution.

The first of the two egalitarian views of freedom of speech offers a justification of freedom of speech grounded in a project of equal status under law. The second, an antisubordination view of equality of outcomes associated with critical race theorists such as Mari Matsuda and Charles Lawrence and the antipornography argument of Catharine MacKinnon, seeks to carve out an exception for hate speech and pornography from the protection guaranteed by the libertarian justification of freedom of speech. The key difficulty in the second view is that it is not in itself a justification of freedom of speech. In addition, it does not address the kind of substantive inequality identified by the antisubordination writers as one of the consequences of restrictions on state action to address inequality. In the end, there remain many questions about an egalitarian justification of freedom of speech and whether such a justification can ever be compelling.

We are left with what should seem like unsatisfying conclusions for those hoping for a strong, internally consistent egalitarian justification for freedom of speech. There is no resolution to the difficult controversy surrounding hate speech and pornography here. Egalitarians who take up the project of equality of respect are left with an inconsistent argument for an exception to consequentialism or else an egalitarian justification that promotes equality of status and not equality of respect. Free speech egalitarianism, like libertarianism and expressivism, falls short of a comprehensive justification of freedom of speech.

CHAPTER FIVE

A Model of Free Speech Justifications

Free speech libertarianism, expressivism, and egalitarianism differ a great deal in terms of which free speech value they regard as overriding, but each identifies a single, ultimate value by which to judge and evaluate a speech event. Each of these approaches to the justification of freedom of speech is methodologically individualist, and each provides an account of the social relations in which individual speech is embedded. In all three schools of thought, free speech is seen as progressive in terms of promoting social and political development in a positive, forward-looking direction. Free speech libertarians grant primacy to truth, expressivists to self-realization, and egalitarians to equal dignity. The sharp differences between libertarians, expressivists, and egalitarians are not methodological or structural. Instead, these differences stem directly from their varied focus on basic but incommensurable free speech values.

Monism

Each of the approaches to the justification of free speech is monist in that each grounds its defense of free speech in a single, unitary value to be promoted through the protection of speech. The supporters of each school use these unitary values to establish the importance of speech in relation to other competing objectives. Theorists rely on unitary values to provide a common basis on which to compare and evaluate competing free speech claims. For instance, egalitarians identify free speech claims as valid where state action infringes upon status equality (such as direct acts of censorship) as opposed to faulty claims where the value is not infringed (such as the effects of unequal material resources on the opportunity to speak).

The role of unitary speech values in the libertarian, expressivist, and egalitarian justifications of free speech parallels monism in ethical theory. Monism posits that all value conflicts ultimately can be evaluated against a universal, primary value commitment.[1] Monists believe that all values can be rank ordered by application of a common denominator, such as utility, and that this ordering can then be used to make ethical and political judgments between competing values or political positions. Monism makes it easy to measure progress because one value provides a single metric.[2] For example, utilitarianism is a monist philosophy that measures all ethical and political questions against the single value of utility. Values such as equality of status or self-realization can be the basis of ethically monist theories, as they are for some theorists of speech. Nonetheless, many of these theorists might not extend the unitary value that forms the basis for their defense of free speech to the defense of all of their ethical and political positions. My use of the term "unitary" to describe the values of truth/democracy, self-realization, and equality is meant to indicate that within speech arguments, these values serve the function and have the characteristics of monist values in broader debates.[3] The unitary values may or may not be used by these writers to justify broader ethical conclusions, however, and therefore may not be truly monist.

Certain common characteristics of the schools of justification reflect the nature of unitary values. The most prominent of these characteristics is the tendency for justification of free speech to identify a core and periphery of protection of speech. Versions of the two-tier theory of the First Amendment favored by Meiklejohn, Sunstein, and Bork offer the clearest example of this. The unitary value driving their approach is truth/democracy, which places certain kinds of cognitive speech about public issues at the core and pushes other kinds of speech to the periphery. Meiklejohn and Bork would offer the strongest legal protection to political speech, while offering reduced levels of protection to art or commercial speech that is only tangentially political. The categorical approach of First Amendment law makes the same kinds of distinctions. Conversely, expressivists who focus on the creative speech that leads to individual self-realization identify art as the core and relegate political speech to the periphery of speech protection.

The prime advantage of ethical monism and of unitary justifications of free speech is that these approaches offer definitive answers to questions about whether a particular kind of speech ought to be protected. This definitiveness is especially important to the lawyers who write on the First Amendment because, after all, they want to win arguments in court, which requires definitive, determined answers. Similarly, monism dominates ethical theory because the potential to identify "right answers" appeals strongly to people who often dismiss pluralism as unsatisfactory relativism. Theorists in all three schools of justification share a common impetus to provide the kinds of definite answers and rank orderings of speech required by monism, but this impulse necessarily leads to exclusion of some speech from protection. Furthermore, as I show below, unitary values lead to irresolvable conflicts between justifications of free speech.

Social Relations

Justifications of freedom of speech are concerned with the nature and quality of social relations. Accounts of most kinds of freedom are about social relations in one way or another, but the liberal focus on negative liberty combined with the basis of civil rights and civil liberties under the Constitution limits the extent to which the issue of freedom is understood to implicate social relations. This is one of the crucial difficulties with the First Amendment framework that currently structures debate over freedom of speech. The prevailing First Amendment framework for freedom of speech focuses on freedom from state interference because that is the way the constitutional text reads and the way that the case law has developed over the last century. However, the First Amendment framework is not universal or eternal. Freedom of speech is, and has been, debated outside of the context of the First Amendment. Obviously, those debating freedom of speech outside of the United States are not likely to be conditioned by a First Amendment framework.[4] In addition, American thinkers on freedom of speech were not always bound by the First Amendment.[5] The first significant First Amendment cases were heard by the U.S. Supreme Court only in the twentieth century, so this constitutional doctrine is relatively recent.[6] Many ideas about what the First Amendment required circulated before the

Court heard any cases, but such doctrinal arguments did not have the practical effects that current arguments have had.[7] It is only in the last thirty to forty years that First Amendment doctrine has approached the broad protection of speech that many seem to think has always existed.

What at first clearly appears as a strictly individual, negative right with little social character is actually very much a matter of social relations. As I argued extensively in chapter 2, even the free speech libertarianism that dominates First Amendment thought is marked by social justifications of an individual liberty to speak. The most obvious, and possibly most important, social relationship created by speech is that between the speaker and the audience.[8] All schools of justification of freedom of speech agree on this, as it is part of the definition of speech itself. Speaking involves an act meant to establish a relationship, while listening is an acknowledgment of a relationship with the speaker. The simplest case of this relationship is the two-person conversation involving the exchange of greetings. Even a brief conversation consisting of "Hello, how are you this morning?" and the reply "Fine, thank you, yourself?" rests upon social foundations and provides a tangible relationship between two people who, at that moment, interact with each other by exchanging language, nonverbal cues, and comprehension of the other's speech acts. The relationship between a single speaker and a large audience is more complicated. The speaker usually seeks out that relationship for some purpose, such as the exchange of information, political persuasion, commercial gain, or artistic expression. Noncaptive listeners also enter into a relationship with the speaker for similar kinds of motives.[9] Motives for captive audiences (and captive speakers) may not exist, other than to avoid penalties of noncompliance, but the (coerced) relationships still exist.[10]

The most important fact of free speech practice is that there is no speech without social relations, therefore we must always consider social relations when making any justificatory argument for or against free speech. There is no such thing as purely self-regarding speech, and all persons involved in the relationship must be taken into account. It is not sufficient to look only at the relationship between the individual speaker and the state while ignoring the relationships between the speaker and other individuals. While the state may be the actor infringing on the individual's freedom to speak (through an act of censorship, say), this does not mean that the individual's relations with others are not part of the equation. While the state may have reasons of its own for engaging in censorship (such as an effort to cover up embarrassing state actions in the past, to avoid criticism of state policies, or to act against the public interest), many of these reasons have to do with the relationships between citizens rather than between citizen and state. In democratic regimes, for instance, there may be popular support for efforts to ban or restrict the speech of members of some groups. Efforts to suppress communism in the United States in the first half of the twentieth century are one example of this. Other examples include acts of state censorship based on moral condemnation of a political or artistic work. These represent state interference in relationships between citizens. It makes very little difference to the state, as an agent, whether pornography is widely available, but there may be substantial popular pressure expressed through democratic channels to eliminate it.

Censorship automatically places the focus on the relationship between the state and the individual speaker, but any given case of censorship will not be properly understood unless all of the relationships involved are considered. In addition to the relationship between the state and speaker, relations between speakers and audiences as well as relations within the audience are important. On the one hand, the state has great power to enact censorship. States have done so throughout history with obvious effects on freedom of speech. On the other hand, relationships between individuals affect what individuals can and do say in many ways. At the most basic level, the linguistic conventions that allow speech acts to occur constrain what people are able to put into words, setting bounds on the available vocabulary for speech acts. Also, the type of audience, choice of medium, and forum for communication involve different kinds of social relations and lead to a different calculus of speech concerns. Hierarchies among audiences as well as between speaker and audience affect what speech acts are comprehensible, the meaning of the speech, and the prospects for continued opportunity to speak.

Speech takes place within relational environments conditioned by state policies, constitutions, and legislative rules. Who is allowed to use certain kinds of media, is permitted to speak in certain places or times, and has the resources to engage in speech are a product of state action.[11] The state grants television licenses, and by design these exclude general access to the use of broadcast frequencies. Labor laws regulate where and when speech relating to union activities can take place.[12] Local franchise agreements determine from which one of several large cable companies individuals can purchase programming. In each of these cases, state action mediates the individual's relationship with the speaker without directly affecting the content of the speech in question.[13] The state often mediates the relationships between citizens relevant to freedom of speech. Rather than focusing solely on the state as the agent of censorship, we might also examine the kinds of relationships that lead to the state's interest in acting as censor. As mentioned earlier, the state has a motive to censor to protect itself, as in the case of seditious libel, but state survival rarely hinges on the suppression of blasphemy, pornography, or hate speech.

While freedom of speech implies a number of things about the social relations that allow speech acts to occur, it also suggests a number of things about the social construction of the individual personality. For instance, one implication of freedom of speech is the social mutability of the individual. Speech acts and the relationships they create change the people who are involved. This social mutability takes different forms within different schools of thought on speech, but is a necessary implication of freedom of speech.[14] Free speech is not simply the elimination of barriers to the expression of specific ideas that a speaker already holds. It also provides the opportunity to engage in dialogue and other expressive experiences that change the ideas that one has and to contribute new ideas to one's thinking (or feeling). The traditional focus on rational dialogue rests upon the notion that ideas can and should change. Freedom of speech is justified by libertarians to protect a speaker's efforts to change the minds of others and to provide the opportunities for audiences to alter their thinking in ways necessary for democratic governance to flourish. Expressivists justify freedom of speech to protect individual creative activity that transforms the speaker through the speaker's striving after self-realization and transforms the audience through cultural development. Egalitarians also rest a great deal on social mutability. Racist speech constructs individuals who hate and who practice racism while at the same time reinforcing a variety of insecurities in its targets. Positive, antiracist speech can have the opposite effect by helping to moderate the racist views of some individuals or groups.

Free speech libertarians use social justifications for freedom of speech. The most prominent of these is expressed in the marketplace of ideas metaphor of robust public discourse. Libertarians have a social project that aims at the discovery of truth. This good is socially valuable and thereby benefits the individual members of society, but it is not an individual good per se. Public discourse in the marketplace of ideas is an adversarial process whereby social benefits flourish through the constant introduction of new ideas to compete with established ideas. Individual speech is instrumental to the functioning of this social process and therefore must be protected. The more individuals who speak, the greater the diversity of the marketplace and the better the chances that the best ideas will be introduced and gain preeminence.

In addition to their social project, libertarians focus on social relations in several nonobvious ways. First, libertarianism provides for certain kinds of relationships between individuals and the state and allows a broad range of relationships between citizens.[15] While the individual may perceive his or her demand for negative liberty, for the state to "get off my back" (out of my wallet, out of the schools, off my body, for example), as the staunch denial of a relationship with the state, "get off my back" is a specific, albeit distant, social relationship. The individual and the state must already be in a relationship of some kind before the person can make a claim against the state. Claims against the state prove that the individual is aware of, even fears, the state. Awareness and fear are characteristics of social relations rather than conditions of atomistic individual existence. The relationship between the individual and state may not be voluntary—in fact, the "get off my back" claim proves that it is not—but it is a relationship nonetheless. The person who says "get off my back" means that individual will not associate freely with state power and prefers to make his or her own relationships. A "get off my back" claim is a demand to be allowed to form the relationships of one's own choice, not a claim to be left totally alone without any social contact. Theodore Kaczynski, perhaps, makes such an absolute claim, but "get off my back" usually means get off my back so that I can set my own agenda and make my own friends, business partners, and acquaintances. These are negative claims to freedom from the state and to the freedom to form associations of one's own choosing. This type of negative liberty does not deny the social world; it may decentralize it or make it more chaotic and less predictable, but these claims are affirmations of the social sphere within an environment of relationships between the state and the individual.

As in the other schools, the social process of the search for truth and better social policy framed by libertarians presumes that each of us is affected by social debate and dialogue. The procedure is worthless if everyone will remain unconvinced by the speech of others. Participants and adherents to this view must believe in their own social mutability if libertarianism is to make any sense as an account of free speech. Of course, such mutability is not often cited as a constituent part of libertarian theory. Instead, some libertarians assume that the point of free speech is to allow everyone to speak, hear, and consume speech according to their own a priori preferences or essential nature. To the extent that preferences are a priori, there is no point in attempting to convince others, and the public debate model flounders in its own self-centered orientation. Reasonable libertarians understand that social debate leads to individual change and embrace the outcome. They may suggest that everyone speaks in order to advance their own interests, but the assumed outcome is better policy and a more accurate appraisal of the truth made possible by individuals' changing views.

At first glance, expressivists are obsessed with the needs of the individual to an extent unmatched by even the most absolutist libertarians. Social goals are not an explicit part of their justifications for individual freedom, and it is not clear that they think that free speech contributes to society in substantial ways. The apolitical elitism of the most ardent expressivists appears in the form of a strong inclination against social or political objectives. Upon closer inspection, however, the cultural development strand of expressivism ties it directly to social objectives. While infinite striving after self-realization is central to the life of the expressivist, this striving is a necessary part of cultural development and hence of the individual development of others. Cultivation is a social process that benefits the person qua individual, but this individualism is necessary to realize cultural growth and development. Expressivism aspires to promote individual development in order to release the cultural genius of a people as a whole.[16] Social relationships are crucial to the working of expressivist arguments. The cultivation or development of the individual requires social relations. Only through expression can the individual engage in infinite striving necessary to achieve moral freedom. While an audience does not always need to be present, this expression requires at least the presumption of a possible audience. Expression and striving are even better served by the active engagement of a group of people in a shared creative experience. The group may act to buttress the expression or as a foil for the speaker. The social relations create the individual, and the individual acts in turn create social relations (and thus other individuals).

Social relations are of obvious importance to egalitarianism. Egalitarians seek to reconstruct the procedural understanding of freedom of speech associated with libertarianism in ways that would advance the goal of equal treatment. For instance, the call for regulation of hate speech is grounded in the empirical claim that racist speech harms the social relations between individual members of racial groups through a combination of reinforcement of racial inequalities and a denial of participation for racial minorities. Equal participation is a social project, one that seeks a specific state of affairs for interpersonal and group relations.

The benefits of the realization of this project accrue primarily to individuals, but the benefits should extend to all members of society as well. To the extent that egalitarians calling for regulation of hate speech adopt the marketplace of ideas metaphor common in libertarian thought, they also accept the value of truth and good policy.[17] That is, not only is free participation in social debates a good for those citizens currently excluded on the basis of race, but it is a good for all citizens who benefit from the widest possible dialogue. If one believes in the process view of the marketplace of ideas and that the more varied the marketplace is, the better the results, then reducing barriers to participation leads to shared social benefits. In the egalitarian view, social development requires that groups (or individual members of groups) be full participants in the process of social and individual growth. Egalitarianism seeks to reconstruct the speech relationships that constrain broader social relations between groups.

Individualism

For many people, freedom of speech immediately highlights emotional commitments to individualism, but this is more than just a rhetorical stance taken by different writers on freedom of speech. One of the least surprising things that I could argue is that individualism is strongly associated with arguments for freedom of speech. It is difficult to imagine an argument for free speech that did not emphasize individual freedom. Many writers on speech begin with a commitment to individualism that is reflected in a specific unitary value. Individualism is a pervasive and familiar characteristic of both popular beliefs about the First Amendment and the First Amendment framework for debate. The institutional structure of that framework determines, in large part, the explicit individualistic features of many free speech theories. Constitutional guarantees of freedom extend to individuals, not groups, through judicial procedures designed to allow them to seek redress of their grievances against the state. The rhetoric of the First Amendment is also responsible. Within the First Amendment framework, arguments are emotionally compelling when they set the controversy as one of the lone individual faced with censorship at the hands of the overwhelming power of the state.

If one takes this emphasis on social relations seriously, then the individualistic focus of free speech theory is surprising. Writers rarely justify freedom of speech solely on the basis of individualism or as a good in itself. Few people expressly found their arguments for freedom of speech on the strength of their belief in the normative value of individual liberty.[18] The pure individualist argument is not seen to be very convincing in the face of competing values and social projects such as equality or public debate.[19] One of the most interesting problems in the examination of the schools of justification of freedom of speech has to be that they share an emphasis on individual liberty while still placing social relations at the core of their justificatory arguments. It would seem, at first, that contradictions between individualism and social relations would be inevitable. If freedom of speech is meant to protect certain kinds of social relations, then strong individualist claims for freedom appear harder to sustain. If social relations are primary, then we should be willing to trade off some portion of individual speech for greater realization of the kinds of social relations favored by the projects of libertarians, expressivists, and egalitarians.

One example of the possibility of such a conflict between individualism and social relations is the first objection to free speech libertarianism that I dealt with in chapter 2. Free speech libertarians justify individual freedom of speech as a means to advance the search for truth or good policy. Their argument relies upon group processes and social goods that are realized most efficiently through a system of free speech and open dialogue. Individual freedom of speech is good because it generates truth and democratically derived, good public policy. The libertarians' exceptions to broad, individual freedom for cases of libel, bribery, and incitement to illegal action, for example, are made in response to direct demonstrable harms to individuals or society, but these cases also fit within the libertarian justification because the ultimate value of truth and good policy is not furthered by these kinds of speech. The state may interfere in these specific types of speech acts, because there is a clear-cut violation of the instrumental value of individual speech to the realization of social ends. By justifying free speech as a means to social ends and demonstrating with these exceptions that free speech may be constrained in favor of those ends, libertarians indicate that social ends have priority.

Here lies the possible conflict. If social ends have priority, then it seems likely that we would be willing to trade off some of the subordinate good, individual free speech, to realize the primary good of truth and good public policy. This is already accepted for bribery and libel. Lines must be drawn and boundaries set between the primary goods and allowable restrictions on secondary goods. Constitutional doctrine draws these lines between acceptable infringements on individual freedom of speech (as in these cases) and unacceptable limits (such as prior restraints on the press to promote national security) in the legal practice of hearing First Amendment claims. Just because these lines are drawn in legal practice does not mean that they are theoretical necessities. The Supreme Court must constantly wrestle with the proper balance to draw between social ends and individual speech rights. Free speech absolutists may not accept the existence of such boundaries, but most others argue for some form of balancing of the social ends and individual freedom. The bulk of the speech cases before the courts involve identifying the relationship between the facts of the case, social ends, and the individual speech infringed upon by the regulations in question. The basic constitutional theory of the First Amendment is relatively stable, it is the practice of that doctrine that continues to be controversial. We may have come to politically acceptable accommodations of individual freedom of speech and social ends, but the fact that the Supreme Court hears a number of free speech cases every term suggests that these accommodations are contested. Conflicts between individualistic justifications and social projects persist both in practice and in theory.

In chapter 2, I argued that this contradiction dissolves because the public debate promoted by libertarians suggests that there should be free speech about free speech. The rules of the game, so to speak, require that even the rules be open for debate, otherwise freedom of speech is hollow. Free speech libertarians do not abandon their commitments to individualism in favor of the social benefits of free speech. As in egalitarianism and expressivism, individualism is as important a part of the justification of freedom of speech as the socially oriented objectives highlighted by other schools of thought. Individual freedom is a secondary good used instrumentally to provide for primary social ends. Libertarians have social objectives and focus on individualistic projects to attain those ends, as do egalitarians and expressivists. Personal liberty is instrumental to social processes in libertarian justificatory arguments that consider individuals in their roles as speakers, audiences, and consumers.[20] Their arguments protect the speech acts of speakers, audience members, and consumers, taken individually, from interference by the state. The common metaphor of the marketplace of ideas results from many individuals exercising the freedom of speech in some combination of these social roles. The traditional examples used in libertarian arguments include street-corner speakers, attendees at a political rally, and television viewers secluded in the privacy of their homes.

In another sense, libertarianism is methodologically individualist in that it sees individual persons as the proper unit of analysis for the discussion of social relations. Of more importance than the relations between large-scale social groups are relationships between individuals. Freedom of speech is guaranteed to individuals so that they may relate to other people in specific ways as speakers, hearers, and consumers. Those who wish to engage in political speech, for instance, enjoy broad protection so that they may participate in a political process of self-determination of policy and direction. Other social relations are tolerated as an unfortunate by-product of the individual freedom. For example, an undesirable effect of allowing individuals to perform racist speech acts is that these reinforce the hierarchical social relations signified by that racist speech. Much of libertarian theory protects the rights of audiences to be exposed to various ideas expressed by individual speakers. However, we analyze an audience not as a single entity but by looking at its component parts, the people who make up the audience. The idea is that, as a member of an audience, the individual is exposed to ideas that contribute to the development of his or her own political views. This in turn leads to voting choices and perhaps even participation as a speaker.

Egalitarians frame many arguments in terms of the status of groups, but the ways that individuals are treated drives egalitarianism. Egalitarians focus on the individual as the basic unit of analysis, much as libertarians do, rarely emphasize group speech, and are more concerned with individual speech acts. There is no meaningful way to understand or define a "group speech act." Groups do not speak, individuals do, even when they represent groups. Egalitarians who want to regulate hate speech are not concerned with the speech of groups or even with the relations between social groups on a macro scale. Rather, their concern is the way in which speech acts by individuals rest upon, replicate, and use social hierarchies to create an undesirable relationship between two people. The person who performs an act of hate speech relies upon the social meaning of racist epithets and the relative status of his or her social group compared to that of the target of the hate speech to create (or attempt to create) or emphasize a relationship of dominance over another. Also consider the supervisor in a workplace setting who uses speech acts of sexual harassment to attempt to extend the legitimate social hierarchy of the management-employee relationship into the illegitimate relationship of sexual dominance. In these speech acts of importance to egalitarians, the social relations of interest are between individuals. The freedoms implicated are individual (whether freedom of speech or freedom from harassment), while the relations themselves are socially situated. For status egalitarians such as Ronald Dworkin, individualism is even more clear. Dworkin argues that what matters is the status of the individual speaker in relation to state power. Dworkin's egalitarianism requires that each individual, taken as an individual, has equal status before the law and equal treatment by the state.

Expressivism is the most overtly individualistic of the three schools of justification of free speech, both in terms of method and in its rhetorical elements. Expressivists see individual speech acts as the basis for social development. While the social project of cultural development is primary, that project advances through the speech acts of individuals in the form of artistic and cultural expression. Each individual, in striving for self-realization or self-development, engages in expressive activity that contributes to the cultural development of the community. At the same time, the individual draws on the cultural development of others as a part of his or her own self-development. The process is communitarian, but the experience of the process is individual. To the individual member of the community, expression has few boundaries, and the end of this speech is highly personal. The process moves forward as a result of the creative achievements of individuals. In the most purely expressivist arguments, those of the German romantics, the creative efforts of a few individual geniuses synthesize the culture and move it forward for all. Freedom consists not only in belonging to the culture and community but also in one's individual efforts to attain self-realization. In the modified expressivist view represented in current debate, one need not be an artistic or poetic genius to benefit from individual expression, nor must the community rely solely upon a few individuals of the creative caliber of Goethe or Shakespeare. The benefit of expressivist freedom of speech accrues first to the individuals released to pursue their own self-development but eventually flows to all members of the community.

Progressivism

An optimistic and future-oriented view of freedom of speech as progressive social development is a common feature of these three schools of thought. By "progressive" I do not mean to imply that freedom of speech always favors "liberal" or left-wing political changes, rather, freedom of speech is progressive in that it favors positive social development toward some better future state of affairs. Writers do not always specify exactly what this future holds because the point of freedom is to protect a process that could lead almost anywhere along all kinds of unanticipated lines. Actors across the political spectrum support various theories of freedom of speech, hoping that it will lead to progress in agreement with their own predispositions. Few people speak out publicly in opposition to progress (even political conservatives like to talk about their "radical" vision of social change for the future), so the optimism of free speech theory may at first seem unremarkable. However, freedom of speech is distinctive because of this progressive outlook. Other liberties considered to be equally fundamental to liberalism are not necessarily progressive. Basic restrictions on state power such as criminal due process rights attempt to maintain a certain status quo power balance between citizens and the state, not to promote the struggle for social progress.[21] The right to be left alone, in this context, may simply reflect the desire to be left alone for its own sake. One can be a strong supporter of due process rights without hoping for any change in the status quo. Few who favor freedom of speech fail to see in that freedom a hope for, or a faith in, positive social change.

Freedom of speech is progressive, but most of the writers I have considered do not believe that its objectives will ever be realized. In contrast, the progressive view of equal protection jurisprudence considers equality to be an achievable goal. Those who argue for equality have a clear objective—meaningful equality along race and gender lines. The substantive results of such a system of equality are not as clear, but the assumption is that substantive equality can be reached and that once it has been, it can be maintained. On the other hand, these arguments for freedom of speech see progress in open-ended terms. That is, the projects pursued through protection of speech are more procedural than they are substantive. While libertarians, for instance, set the discovery of truth or good public policy as projects, the specifics are not—in fact, cannot be—specified. Whatever counts as the truth today, or as the correct policy, will undoubtedly change in the future, and we should be prepared to embrace that change as the outcome of the process that gave us today's version of truth.[22] At the core of the pluralist framework of freedom of speech is the understanding that whatever our particular project is, speech will help advance it.

The progressive outlook is due in part to the skepticism common in free speech theories from the seventeenth century to the present. Those who favor freedom of speech (whether libertarians, expressivists, or egalitarians) are skeptical not only of the current status quo but of future arrangements as well. Again, these progressive aspirations may at first seem unremarkable. However, a contrast with conservative theories of speech, or the defense of state authority over speech, should indicate that there are those who do not share such hope for social development. In some conservative theories (but not all), the state must place limits on speech in order to enforce adherence to an ideal past state or traditional order. Robert Bork reads the First Amendment to protect overtly political speech (that is, speech of, or regarding, political institutions) to allow for political development in accordance with his understanding of the original understanding of the U.S. Constitution, but he would limit speech that challenged a traditional moral order. Those who would use state power to enforce their own particular understanding of the truth are always present, arguing that on at least some issues, no social development or change is either possible or desirable. For example, a plank in the 1996 Republican Party platform called for a constitutional amendment that would prohibit abortion as well as advocacy of abortion by anyone who receives federal funds.[23] As an amendment to the Constitution, such a restriction on speech could not be overturned by appeal to the First Amendment. Whatever one's views on abortion rights, it is obvious that such an amendment would eliminate most discussion of abortion by medical personnel and social service agencies. Doctors would be prevented from disseminating information about abortion to patients, even those whose lives might be at stake. Furthermore, it would prohibit most academics from discussing abortion, since universities receive federal funds from many sources.

The progressive outlook is also due to a shared (but rarely articulated) romantic belief in the importance of striving. Free speech progressivism is an ideal of social development as the pursuit of an unrealizable perfect state of freedom. This pursuit of perfect freedom is the characteristic feature of expressivism, but something similar is present in the other schools as well. Libertarian speech theory since Mill has treated the struggle for self-realization as an important (albeit secondary) part of freedom of speech. Mill himself adapts this view from his reading of the German romantic and libertarian thinker Wilhelm von Humboldt. Contemporary libertarians place a great deal of weight on artistic expression for its value to the individual artist as well as its role in helping audiences understand the world in ways that further the libertarian project of good public policy. The infinite-striving argument takes the form of social process in egalitarian and libertarian arguments. The notion of self-realization is often referred to, in a rhetorical way, by contemporary free speech writers who draw on what Charles Taylor identifies as a romantic theme in the modern understanding of the self.[24] These romantic themes color liberalism itself, as they find expression in all justifications of freedom of speech. In addition to the rhetorical commitment to the struggle for self-realization by libertarians, the infinite process of the marketplace of ideas represents freedom itself (as infinite striving after self-realization represents freedom for expressivists). These schools of thought are nonutopian in that they are not premised on the idea that the social process aims at an ideal or utopian set of social arrangements. For example, the libertarian marketplace of ideas is not really about an efficient means to get to a specific, predetermined point but instead about the potential for the progressive process protected by freedom of speech.

The most compelling egalitarian arguments focus on social goals and well-functioning democratic processes rather than on assaultlike harms to individuals. The critical race theory argument that a racist epithet harms the individual target of the insult identifies a real problem, but the deeper argument about the exclusion of racial minorities from equal participation in social and political relations identifies an aspiration for unfettered, progressive social development. Egalitarians suggest a specific and plausible social objective, but they offer no predictions as to when or if the objective of social equality will ever be realized in practice. Instead, egalitarians strive for ever closer approximations to this ideal. Even if the process is not an efficient means to the realization of equality and will never be completed, progress counts as a kind of freedom. There are different opinions as to what counts as progress depending upon the objectives of those making the definition. The point is that adherents of all three schools of thought perceive their own view as progressive.

Incommensurable Values

We have seen that there are four primary dimensions to a justification of freedom of speech acts: unitary values, social relations, individualism, and progressivism. The three schools have distinct justifications of freedom of speech with different emphases that are often in conflict as to what free speech policy is best, yet the different schools have much in common. The obvious question, then, is how or why these schools are so different in their emphases and in the kinds of arguments made for the protection of freedom of speech.

Every theorist of freedom of speech has objectives, preferences, and values that he or she attempts to promote through free speech. Some of these values are justified by normative or legal arguments that are logically prior to those that justify freedom of speech. For example, egalitarians justify equal status with arguments that are prior to, and independent of, their case for freedom of speech. Similarly, the value of self-realization exists as a value logically and historically prior to the expressivist justification of freedom of speech. Free speech libertarians value truth for reasons that are independent of the argument for free speech as well. In each case, the justification of the underlying unitary value, if such a justification exists, is absent from the argument for free speech. Few libertarians tell us why truth is better than falsehood. Only a few expressivists make an effort to explain why one should value self-realization, which requires intense effort and sacrifice, over a life of lazy, contented ignorance of one's essential self. Nonetheless, attachment to these values is the source of the differences between these free speech justifications and accounts for the conflicts between what are otherwise similar schools of thought.

The structure of each of the three schools of free speech justification is similar, but the values they promote are very different, thus leading to different conclusions. None of the three justifications is truly comprehensive, as each emphasizes different kinds of speech in relation to the unitary value on which they focus. One possible response to this would be to attempt to harmonize all three justifications by reducing them to some common primary value thought to cover all speech situations.[25] However, these values are incommensurable and cannot be reduced to a single, coherent common value. Inescapably, these values come into conflict, and they cannot be melded easily into a "system of freedom of expression" that is both logically consistent and comprehensive.[26] The most we can do is to illuminate these differences. To move forward with the project of a comprehensive justification of freedom of speech requires something different. Since the unitary justifications fail to provide the comprehensiveness long sought by free speech theory and these arguments cannot simply be added together, I propose a pluralist framework for freedom of speech that draws on the strengths of the unitary justifications to provide a more comprehensive defense of freedom of speech.

CHAPTER SIX

Speech Acts

The unitary justifications of free speech define speech by direct reference to the value served by free speech. Expressivists, for instance, rely on implicit definitions of speech that are dependent on their overall argument that free speech promotes self-realization. In these schools of thought, there is no phenomenon of speech prior to the question of freedom of speech. At least they do not describe or articulate speech acts independent from their other concerns. This presents two key problems. First, many of the most interesting questions are about what we mean by speech. Second, by making their definitions of speech dependent on their overall arguments for free speech, current approaches stack the deck against alternative understandings of free speech. If, for example, we define speech as inextricably linked to the democratic procedure of truth finding, there will be little room to consider the role speech plays in self-realization. A pluralist framework for free speech requires an independent definition of speech that does not have built into it concepts or arguments that privilege a single value over others. It would also be helpful to avoid the false and unworkable dichotomy of speech and conduct found in Hugo Black's absolutism and later constitutional approaches to speech. In practice, absolutism breaks down quickly and provides little protection of controversial speech. Speech exists in the real world logically prior to, and independent of, our attempts to make it free or not free under the Constitution.

While it seems obvious that every theory of free speech or empirical account of a specific practice of free speech ought to begin with a definition of speech itself, it is rare that such a self-conscious definition is offered. I begin with the assertion that there is no essential or foundational definition of speech as a concept and propose to work with a definition of speech as a contextually situated phenomenon.[1] The definition I rely on is based upon speech act theory and grounded in the practice of speech.[2] Speech act theory is independent of constitutional structures like the First Amendment, situates each speech claim in the context in which it occurs, and says nothing about whether speech is or should be free. While I see speech, and freedom of speech, as situated in certain practices, I do not agree with radical relativists or free speech absolutists who would refuse to set any meaningful boundaries on the definition of speech. Just because there is no essentialist concept of speech or freedom of speech does not mean that we cannot develop a useful definition based in practice and the context in which speech takes place. Free speech libertarianism, expressivism, and egalitarianism provide grounds for the articulation of a relatively stable, but not universal, definition of speech, even if theorists within these schools rarely offer such a definition.

A pluralist approach to free speech should start with a definition of speech that is logically prior to specific justifications of free speech. First, this will maintain the definition's independence from any particular unitary value favored by different schools of justification. Otherwise, speech as a phenomenon is too easily conflated with arguments for freedom of speech. Second, a contextual definition of speech accounts for the plurality of kinds of expression already emphasized by different theorists while being open to additional types of speech as well. The choice of definitions makes a difference in the kinds of justificatory arguments that one can make and the implications of those arguments for speech situations. To bury the definition of speech as a phenomenon in ambiguous or implicit assumptions surrounding one's defense of freedom of speech does not solve the problem of choosing a definition; it exacerbates the problem. A post hoc definition of speech that is subordinate to an argument about freedom of speech is likely to reflect only the primary concerns of the theorist and stack the deck in favor of those concerns. Third, we can dispute the meaning of speech, but our disagreements cannot be aired unless we first make our own definitions explicit. We cannot take for granted a commonsense, but empty, definition of speech as "only words." A detailed account of the concept of speech is a necessary prerequisite to a rigorous theory of freedom of speech. Fourth, current theory structured by the First Amendment framework provides little in the way of a definition of speech. There are ascriptive laundry lists of what counts (or, more accurately, what does not count) as speech, half-formed judgments (such as "I know it when I see it"), and a distinction between speech and conduct. To counter this vacuum, I ground the pluralist framework for debate in the speech act theory developed by philosophers of language such as Austin, Searle, and Grice.[3]

The definitional approach to speech has a number of advantages over the ascriptive approach used by some theorists. Many arguments about freedom of expression, especially legal arguments over the First Amendment, take the position that all speech should be protected from state interference. Enumerated exceptions to this universal rule then exclude certain kinds of speech from protection. For example, the categorical approach of *Chaplinsky v. New Hampshire* argues that certain kinds of speech such as libel, obscenity, and fighting words can be regulated because they lack ideational content and really are not speech.[4] However, this case offers no explicit definition of "idea" as a concept or other explanation of the nature of speech. Another ascriptive account is seen in some contemporary arguments about hate speech that neglect to define speech but hold that racist insults should not be protected since they are like physical assaults.[5] Many interpret Catharine MacKinnon's call for restriction of pornography to be based upon the identification of pornography as a regulable sexual act rather than as nonregulable speech.[6] One problem with ascriptive approaches to the definition of speech is that these are wholly dependent on the outcome of political struggles that reflect the temporary relative power positions of those participating in the argument. There is little or no room for constructive dialogue about the theoretical meaning and content of the concept of speech within these ascriptive accounts. I have nothing against the notion that the definition of speech should be, and always will be, the subject of political debates, but the ascriptive approach is retrospective and usually only used to explain past practice.[7] It offers little guidance for how we should deal with new modes of expression or the speech situations created by emerging technologies. The ascriptive approach provides only the weakest of foundations for a clear, rigorous investigation of freedom of speech. A clear definition of speech is required before we can begin to discuss which speech should be considered free.

Pervasive in public opinion and theoretical writing on freedom of speech is the idea that if an event qualifies as speech, then that speech should be free. This attitude is partly represented in the series of First Amendment cases capped by *United States v. O'Brien* and *Texas v. Johnson*, which develop a distinction between speech and conduct.[8] The dichotomy is of great importance since, many argue, speech should be free, while conduct can be regulated through standard criminal legislation as long as such laws are not motivated by a state effort to control the expressive component of the conduct.[9] With a speech/conduct distinction like this in place, free speech argument takes the form of proving that an act or form of expression counts as speech. If one makes a convincing case that the act in question is speech, then one concludes immediately that the act should be protected. That is, the argument holds that most conduct may be regulated by the state under a lower level of judicial scrutiny, while all speech is off limits to regulators.[10] Such an argument reduces debates over freedom of speech to arguments about which kinds of utterances qualify as speech, but it still offers no general definition of speech. The speech/conduct distinction rests entirely upon the legal practice of freedom of speech, which is especially ad hoc when it comes to this dichotomy. Definitions of speech and conduct are legally and politically contested. They represent extremely slippery ground on which to rest theoretical justifications of freedom of speech beyond simple absolutism.

It will be more useful to consider that all speech acts are a form of conduct, some of which is regulable, rather than relying upon the illusory speech/conduct dichotomy. The common distinction between the two is not only illusory, it is unhelpful at best and dishonest at worst. Speech and free speech are not coterminous categories. Many categories of speech are prohibited with the First Amendment blessings of the U.S. Supreme Court. Categories of speech acts exist that are excluded from freedom of speech, therefore it makes no sense to argue that all speech is free while conduct is open to regulation. Libel, bribery, and incitement to illegal action are categories of speech that express ideas but that we wisely restrict by law consistent with the Constitution. At the same time, as Schauer correctly points out, the First Amendment protects nude dancing, which conveys little in the way of ideas or as a kind of speech. Maybe these are the correct legal outcomes, but they demonstrate the hopeless muddle of the speech/conduct distinction as a basis for normative theory about speech. The ways in which speech and conduct are distinguished in First Amendment law and by individual theorists of free speech do not reveal a clear definition of speech. This distinction does not provide a justificatory argument for why speech should be free, nor does it offer guidance as to how to resolve difficult cases.

Speech Act Theory

The concept of speech act is already well described outside of debates about freedom of speech and therefore meets the independence condition mentioned earlier. Speech act theory belongs to the philosophy of language and philosophy of mind. It says nothing about whether speech should be free or whether anything in the definition of speech is relevant to freedom of speech. At the same time, it gives a thorough and structured phenomenological account of what happens when we speak and offers a firm foundation for a pluralist framework for free speech.

John Searle writes that "talking is performing acts according to rules."[11] He contrasts speech acts with simple utterances that are no more than strings of sounds, words, or marks on paper that fail to transmit meaning or cause effects on hearers. "Utterance" describes the simple, physical act of creating sounds or gestures.[12] Utterance does not tell us anything about the intentions or mental state of the actor or of the communicative properties of the utterance in question. We can think of utterance as a prerequisite for all speech acts. Speech acts are the class of utterances that meet certain conditions of performance and meaning. They involve the uttering of words or symbols that have "a certain more-or-less definite sense and reference."[13] A speech act occurs when words from an existing vocabulary are linked in sentences with accepted grammar to give effect to certain meanings that could be (but in any given instance might not be) understood by a hearer. Speech acts generally represent attempts at interpersonal communication. They may also be attempts to bring about consequences beyond communication.

In *How to Do Things with Words*, J. L. Austin describes four conditions that define a performative utterance (or speech act) as well as the categories into which such utterances may fall: the utterance must follow a conventional procedure and have a conventional effect; the appropriate persons and conditions must be involved; all those involved must execute their roles in the procedure; and the participants must intend to participate and then do so.[14] Searle conveniently summarizes these primary conditions: "Illocutionary and propositional acts consist characteristically in uttering words in sentences in certain contexts, under certain conditions and with certain intentions."[15] The criteria that define context, conditions, and intention establish the rule-governed nature of speech acts. The crux of speech act theory is that there is quite a bit more to saying something successfully than an individual just stringing together some words (an utterance). The vocalization (or writing) of words is a speech act only when the circumstances surrounding the act are such that all participants (speakers, hearers, and relevant third parties) can recognize that the act has occurred. Austin emphasizes "that the illocutionary act is a conventional act: an act done as conforming to a convention."[16] The speaker must intend to achieve certain effects, such as the communication of meaning or the making of a contract, within a context such that those effects are possible. The illocutionary act must also result in "uptake" by the hearer, the recognition of what the speaker was doing in performing the act.[17] Searle states, "In speaking I attempt to communicate certain things to my hearer by getting him to recognize my intention to communicate just those things."[18] A speech act is successfully performed when there is a connection between what a speaker means (intends) and what the words spoken mean.[19] Speech act theory brings together the experiences of both the speaker and hearer by considering the intentions of the speaker and the meaning taken by the hearer in a single analysis. The relationship between speakers and hearers is crucial to understanding the speech act. Speech theories that look only to consequences on hearers fail to understand the act performed in speaking, while theories that look only to the expression by speakers fail to understand the extent to which no act can be said to have occurred unless some hearer (or potential hearer) secures uptake.

Social conventions play a significant role in the successful performance of speech acts. Meaning rests upon conventional rules as to what words signify in particular circumstances. Sentences do not have absolute meanings independent of their context, the conditions pertaining to the act, and the intentions of participants. Words reduce to gibberish absent these conventions to order hearers' interpretation of what speakers mean. Language is a social construct, and meaning rests upon social relations. The freedom to speak is useless unless it includes the ability to communicate the meaning of the sentences uttered. Language develops, grows, and changes in meaning as a result of social relations. Children learn language from other people (or television and computers programmed by people) and develop their skills through use of language with others. This does not seem controversial. Given that language develops in social relations, the speech acts made with language are ultimately dependent upon those relations. Individuals may choose to say this and not that, but what they say cannot stray far from the socially constructed language, shared meanings, common knowledge, and power relations within which they exist or else the rest of the community will fail to understand what they say.[20]

There are always parties to a speech act. To say that a speech act has occurred is to imply the existence of a speaker and one or more hearers. Furthermore, the speaker and hearer are bound in a relationship created by that expression. To say that a speech act has occurred is to say that a social relation exists, even if the nature of that relation is not immediately clear. When an individual speaks, there is always a hearer to whom he or she speaks. This may be another individual, a group of individuals, or a large collective body. The speech relationship may be direct, as in the case of actual conversation, lecturing, stump speeches, making a demand or request, or answering a question where the parties are immediately aware of each other. The speech relationship may be indirect, where the speech act is performed but the hearing or recognition takes place in a different time or place, as in the case of written communications, speech recorded through electronic means, or some form of Internet communications where the parties are not in contact. The parties to the speech act may voluntarily agree to the relationship formed (as when each seeks out a conversation) or may find themselves in a relationship they do not seek out.[21] In these indirect cases, the speech act is still performed with some hearer in mind, even if that person is not immediately present or even identifiable.[22] The speaker must have specific listeners in mind or presume the existence of a possible, unspecified audience. For instance, writing in a journal might represent a speech act that does not presume a reader in the present or future. However, the writing of the journal requires a background of social relations that provides the journal's language and meaning. In addition, while the writer may believe that the text will never be read, to write sentences with meaning that qualify as speech acts requires, at minimum, some kind of presumed audience.[23] This presumed audience might be one's own alter ego, a specific individual, or an amalgamation of people important to the writer for whatever reason. The journal may even be written as a record of current events, with the writer's future self in mind as the hearer of the speech act.

Speech creates social relations. Such relations often are intentionally sought out by both parties, as in contracts, for example. Individuals create the contractual relationship when they perform specific speech acts such as "I agree to deliver X goods on Y day in exchange for Z dollars." Conventional speech acts performed by each party create a contractual relationship between two people that would not otherwise exist. Some relations created by speech acts are less intentional, for example, I strike up a conversation on the street with someone whom I have not previously met. My speech act forms a relationship (albeit temporary) between us. Speech acts create many kinds of relationships and change the meaning of most others. Tomorrow, on my way to the office, I may find myself relating to a man preaching on the library mall, and that relationship will be constituted by his speech acts (declaiming against the seven deadly sins) and my possible response (a hasty but impassioned defense of gluttony). Our unavoidable physical proximity provides an opportunity for a social relation to be created. Were I to pass by out of earshot or during the preacher's coffee break, we would never have any relationship at all. The social relations involved are not of great consequence, and each of us may forget the other quickly, but the connections exist and are created by speech acts.

There are many important relationships created through speech acts. Political candidates form social relations with their followers through the speech acts involved in campaigning. While many factors induce someone to support a candidate, such as shared interests, common background, and similar political objectives, it is only through speech acts that a candidate communicates such information to people and develops a connection with supporters.[24] Supporters register their approval through speech acts, such as attendance at rallies, cheering, contributions, answers given to pollsters, and conversations with other people. A relationship of allegiance forms between supporter and candidate, which leads to certain kinds of speech acts by the supporters. In turn, these elicit further social relations between supporters and uncommitted citizens they hope to convince, as well as adversarial relations between supporters of different candidates. The entire web of social relations is linked together by the speech acts of parties to these social relations.

Speech always takes place in some kind of social relationship. Campaign speech involves speakers and audiences in some combination. A political candidate speaks to an audience of citizens, and that speech is a social act resting upon shared language, shared conventions for political speeches, and perhaps a shared understanding of each participant's interests. While the candidate probably has no personal connection with each member of the audience, he or she has ties to the audience as a group. It may be very difficult to specify the nature of that relationship; in fact, each individual in the audience probably perceives it somewhat differently or might even deny the existence of such a relationship. Nonetheless, no speech could occur without the background of social relations. There are common features we might recognize in the candidate-audience relationship. Candidates play up to audiences. Audiences (especially at political conventions) play up to the candidate. Candidates make speeches punctuated with lines meant to inspire applause and positive reinforcement. Some kinds of speeches, at a town-meeting style debate, for instance, allow for audience questions.

The political speech of protest also takes place within social relations. The dissident has a relationship with his or her supporters but also with the opponents in power. The adversarial relationship is one that involves shared language at a minimum and might include shared allegiance to a basic document.[25] Protest is useless unless it follows conventions understood by the groups it criticizes such that those groups understand what is said. Flag burners destroy flags less out of revulsion at the flag than out of the understanding that a burning flag sends a vibrant message. When dissident action strays too far from shared conventions and relations, it ceases to be comprehensible and fails to promote social change.

Speech often takes place within hierarchical relations, as in the case of discussions between managers and workers. These discussions are marked by different conventions than political speeches. In addition to shared language, workers and managers are linked by the employment relationship, financial responsibilities, and common purposes (completion of a product), as well as adversarial purposes (the negotiation of a collective bargaining agreement). The hierarchy itself conditions the speech that takes place. Workers cannot say the same things to managers that managers can say to workers ("You are fired," addressing one another by first name, harassment).[26] Speech between members of the management group and the worker group will be scrutinized for adherence to the norms of the hierarchical social relationship. Workers who "show up" the boss may be censured or fired. Managers who engage in racial or sexual harassment may be subject to sanctions (civil suits, criminal complaints) initiated by workers.[27]

Relationships of authority are an important part of the circumstances that establish the existence and meaning of a speech act. For instance, "Get me some coffee" has a very different meaning when said by a superior to a subordinate than it does when said between peers. It is not an act at all if said by a subordinate to a superior whose response is "I don't take orders from you," thus nullifying the statement.[28] Because the superior does not recognize "get me some coffee" as something that a subordinate can say in this context, the statement either reduces to meaningless gibberish or else is seen in a different way as rank insubordination. "Get me some coffee" may come across to the boss as "I desire that you fire me" if the offense against hierarchy is serious enough. There is more to this than mere misunderstanding. The speech act of ordering has not been successfully performed in the sense that what was said is not what was heard.

There is a problem with defining speech acts according to one's particular interpretation of the social relations between speakers and hearers. Such a definition allows the dominant party to the relationship to determine when a speech act has taken place. For an utterance to be a speech act, Austin requires intent to communicate on the part of the speaker and recognition by the hearer that a speech act has been attempted. He defines a "performative utterance" as the saying of something within procedures and circumstances such that all parties recognize the saying as an act.[29] Austin's condition of mutual recognition of the speech act must be relaxed, otherwise too much power is left in the hands of the addressee of the utterance to deny the existence of the speech and to deny the relevance of the speaker. For instance, the possibility of political dissent is sharply curtailed if those in power simply may choose to deny that the dissenter speaks by refusing to acknowledge that the speech acts of protest have meaning.[30] Protesters could find that their expression has been relegated to the dustbin of nonsensical utterances by the active refusal of the authorities to recognize that their speech acts have occurred. There is a danger that if we limit the definition of speech to specific social relations between speakers and audiences, the power relationships will overwhelmingly determine the range of allowable speech.[31] Instead, the definition of speech acts, while based in social relations, must allow for the speech act to be recognized in spite of specific power relations.

A modified version of Austin's account would recognize the occurrence of a speech act when his conditions of shared vocabulary, grammar, sense, and reference are met not by the general agreement of all parties to the speech act but within the context of possible satisfaction of these concerns. The condition of intentionality must be relaxed to no longer require the hearer's actual intention to receive the speech act. That is, in my formulation, the specific relationship between speaker and hearer is important to describe the kind of speech act that has occurred but does not in itself determine the occurrence. Instead, the broader social relations within which the speaker and hearer are embedded ultimately determine whether an utterance was a speech act or merely senseless gibberish. This requires an external standard to determine speech acts rather than allowing for this determination wholly within the relationship between utterer and hearer. Such an external standard is necessary, otherwise the powerful can always ignore dissent. In this way, the theory can also extend to speech acts that do not directly involve parties other than the speaker, for instance, in the writing of texts or in talking to oneself.

There are several ways in which speech acts are socially embedded, thus suggesting their centrality to an understanding of freedom of speech. Most important, the language that we use when we speak is social in that it is shared by others whether they are audience members or not. We cannot speak unless there are words, symbols, or gestures with shared meanings that we can use to perform a speech act. There are wordlike sounds, symbols, and gestures without shared meanings that human beings can and do utter, but these do not make speech unless someone could recognize these words as having meaning.[32]

Let me illustrate with examples of what does and does not count as speech. Astrid performs a speech act when she walks into the rathskeller, approaches the bar, and utters the words, "I would like a bottle of Rolling Rock, please." This is a speech act because both Astrid and the bartender understand something similar by these words, and Astrid leaves the bar with a beer in hand.[33] Astrid probably would also have left the bar with a beer if she had entered with "Una cerveza fria por favor," even if the bartender did not speak Spanish, since there are shared patterns of gestures involved in requesting a beer, a limited number of reasons that Astrid would be at the bar with cash in her hand, and a general understanding of what each individual's role in their limited relationship is. On the other hand, a lunatic screaming on a street corner often fails to perform a speech act. Bystanders draw meaning from the raving ("Wow, this person is disturbed"), but this probably is not the conventional meaning of the words being used. In this second example, there is a disjuncture, either because the condition of intention on the part of the speaker is absent or because reception (uptake) fails. Sensible-sounding nonsense also fails to be a speech act, on its own, but does constitute a speech act in certain circumstances. Alone, a string of made-up words that resemble an actual language fails as a speech act. However, when a comic strings together made up words along with certain gestures and cadences, a speech act of humor is achieved.

In addition to shared language and power relationships, the circumstances of a speech act are also marked by relationships of shared knowledge of certain facts. Much of what we mean when we speak rests upon the assumption that others know something of the world we are discussing. Some of these are facts about the physical universe that are so obvious or well known that we rarely consider them. For example, Earth is round and gravity points us down. John Searle refers to these as "brute facts," and they are independent of our descriptions and depictions of them. Some shared knowledge is more complicated. Searle says that there are "objective facts in the world, that are only facts by human agreement."[34] These "institutional facts" are dependent upon convention and institutions. Not only do these facts rest upon human relationships and institutions, but they also serve as context for the meaning of speech, the context that allows an utterance to qualify as a speech act. These institutional facts can be altered by speech acts oriented toward changing the conventional meaning, however, thus affecting the meaning of future speech acts that will occur in the new social context of institutional facts.

Speech Categories

To this point, speech act theory cannot tell us how we might differentiate between categories of speech. There are frequent efforts within the First Amendment framework to categorize speech with an eye to excluding certain categories of speech from protection. Categorization for this purpose is problematic because, like the speech/conduct distinction, it is ad hoc, is retrospective, and offers little guidance as to how new free speech situations should be addressed. The categorical approach seen in a case such as *Chaplinsky* merely sets in stone a contemporary political preference for certain kinds of speech over other kinds without contributing to an overall understanding of what speech is. We can rethink categorization in a way consistent with speech act theory in order to improve the contextual definition of speech. Some definitions of different categories of speech are necessary in addition to the general description of speech acts.[35] This categorization depends on the same kinds of contextual factors that identify speech acts, therefore the distinctions we make between different kinds of speech are compatible with speech act theory. Such categorization better describes a particular speech act by indicating contextual factors in addition to the conventions of intent and recognition that differentiate a speech act from a mere utterance. The additional context helps to reveal the distinct character of different kinds of speech. Furthermore, since speech act theory does not recognize a speech/conduct distinction, some means must be used to distinguish between different kinds of speech for the purposes of deciding what speech should be protected. Speech act theorists have not had to make such distinctions because they have not been concerned with the legal practice of freedom of speech or free speech policy. Without a categorization of speech, it would be very difficult to draw boundaries on freedom of speech. The kinds of categories that are most relevant include political, artistic, scientific, emotive, and religious speech.

Political speech is the most important category under the current First Amendment framework. A great deal of debate about speech is over the boundary between political and nonpolitical categories. Political speech is at the core of free speech theory as structured by the First Amendment framework and has the strongest claim to protection given the language and history of the Bill of Rights. The more inclusive the category of political speech, the more speech the First Amendment protects. Alexander Meiklejohn's two-tier approach to the First Amendment is the clearest example of a political/nonpolitical dichotomy.[36] Meiklejohn construes the First Amendment narrowly and argues that the text and history of the Constitution mandate an interpretation of the First Amendment as protection of political speech. Article I of the Constitution includes rules to protect free speech for members of Congress in order to secure an open process of debate within the legislature. Meiklejohn argues that since the people are ultimately sovereign under the Constitution, they must be guaranteed the same speech rights. They are members of the sovereign body, and the same sort of open process called for in Article I for the legislature should extend to the democratic debate carried on by citizens. On the other hand, nonpolitical speech does not relate to the process of self-government and does not fall within Meiklejohn's interpretation of the First Amendment. Instead, he sees all other speech as regulable, with consideration for conventional due process under the Fifth Amendment.

Political speech has absolute protection; nonpolitical speech may be regulated like any other conduct. For instance, Meiklejohn originally saw nothing in this interpretation of the Constitution that would call for the protection of commercially produced speech such as radio broadcasting or advertising.[37] He was forced to modify this position as he realized that limiting First Amendment protection to a narrow understanding of political speech excluded a number of categories of speech, such as artistic expression, that he and others valued highly.[38] To retain the structure of the defense of freedom of speech as a requirement of self-government and to include artistic expression and other valued categories of speech, Meiklejohn had to expand his definition of political speech to encompass these other categories. Sunstein's version of the two-tier argument, while it abandons Meiklejohn's dichotomy between First and Fifth Amendment speech, also expands the category of political speech to encompass other categories deemed worthy of protection while relegating "low-value" speech to a reduced standard of protection.

There is no consensus on the definition of political speech, and it is difficult to determine how extensive such a definition can be and remain workable. The best we can do is to use a moderately broad definition of political speech that falls somewhere between the too exclusive (Bork) and the overly inclusive (Sunstein). Recall Sunstein's definition: "For present purposes I mean to treat speech as political *when it is both intended and received as a contribution to public deliberation about some issue*. This is a broad standard. It categorizes all speech that bears on potentially public issues as falling within the free speech core."[39] There are two problems with Sunstein's approach. First, he does not define the concept of speech, so it is unclear what breaks down into categories of political and nonpolitical. Second, his definition appears to include all speech that we value for any reason, thus making this useless for the categorization of speech. Some kinds of valuable speech must be nonpolitical, and the trick is to usefully articulate the boundaries of political speech.

The two problems in Sunstein's definition can be alleviated through recasting his two conditions of intention and reception in Austinian terms to make the definition somewhat less inclusive and thus more manageable. Sunstein's second condition, reception, is parallel to Austin's "uptake" (in this case, the listener must understand that the utterance is a political speech act). For a speech act to be political, it is necessary that the speaker intends it to be a political speech act (Sunstein's intention condition), demonstrating this intent through the use of linguistic conventions associated with political speech (the modified reception condition). This does not mean that the speech act must be conventional in the sense of "acceptable" or "mainstream," only that it is potentially comprehensible by an audience, in other words, that the political speech act is an utterance that has "a certain more-or-less definite sense and reference" that is taken to be political. The reception condition suggests that only a few people need to understand the speech as a contribution to public deliberation, which they will do through consideration of the conventions of political speech acts. By no means is it required that everyone understand the speech as such a contribution for it to count as political.

Let me offer examples of how this modified definition would categorize several different speech acts. An easy case would be that of a peaceful protester (call him Bjorn) carrying a picket sign and an American flag on a public sidewalk in front of an army recruitment office to protest military spending. This is a wholly conventional act readily accepted by most people as political speech. Bjorn gives notice of his intentions by choosing a means of protest that adheres to conventions of political speech acts. His action also meets the intention and reception conditions for successful performance of a speech act. If Bjorn decides to burn his picket sign and the flag, the case becomes more complicated. Under the First Amendment framework, we might ask several questions about Bjorn's action. First, is this speech or is it conduct? Second, if this is speech, does it fall within the categories of speech receiving First Amendment protection? Third, was the state motivated in prohibiting the conduct by a desire to suppress speech or by a neutral, nonspeech motivation?[40] Within the definitions of speech act and political speech act that I have offered, Bjorn's flag burning is a political speech act. While it does not involve words or even an utterance in the literal sense, flag burning meets the conditions of intention and reception within current practices of freedom of speech.[41] When Bjorn ignites his flag in front of the recruiting office, we know what he means and he knows that we will know.[42] Finally, in a different case, flag burning could be scientific speech rather than political speech. If Bjorn is a safety tester by profession, he may ignite flags to collect data on ignition temperatures and combustion time. If he does this work in his laboratory and reports his results in scientific journals, both the flag burning and the reports will unambiguously belong to the category of scientific speech. If he chooses to do these experiments on the sidewalk in front of the recruiting office, there will be some confusion.[43] As observers, we would have a choice of several categories in which to place the act.

The conventions followed (artistic, literary, political, scientific) count heavily in assessing in which category to place a speech act. Of course, this places a great deal of weight on the identification of those conventions, something neither Austin nor Sunstein does. In my view, the linguistic conventions that identify a speech act as political, artistic, religious, or scientific are known from the context in which the act takes place. There is no way that one could simply or definitively identify the context required such that an act could be known, without a doubt, to be political speech. Bork's statist definition of political speech certainly is a start. Expression involving clear statements about government policies and personnel would fit the conventions of political speech because almost everyone could recognize the political quality of these statements. On the other hand, flag burning as a political statement is more ambiguous, although many people do understand the symbolism that makes flag burning political speech. The most controversial identifications of speech acts as political tend to occur at the boundaries of categories where speech acts follow the linguistic conventions of artistic, emotive, or scientific speech categories.

The contextual definition of speech acts is well-suited to form the basis of a pluralist framework for freedom of speech. Speech act theory provides an independent definition of speech as a phenomenon that is logically prior to any specific justification of free speech. This definition does not privilege one kind of speech over another, thus allowing for the examination and justification of free speech apart from the loaded categories of the First Amendment framework. The pluralist framework takes advantage of the independence of the contextual definition of speech to put the focus in debates over any particular free speech claim or speech situation on the values most relevant to that particular claim. While the pluralist framework cannot settle every disputed free speech claim by bringing to bear a single, general free speech principle, it does allow us to examine conflicting values more easily. We can consider politically the relative position of these values free from the confusion of poorly articulated definitions of speech and justifications built around unitary but exclusive values.

CHAPTER SEVEN

The Pluralist Framework for Freedom of Speech

Most free speech theorists seek a comprehensive justification of freedom of speech that protects many kinds of speech across a variety of political, legal, and social circumstances, but the three prominent schools of thought on free speech all fail to provide such a comprehensive justification. Were we to adopt any of these justifications as the sole argument for freedom of speech, some quantity of important speech would be excluded from protection. The dominant First Amendment framework for debate about freedom of speech may help with the problem of the absence of a single free speech principle, but it has problems of its own. That framework organizes and structures American debates about the meaning of free speech, but in doing so it sets strict parameters on the scope of what counts as a valid free speech claim, and on how these claims may proceed, and creates obstacles to new free speech arguments. If the First Amendment framework for debate cannot be used to address a significant number of the claims that many would like to make and no general principle of free speech exists, then our debates about freedom of speech require an alternative framework within which new arguments can be made, speech claims can be reinforced or made for the first time, and new circumstances addressed. Such a framework would supplement the legal processes of the First Amendment with political advocacy, argument, and deliberation.

I propose a pluralist framework for free speech that is broader in scope and more general in application than the First Amendment framework. Frameworks for debate are general features of social and political life. We operate within these frameworks all the time, even though we are often unaware of them. Only when we critically examine these frameworks and begin to rethink them do the consequences that they have for various problems and claims become clear. The First Amendment framework is comprised of a set of legal, political, historical, and cultural factors that constrains the kinds of free speech claims that we can develop and recognize, while it also conditions the response to new speech situations. In particular, it limits individual free speech claims to those against state action that restricts speech. Also, obviously, this framework can only be used to describe free speech claims in the United States. The pluralist framework, which is more general and less restrictive than the First Amendment framework, builds on the different free speech values exhibited in the libertarian, expressivist, and egalitarian justifications of freedom of speech. It follows context-driven speech act theory in its identification of speech claims and is not limited to the specific legal-political institutional domain of First Amendment law. It is more political and much less concerned with technically correct legal responses to speech claims.

While the pluralist framework is more open to new speech claims and varied speech values, it is not simple, unmoored relativism. Frameworks for debate, in general, provide the possibility of evaluation and judgment. The pluralist framework recognizes that there are many values relevant to speech and that a variety of different goals and objectives can be advanced by freedom of speech across a range of speech situations and contexts. Like the First Amendment framework, the pluralist framework allows individuals to evaluate free speech claims and make judgments about which speech should be protected. The pluralist framework also helps individuals identify the speech that they believe should be controlled through law, moral suasion, social sanction, or protest movement. It does not offer the possibility of technical legal solutions for use in court challenges against state action, nor does it make authoritative judgments about the Constitution. Instead, it presents a set of questions and evaluative criteria with which to make political judgments. That is, it establishes the groundwork for a politics of free speech. The next wave of new free speech claims will not be found in the legally creative solutions to speech problems favored by legal scholars but rather through the work of social and political movements. Like other important liberal values, such as justice or equality, free speech should be subject to political deliberation. The pluralist framework helps define what the parameters of such political debates should look like.

Pluralism

The pluralist framework that I develop is grounded in the pluralism of Isaiah Berlin, Charles Larmore, John Kekes, William Galston, and others. This is the pluralism of liberal political theory rather than the adversarial interest group pluralism of contemporary political science. Berlin's pluralism is by no means the dominant version of liberal theory, but it is compelling, and the value conflicts at the heart of many free speech disputes strongly indicate that we must take pluralism seriously as a descriptive and normative theory.[1] Larmore offers a clear definition of pluralism: "In its broad form it asserts that the kinds of moral claims upon us and the forms of self-realization we can admire are in the end not one, but many. It is, in other words, a doctrine about the sources of value. Moral pluralism, in one plausible version, is the view that our moral convictions cannot all be conceived in terms of the consequentialist principle of bringing about the most good overall."[2] Pluralism is not especially popular with those who hope to solve problems through legal procedures that offer unique solutions to social problems. Such procedures require what pluralism denies, namely, the existence of a single principle by which to judge all outcomes.

Political and legal theorists concerned with determining specific policy solutions for social conflicts find monism much more appealing. It holds out the promise of a single solution for each conflict through logical appeal to a common value. Utilitarians, for instance, promise to solve every problem by reducing conflicting positions to expressions of the underlying value of utility. To resolve a conflict, they calculate the utility of each position and set policy according to that calculus. Utilitarianism is by no means the only monistic theory within liberalism, but it is the most familiar, common target of pluralist theory. There are two general characteristics of monist theories of value. "A theory of value is monistic . . . if it either (a) reduces goods to a common measure or (b) creates a comprehensive hierarchy or ordering among goods."[3] There are no "ties," "do-overs," or conflicts that defy a measured and calculated response. There may be unfortunate results for monists when some lose in a policy dispute, but there are no tragic choices between incommensurable goods. Appeal to the monistic value always provides a definitive answer. This does not mean that monism always provides the right answer.

Pluralism presents certain difficulties for us as citizens because it means there are no easy answers and no simple procedures for resolving value conflicts by reference to a common denominator such as utility.[4] For pluralists, the good life is all about how we deal with the inevitable conflicts presented by the plurality of values around us.[5] Pluralists have no simple yardstick for progress. Instead, for pluralists, "the ideal is of a framework that fosters the realization of plural, conditional, incompatible and incommensurable values; it is not the advocacy of some specific value."[6] Pluralists follow Berlin in recognizing a plurality of values that are not reducible to one or the other.[7]

Pluralism has distinct descriptive advantages over monism because it recognizes that there are values that cannot be reconciled. Values are incommensurable when they are characterized by an "incomparability of valuable cultural objects, activities, reasons for action or forms of life."[8] There are simply some values that cannot be reduced to common terms for comparison.[9] These conflicts are, in a sense, built into moral expressions themselves.[10] Utilitarians and other monists deny this, of course, but the monist project of being able to aggregate, rank, or compare all values leads to mischaracterization of the reasons for why people care about various values. In the speech context, for instance, monists have to explain artistic expression in terms of its political value even when that expression is neither intended nor received as political. In order to compare the artistic worth of one speech act with its political consequences, monists try to translate these into a common metric, despite the fact that they are distinct expressions of two different values.

Incommensurability does not mean incompatibility.[11] We can value both artistic speech and political speech even if we cannot rank order them in a hierarchy according to a common denominator. Art does not preclude politics (or vice versa), so while these values are incommensurable, they are compatible. At the same time, pluralism is not relativism. Relativists would argue that incommensurable values were also incomparable, that we could take no position favoring one incommensurable value over another. Pluralists, however, recognize that there are a variety of ways that we compare the incommensurable. For instance, instead of ranking two values that are in conflict, we can rank the options or policies that arise from those values.[12] Such a ranking is not a technical exercise in reduction to a common metric. Instead, it is a political process of advocacy, argument, and deliberation.

The first step to resolve conflicts between incommensurable values is to articulate those in question. One of the problems with monism is that it leads adherents to misidentify values. That is, the structure of monist arguments requires that values be reduced to a common metric, with the result that the distinctions between them are often submerged or papered over. A pluralist can describe conflicting values in their own terms because there is no imperative to reduce them to a unidimensional rank ordering.[13] This allows for clear statements about what the values are before deliberation begins about which takes precedence in a given situation. We can distinguish pluralism from relativism along these lines. When pluralists see incommensurable values, they can still argue in favor of one over the others. Pluralists defend or justify their favored values politically by reference both to a background of shared social values as well as by reference to those they consider part of the minimum requirements of the good life.[14] Pluralists accept that there is no single universal rank ordering of all values, while at the same time they argue for specific outcomes in particular cases. This is why negative liberty is so important to Berlin. Given the fact of "unavoidable loss among rivalrous goods and evils," we need negative liberty so that social interference in the choices we make according to our values will be kept to a minimum.[15]

I propose a framework that is pluralist in three senses. First, the framework is at its core value pluralist and opposed to universalist claims. No single principle can serve as an ultimate criterion or common metric for all free speech questions. While self-realization, equality, and truth/democracy each fall short as comprehensive solutions to free speech problems, the framework is open to a wide variety of values that underpin freedom of speech, including these. The pluralist framework need not be limited to these values, although such values are those most often discussed in relation to freedom of speech. The pluralist framework allows us to make judgments about competing free speech claims, but these judgments will not be made by reference to a single value that ultimately trumps all others. As I showed earlier, unitary values often come into conflict in especially difficult free speech cases such as hate speech or arts censorship. Universalists must either deny the existence of these value conflicts or else redefine the situation in ways that obscure the conflict. For instance, in the conflict between truth/democracy and expressivist self-realization, monists such as Martin Redish and Cass Sunstein redefine art as a contribution to public debate, thus indicating that when conflicts arise, self-realization will be treated as a secondary value. They do not protect artistic expression for its own sake and promote self-realization only to the extent that it leads to the policies that a focus on truth/democracy would have. Such acts of redefinition do not always work, and if art is only protected insofar as it is a contribution to political debate, self-realization may be sacrificed. The pluralist framework does not require these instances of mutilating acts of redefinition or obfuscation.

Value pluralism allows individuals to promote a variety of different values associated with freedom of speech within the parameters of the framework. The pluralist framework itself does not necessarily attach more importance to some values than others. The framework creates room for a politics of free speech as opposed to the rank ordering and aggregation of values favored by monists operating under the First Amendment framework. This is not to say that all potential values are acceptable under the pluralist framework. Instead, a number of values such as those promoted by libertarians, egalitarians, and expressivists could be seen as compatible with freedom of speech, while others would prove to be incompatible. In this sense of pluralism, then, debates over the meaning of freedom of speech are not an effort to find a single ruling principle to decide all cases. This means there will be some hard cases with ambiguous solutions, but there already are many free speech problems with ambiguous solutions under the First Amendment framework. Hard cases are a fact of life, and the goal should not be to eliminate them but to come up with better ways to debate solutions for them. Pluralism does not mean that all parties to the political debate over a free speech claim will be satisfied with the outcome of that debate. Rather, openness to a variety of political values creates an environment for free speech debate similar to what Larmore calls modus vivendi liberalism in the broader political context.[16] The framework privileges no particular value but allows clear arguments about free speech values to take place.

The framework is pluralist in the second sense that it is open to multiple speech justifications. The framework's pluralism rests on the understanding that some values and preferences are incommensurable. Thus, arguments based on incommensurable values are likely to conflict. Freedom of speech is part of the bedrock of liberalism, but the arguments in support of freedom of speech represent different, not always complementary, values. The pluralist framework requires us to recognize this variety rather than submerge it. While the First Amendment framework constrains the kinds of arguments that can be made to justify freedom of speech, it still allows a limited number of different arguments to be made. Similarly, the pluralist framework does not promote any one "best" justification of freedom of speech. Instead, it supports a larger number of different justificatory arguments for free speech, providing two important advantages over the First Amendment framework. First, no argument itself is privileged by the terms of the framework in the way that the First Amendment framework favors free speech libertarianism. Second, by considering the context in which speech acts occur, the pluralist framework allows us to apply the arguments most appropriate to a specific kind of speech act or speech situation rather than shoe-horning different kinds of speech into an all-purpose, unitary justification of free speech. Essentially, recognition of the diversity of free speech values requires the further recognition of a plurality of justifications of freedom of speech.

The framework is pluralist in the third sense that it recognizes the diversity of speaking subjects. The pluralist framework recognizes that there are always several parties to a speech act. The calculus of their freedoms will vary depending on the nature of the speech act, the relative social positions of the parties, the relationship of the parties to the speech act, and the context in which the speech act occurs. Speech acts always require speakers and listeners (or potential and perceived listeners). Free speech theory usually focuses on the speaker, but the freedom of the listeners conditions what they hear, their opportunity to speak in response, and the kinds of speech acts that may be performed both at the time of the original speech act and later. Free speech theorists carry ideas of whose speech is to be free along with the values that they promote through freedom of speech. Unitary justifications of freedom of speech privilege certain kinds of speech and certain kinds of speakers. The pluralist framework requires that in the analysis of a speech claim or a speech situation, the position of all potential parties must be considered.

Often, the threats to free speech identified by a theorist also tell us a lot about whose speech is to be protected and whose freedom is to be promoted. Unitary justifications usually specify who is to be free in terms of a universalist claim that free speech is for everyone, with a few modest exceptions. It would be surprising to encounter a free speech theory that overtly excluded certain classes or social groups from free speech protection.[17] While universalist claims for freedom of speech are the norm, restrictions on those who are to enjoy freedom of speech may lie hidden in the caveats and boundaries of the argument rather than in overt declarations. For instance, the marketplace of ideas metaphor of public discussion leading to beneficial social policy rests upon assumptions of rational individuals participating in a grand social process. This theory of freedom of speech excludes nonrational individuals. The definition of "person" is actually a restriction on who shall benefit from a particular justification of freedom of speech.[18] The limitation of freedom of speech to rational individuals does not explicitly exclude whole classes of people, but the definition of rationality may have many built-in biases that exclude groups of people and categories of speech. Rationality is a hotly contested concept, and it is unlikely that we will soon agree to a neutral and inclusive definition of it. Political theory lacks generally agreed upon definitions of rationality. Since rationality carries great political weight in the identification of who has freedom of speech, free speech theorists need to be aware and explicit about the implications of their definitions of rationality on the question of which speakers receive free speech protection.

The pluralist framework encompasses plurality of values, justifications, and speaking subjects in direct contrast to the First Amendment framework that favors value monism and unitary justifications while privileging the speech of particular kinds of speakers. These three senses of pluralism are advantages in the description of the universe of potential free speech claims and allow for more inclusive debates about free speech. However, these descriptive dimensions do not in themselves tell us how the pluralist framework allows for judgments and evaluation of competing free speech claims. Pluralism makes room for a politics of free speech, but this politics is not a free-for-all. Pluralism should ask specific kinds of questions and apply explicit criteria to evaluate free speech claims made by a variety of speakers.

Context and Speech Acts

Consideration of a speech claim or speech situation under the pluralist framework begins by reference back to the definition of speech act and its conventions of intention, condition, and reception (uptake).[19] The contextual approach to the definition of speech is a natural fit with pluralism because the speech act definition of speech does not recognize an inherent ranking of kinds of speech. It defines what counts as speech (as opposed to a mere utterance) but applies no value distinction between one type of speech over another. People who accept speech act theory certainly still argue in favor of some kinds of speech over others, but the definition of speech act only provides a context in which to make those arguments rather than providing an answer to which kind of speech is worth more than another. To rank some kinds of speech as more valuable than others requires that we make political arguments about those kinds of speech that take place after it has already been established that something is a speech act. Speech act theory does not provide for a simple speech/conduct distinction since all speech is a kind of action. We cannot fall back on the simple formulation that all speech acts are valuable and should be protected while utterances that fail to meet the conditions for speech acts are therefore not valuable and not protected. Bribery, for instance, is unworthy of protection because it is harmful and has little value even though it satisfied the conditions for a speech act. The argument against bribery is not about whether it is speech but about what it does and the harms that arise from it.

Speech act theory is inherently pluralist, and the pluralist framework builds on the contextual identification of speech found in speech act theory. Speech act theorists identify speech acts by examining an utterance in the context of the speaker and his or her relationship to the audience, the forms and rules of language, the shared understandings of the facts that govern the environment in which the utterance occurs, and the intentions of the speaker. Monists working within the First Amendment framework are forced by the terms of that framework to turn every speech act into an expression of the unitary value that they believe justifies protection of speech under the First Amendment. Pluralists, on the other hand, can look at the speech act on its own terms and in its own context. Since pluralism is open to a range of values, there is no need to explain speech acts in terms of a single value that may or may not be appropriate to that situation. Speech act theory defines the line between a mere utterance and a speech act according to rules of intention, condition, and reception, but these rules allow for a wide variety of utterances to succeed as speech acts. The theory does not require that every speech act be made according to the strict rules of "proper" grammar or that it even be made in the form of spoken words. Gestures, body language, and facial expressions can all qualify as speech acts as long as they meet the appropriate conditions. The same speech act can take on different meanings in different situations or even fail as a speech act in one situation while succeeding in another. Speech act theory denies a single underlying metric for what counts as speech. Speech acts cannot be rank ordered or understood according to a unitary value. Speech act theory is inherently pluralistic since it requires consideration of the enormous variety of possible speakers' intentions, the complex and multidimensional context of the referents that give language meaning, and the diversity of experiences that lead listeners to be able to receive an utterance as a speech act.

The pluralist framework also seeks to identify the type of speech act an event represents. Is this political, artistic, religious, or scientific speech or some other type? A theorist working within the pluralist framework will have to look at the facts of the event in question and the conventions that normally apply to speech in that context to determine if the event is a speech act. Does the speaker have the intention to perform a speech act of this type? Is the context such that the speech act is possible?[20] Do listeners receive the speech as conforming to the conventions of speech acts in this context? If a speaker misunderstands the conventions appropriate to a certain context and set of conditions, audiences will fail to "secure uptake" of the speech act, and the act fails. As I argued in chapter 6, observers cannot leave the determination of speech acts wholly up to the listener's uptake. It should be enough that potential listeners could secure uptake or that the speech follows the conventions of a speech act closely enough that only a listener biased against the speaker would refuse to acknowledge the speech act.

The identification of the type of speech act also depends upon the conventions of intention and context. A political speech act is performed when an individual utters words that "have a certain more-or-less definite sense and reference" that is political.[21] In other words, the speaker intends to perform a political speech act, the conditions are such that a political speech act is comprehensible, and a listener or potential listener can recognize the political speech act. A typical political speech act might be door-to-door canvassing in support of a ballot referendum. The canvasser approaches a listener and promotes a political position through sentences meant to persuade the listener of his or her view. Failure to perform a political speech act can take many forms. The famous First Amendment case *Cohen v. California* offers an example of an event that in the First Amendment framework is protected and is generally considered to be political speech but under the pluralist framework might not qualify as a political speech act.[22] Cohen was convicted on a charge of disturbing the peace by "offensive conduct" for wearing a jacket that said "Fuck the Draft" in a Los Angeles courthouse where women and children were present. The California Court of Appeals, which upheld the conviction, saw this kind of speech act as "behavior which has a tendency to provoke *others* to acts of violence or to in turn disturb the peace." At the same time, the phrase, under the wartime conditions that included a draft, obviously makes a political statement relevant to public debate. If the message were unintentional on Cohen's part (for instance, if he had borrowed someone else's jacket without looking to see what was printed on it), the phrase would not qualify as a speech act, even though the meaning of the words was clearly received by the arresting officer.[23] In fact,

Cohen is an interesting case because three dissenting justices saw the event as punishable conduct rather than speech. Cohen's speech could be seen as offensive conduct leading to a breach of the peace rather than a political speech act. While the phrase "Fuck the Draft" meets common conventions of offensiveness and would be recognizable as such to almost any listener, offensiveness alone does not preclude protection of this speech.

The pluralist framework also requires that we examine the context of the social relations between the parties to a speech act. A common theme running through libertarianism, expressivism, and egalitarianism is that social relations are an important part of the context that explains the values promoted by freedom of speech. The social relations involved in a speech act vary tremendously, from the informal conversation on the street marked by only the most superficial acquaintance with the other person to the intensely personal relations in a family discussion (or argument). The existence and very meaning of the speech act depend upon the context of these relationships. As in the question of whose freedom a theorist emphasizes, different theorists focus on different social relations. For libertarians, the relations between the state and the individual are most important, and much less emphasis is given to relations between individuals. For many egalitarians, relations between individuals in hierarchical relationships are the most important, and less concern is attached to relationships with the state.

Pluralists recognize the existence and importance of many different social relationships. The relevance to freedom of speech of some relationships is not controversial, for instance, that between the state and the individual. Other relationships are more complicated. Those who want to argue for the relevance of the hierarchical relationship between workers and managers to analysis of freedom of speech have a more difficult case to make. It also may be difficult to convince other theorists to accept the relevance of family relationships to freedom of speech. Some relationships are especially complicated, particularly those between a speaker and a potential audience or between an individual and himself or herself (as in the writing of journals). Unintentional relationships or those between strangers are also complicated. Other kinds of social interactions, such as those found in the "cybercommunity" of the Internet, have emerged so recently that there is no clear sense of what they are really like, let alone the different dimensions of these relations relevant to the questions posed by the pluralist framework. That some relationships are complicated, or new, or poorly understood does not mean that they may be ignored. Instead, the pluralist framework asks that these relationships be explored and fleshed out as a part of a fully specified free speech argument.

While determining who benefits the most from a particular free speech claim seems like the obvious question in any debate that concerns a matter of policy, the question must be asked and an answer specified. It is not that theorists are unwilling or unable to do so, but identifying who will benefit is more often implicit than explicit. The marketplace of ideas metaphor and the arguments based on it suggest that everyone benefits from a regime of freedom of speech through the superior policies that such a regime allows to be introduced and flourish. The macrolevel response that everyone benefits obscures the likelihood that specific people or groups of people end up losers in a reformulated marketplace. Even if there are broad social benefits overall, in specific cases some individuals win while others lose. Also, it is not always clear who the winners and losers are without in-depth analysis of the question. For example, the deregulation of election campaign financing may contribute to the most robust marketplace of ideas, at least as measured by quantity and volume of speech. Or deregulation might further strengthen the dominant position of a few wealthy interests who buy a great deal of speech and dilute the messages of those with restricted means to contribute to campaigns. Whether campaign finance regulation leads to different electoral outcomes than deregulation is a hotly contested empirical question, but any free speech argument over campaign financing must address it. This question of who wins and loses is related closely to the earlier question of whose freedom is emphasized in any given free speech theory.

Pluralists recognize that many different values may be served by freedom of speech and that arguments for free speech only make sense when the context of these different values is specified. The specific values favored by a theorist of freedom of speech must be stated clearly because much of the disagreement between theorists stems from the priority they place on different values. Monism tends to obscure these differences rather than resolve them. Any given school of thought on free speech may promise to provide for the realization of a wide variety of ends, not all of which may be compatible. Explicit identification of the values favored in an account of speech helps to identify the kind of free speech a specific theorist actually defends. It also clarifies debates between different groups of free speech theorists. For instance, some who offer libertarian justifications for free speech may actually be expressivists if their goal is to promote self-realization and self-development. On the other hand, some egalitarians claim to be libertarians and to accept the bulk of libertarian free speech theory, yet the value they place on racial equality may take such precedence in their thinking that they cannot really be considered to be libertarians.

The pluralist framework requires that free speech claimants be explicit about the contexts in which their arguments make sense. Some arguments simply do not apply to every case because of the institutional, political, or cultural context in which the claims arise. The First Amendment framework is the right context in which to resolve some kinds of free speech claims but not others. The pluralist framework allows us to identify institutional factors, such as a constitutional limit on state action or the cultural value of academic freedom in a private university, that are crucial to making successful free speech claims in these different contexts. An expressivist who develops a justification of free speech to further a project of artistic creation in one context will be unable to offer a convincing defense of political speech in a different context. The explicit identification of the parameters of argument called for in the pluralist framework highlights the importance of contextualization of all free speech arguments.

Pluralists also ask claimants to be explicit about the threats that they perceive to freedom of speech. Whatever project someone pursues through freedom of speech, looking at the obstacles he or she identifies is an important piece of evidence as to the objectives or values that have priority. Libertarian free speech writers have diffuse objectives in mind. Their single-minded focus on state interference as a threat to freedom of speech indicates that political speech has priority in their arguments. While state interference threatens artistic expression as well, the threat of state interference is most closely related, historically and theoretically, to the problem of political speech. Libertarian justifications of freedom of speech have developed during the last 350 years in opposition to state interference in the publication of political opinion. Only in recent decades has the question of artistic or emotive speech been integrated into libertarian projects and justification of freedom of speech. Even at that, libertarians include artistic speech because of its political value rather than for its intrinsic value as expression. It is always difficult to interpret the motives of writers and even more difficult to make guesses about the collective motives of a large and diverse group of thinkers. My argument about the leverage that perceived threats gives us on projects is not that writers purposively obfuscate their objectives. Where statements of value are less than crystal clear, overlap, or contradict themselves, perceived threats sharpen our understanding of those values.

Perceived threats tell us a lot about the boundaries of the arguments made in each school of justification. Some egalitarians identify racist speech as the most significant threat to the speech of members of subordinate groups. While the critical race theorists who have argued the public case for regulation of hate speech do not make it explicit, the state also remains a threat to the speech of members of subordinate groups. State censorship sweeps broadly and is just as, if not more, likely to affect subordinate groups. Thus, egalitarian understandings of threat bind the theory to situations where racist speech affects the speech of subordinate group members, holding state action equal. The justificatory arguments of egalitarianism focus on one kind of threat over others and are unable to account for different barriers (such as state interference) to the speech of minorities. Because of this focus, egalitarianism fails as a comprehensive justification of freedom of speech. Some other, external set of justifications must be used to deal with different kinds of threats.

The boundaries of libertarianism are set in a similar fashion, although this is more difficult to see given the size, scope, and history of the threat of state interference that it identifies as of primary concern. State interference can take many different forms, such as prior restraints on publication, punishment after the fact for seditious libel or obscenity, or even restrictive parade permit laws. In many ways, the state must be of primary concern as a threat to free speech given its monopoly on legitimate force, the powers of the criminal law, and the historical interest of states in controlling speech. Absent substantial protection from state interference, it would be difficult to imagine that other threats to speech would even be apparent. Programmatic state censorship generally dwarfs any other restriction on freedom of speech. However, assuming that substantial freedom from state interference now exists, libertarianism does not account for all threats to free speech and requires external accounts of threat, just as do the somewhat narrower egalitarianism and expressivism. Libertarianism has social objectives of truth and good public policy that are threatened by actors other than the state, such as powerful private institutions like churches and schools. Systemic racism and sexism also threaten these goals.[24] Eliminating the specter of state interference through rigid constitutional controls on state power does not alleviate every threat to libertarian objectives. A regime of noninterference is necessary to promote freedom of speech but not sufficient. Noninterference in itself will not secure the libertarian value of truth/democracy.

Individualistic, prepolitical assumptions about threats to nonpolitical speech severely constrain expressivism. In its strongest form, such as in German romanticism, expressivism is antipolitical, and the issue of the relationship between the individual and the state does not arise as a part of its justificatory arguments. Even a milder, contemporary expressivism supported by those who promote state funding for the arts steers clear of identifying the state as a threat to expression.[25] However, state action constitutes a major threat to the artistic speech central to expressivism, even though the nonpolitical nature of expressivism precludes an overt focus on the state. Expressivism, like egalitarianism and libertarianism, requires external arguments in order to identify all possible threats to its objectives and to buttress its justification of freedom of speech.

So far, we have seen that the pluralist framework involves a different set of questions than those asked by the First Amendment framework. The pluralist framework begins by looking at the context that determines whether a speech act has occurred and what kind of speech it is. Arguments made within the pluralist framework must also be specific about what kinds of values freedom of speech promotes and whose freedom is advanced by these arguments. The kinds of social relations involved in freedom of speech must be considered, as should the question of who wins and loses as a result. Answers to these questions are necessary to evaluate free speech claims but by themselves are not sufficient to tell us which free speech arguments are good ones in terms of the pluralist framework.

Free Speech Claims within the Pluralist Framework

Compared to the First Amendment framework, pluralism presents a substantially different framework within which to make free speech claims. Under the First Amendment framework, free speech claims either take the form of actual court challenges or else the form of hypothetical challenges evaluated by the same legal criteria of precedent, history, and evidence. It is very difficult to make claims outside of the strict parameters of the First Amendment framework. The pluralist framework allows for many kinds of claims that do not fit within the First Amendment framework. These new claims could be against the state, against individuals who wield private power to restrict speech, or against organizations or employers who may restrict speech within their legal powers. Also, individuals can make claims that do not fit within well-established categories of rights, such as cross-border claims arising from Internet speech.

The pluralist framework does not preclude First Amendment claims. Where there are clear legal claims to be made in cases that fit well within First Amendment doctrine, a claimant should go to court and use legal procedures to prove the claim. At the same time, speech such as flag burning that is legally protected by the First Amendment may not receive as much support within the pluralist framework. Speech pluralism outlines a very different kind of political process to establish and defend the claims that do not fall under the rubric of the First Amendment. Making a claim under the pluralist framework begins with the identification of the contextual variables that are so important to understanding a speech act as well as to locating the values relevant to the speech claim. The claimant must be able to show that the act or utterance in question is a speech act and relate that act to a value associated with freedom of speech. Some claims are easy and would not require more than this kind of identification. For instance, most people would easily recognize a political stump speech as a speech act, and it would be easy to relate that speech to democracy as a value that commonly warrants protection of speech. In more difficult cases, a speech claimant may have to continue to establish his or her claim along pluralist lines. It may be more difficult, for instance, to show that guerilla street theater is a speech act or a contribution to democratic deliberation. The speaker who claims a free speech right that protects his or her street theater performance may have to prove that the performance meets the intention and reception conditions for a speech act. Such proof may require evidence of the reactions of listeners or the potential reaction of listeners. The effects of the performance may need to be discussed as well.

A speaker claiming protection for speech under the pluralist framework may often have to do more than simply prove that a speech act was performed. Not all speech deserves protection, and not all claims warrant recognition. There may be opposition to recognition of the speech claim. For instance, if the street theater performance includes the burning of an American flag, there will certainly be opposition to claims that flag burning is protected speech.[26] Despite the constitutional protection for flag burning under First Amendment law, most Americans do not believe that flag burning is legitimate expression deserving of free speech protection.[27] Someone who would deny speech protection for the street performance will probably argue that flag burning in the context of a public performance is not speech. The critic might also argue that while the burning of the flag is a speech act because it is intended and received as a message, the act performed here is a terrorist threat or hate speech that ought not to be performed. This argument has merit if performers burn flags in front of a group of military veterans at a Memorial Day parade. Flag burning in this instance will be seen by that audience as a kind of assault and is likely to elicit a visceral response. The emotional effects on the veterans viewing the performance may be as strong as those that racist hate speech causes for members of targeted minority groups.

In this example, we have a clear conflict between the speaker who makes a free speech claim and an audience that denies that claim. Under the First Amendment framework, the flag-burning speaker is protected, and the audience of veterans has no claim to make. Under the pluralist framework, both the speaker and the audience have claims to make, and these may be resolved politically. That the flag burner has a legal right does not mean that it is morally or politically right for the speaker to perform this speech act. While the speaker would not go to jail for the performance, as observers we could judge that this speech act is illegitimate, wrong, or at the very least in poor taste. This may explain why actual incidents of flag burning are so rare despite the legal protection currently extended to this type of expression. The issue of whether flag burning is legitimate is based on consideration of a number of different political values. One of these is the value to the speaker of this form of expression. Is flag burning the best or most effective means to communicate the speaker's political message? Perhaps the speaker intends the flag burning as part of an act of creative expression leading to self-realization, and it has nothing to do with a political message. Either of these values may not be very compelling as compared to the damaging effects on the audience of veterans' speech acts of patriotism, commemoration of those killed in action, and remembrance of their own service. In making judgments about this speech situation, most observers would favor the speech claims of the veterans despite the First Amendment protection for flag burning. There is wide agreement that flag burning is wrong, albeit legal, and that it is not part of the set of speech acts considered acceptable in situations like this example.

Unfortunately, veterans cannot make claims against flag burners under the First Amendment framework. They can make claims under the pluralist framework. Furthermore, the pluralist framework does a much better job of explaining what happens in this kind of case. The First Amendment framework does not tell us anything about why, if flag burning is legal and also an effective way to oppose the state and expressions of patriotism, so few people choose to perform this speech act. The First Amendment framework also does a poor job of describing why flag burning is not considered a valuable kind of speech or why so many Americans would be glad to see the Constitution amended to make flag burning illegal. It is not hard to understand why people oppose flag burning; in fact, it is pretty easy to see why. However, it is almost impossible to explain why within the terms of the First Amendment framework. One has to go outside that framework to explain the opposition to flag burning. Controversies over flag burning are about free speech, and they are politically important even if the act itself is rare. Political candidates often deride their opponents for lack of patriotism if they are not sufficiently supportive of the flag. Various versions of a constitutional amendment to protect the flag are frequently introduced in Congress, and many state legislatures have indicated their intention to ratify such an amendment if it were to pass in Congress. The entire debate about such an amendment is necessarily external to the First Amendment framework. The movement to restrict flag burning is, in essence, a political argument that the First Amendment framework should not apply to the flag. Nonetheless, this debate is still about the meaning and extent of freedom of speech, and the pluralist framework makes that fact more clear. We can see that the opposition to flag burning exists because, in this context, some hold that the value of patriotism or respect for veterans outweighs the value of political speech.

We can examine arguments about specific kinds of speech or particular speech controversies and evaluate those arguments along several dimensions. Evaluations begin with the determination of whether the speech claim being made actually involves a speech act. Does this phenomenon meet the contextual definition of a speech act and the conventions necessary for intention, condition, and reception (uptake)? If no speech act has occurred, there can be no free speech claim. We can go no further, and the argument fails as a free speech argument.[28] As I argued in the preceding chapter, the conditions for a speech act must be relaxed from their original Austinian rigor in order to prevent the power plays of unwilling listeners who, if they oppose certain speech, might simply deny that it met the conventions for reception by claiming that they do not understand the utterance. They thus deny that a speech act has occurred, blocking an opportunity for a free speech claim. Instead, we as outside evaluators can use standards of potential reception and intention.[29] This criterion of whether a speech act has occurred serves several useful evaluative functions. First, it seems obvious that free speech arguments should only concern speech acts and not, for instance, economic markets or abortion rights. By excluding those acts that fail to be speech acts, we simply clear the way for a debate over freedom of speech. Too often, substantive, nonspeech issues are turned into speech claims for the rhetorical benefits that come along with an invocation of free speech or the First Amendment.[30] The pluralist framework properly excludes these issues from free speech debates.

Second, limiting the debate over freedom of speech to speech acts allows us to exclude some of the most egregious overextensions of freedom of speech. For example, acts of terrorism may communicate a message, but they are not speech acts because they go beyond conventions that define speech. Terrorist murder is an obvious case of something I would exclude from the class of speech acts. Clearly, there will be hard cases at the boundary between speech and other acts. Hard cases always exist at conceptual boundaries. In evaluating free speech arguments, it should be possible to be generous in granting that an event is a speech act since there are additional criteria by which to evaluate whether the argument is a good one. That is, in cases where we are unsure that the conventions for a speech act are met, we as evaluators can assume for the sake of argument that speech has occurred and then move on to evaluate the argument in favor of making that kind of speech free. Even if some might grant that terrorist murder is a speech act, it should still be a simple matter to exclude terrorist murder from the categories of protected speech by reference to other pluralist criteria.

Once it is established that we are looking at an argument about a speech act, we need to examine what makes that argument effective. An argument for freedom of a particular kind of speech is much stronger when two or more different justifications agree on protection of that speech. When justifications overlap, we can be more confident about protecting that speech. The least contested kinds of speech are uncontroversial because they can be justified in a variety of ways, and a number of values are served by freedom for these kinds of speech. Libertarianism and Dworkin's egalitarianism both protect political speech, thus reinforcing the argument for freedom to engage in political protest, campaigning, and the publishing of polemics. Arguments in favor of freedom to use offensive but nonracist words are well supported by libertarianism, expressivism, and egalitarianism and thus rarely give rise to a speech controversy. Academic inquiry receives the support of a libertarian defense grounded in the search for truth as well as an expressivist argument that such inquiry promotes the self-realization of the individual.

The evaluation of strong arguments and easy cases does not do much good unless we also have criteria for the hard cases. Several of the most important evaluative criteria in the pluralist framework have to do with the value promoted by freedom of speech in the case at hand. Since different values are the primary source of variation between justifications of freedom of speech, we should expect that evaluations of those arguments should also focus on those values. First, we need to examine the values themselves. If the goal to be advanced by freedom of speech is illegitimate or undesirable on its face, and we can show why this is so, then we need not even address the question of whether that goal leads to a justification of freedom of speech. This is not to say that speech that may contribute to undesirable events, such as the violent overthrow of the government, is automatically prohibited. The goal is not to eliminate "bad speech" but rather to exclude bad values that give rise to questionable justifications. For instance, contemporary American free speech practice protects the advocacy of violence and law violation.[31] This protection is relatively uncontroversial. It would be a very poor free speech argument, however, to defend advocacy of violent revolution on the basis that revolution is a valuable project to be promoted by freedom of speech. To do so, one would have to first make the unlikely case, in a way convincing to many people, for the legitimacy of the project of violent revolution itself.[32]

At the same time, it would be a poor free speech argument to prohibit advocacy of violence merely because we think it is bad speech. Such an argument must instead be based on what makes the speech bad, requiring an examination of the speech act with reference to the justification of freedom of speech. Justifications are more complex than simply judging whether speech acts are good or bad. While the First Amendment protects advocacy of illegal action, it does not protect direct incitement to violence. This practice also can be explained with reference to several of the justifications of freedom of speech. For instance, libertarians protect advocacy of lawless action by portraying it as a necessary part of their project of public debate about legitimate government. Advocacy of law violation puts forth ideas critical of law and government in such a way that these ideas challenge accepted views on government and allow progovernment speakers to challenge critics of government. We may or may not find advocacy of law violation to be desirable speech, but it is protected under the umbrella of the libertarian justification. Libertarians can then draw a line between protected advocacy and unprotected incitement (each of which are speech acts) because direct incitement to violence does not promote public debate.[33] The revolutionary who justifies freedom of speech with reference to a project of revolution cannot draw a line between advocacy and incitement. As long as we believe that such a line is necessary or desirable, such a failure further undermines the revolutionary defense of the speech of incitement.

CHAPTER EIGHT

Free Speech Claims under the Pluralist Framework

The pluralist framework has several key advantages over the First Amendment framework for freedom of speech. The contextual sensitivity of the pluralist framework is more appropriate to speech problems in situations where the First Amendment framework now forces speakers to articulate their claims in the narrow terms of legal categories and vocabulary. The pluralist framework better identifies and defines a variety of emerging free speech claims. Some speakers find it very difficult to identify these new claims in terms of the First Amendment framework, and their claims are too easily shunted aside. Speech claims that cannot be described in the First Amendment framework often go unrecognized altogether. In this final chapter, I raise several claims that have no easy definition under the First Amendment framework. These should be read as examples of the kinds of political dilemmas revealed by the pluralist framework. The examples demonstrate the capacity of the pluralist framework to allow judgments about speech situations that are sensitive to context while promoting a variety of speech values. These accounts do not lead to definitive answers, but they do illustrate what political debate about free speech might look like beyond the constraints of the First Amendment framework.

Speech and the Internet

The development of the Internet raises an increasingly large number of new free speech claims. Some of these are primarily legal claims and can be dealt with by analogy to older, established First Amendment precedents. At the same time, we cannot solve all of the new claims this way.[1] The Internet holds enormous potential for speakers and for the promotion of many different speech values, such as those favored by libertarians, expressivists, and egalitarians. This potential will never be realized, however, if we do not address the unique threats to speech currently emerging as the Internet develops. One claim in this new social and technological context originates from cross-border speech conflicts. Three recent events highlight the difficulties faced by national legal frameworks, including the First Amendment framework, when confronted with a claim by domestic speakers against a foreign state. The cases involve different kinds of speakers, speech acts, and the laws of several countries. American speakers find themselves facing legal restrictions on Internet publication based in the United States. In 2002, Dow Jones Corporation, the American publisher of *Barron's* magazine, a business magazine also available on the Internet, was successfully sued for libel in Australia by mining magnate Joseph Gutnick over material located on its servers in New Jersey.[2] A year earlier, Yahoo!, Inc. was ordered by a French court to take down sections of its American auction site that featured books and artifacts related to nazism. Enforcement of this order in the United States was later rescinded by an American federal district court.[3] Similarly, U.S. law has been used to restrict the speech of foreigners. For instance, the Church of Scientology, using the U.S. Digital Millennium Copyright Act (DMCA) of 1998, forced the search engine Google to remove from its American Web index all sites originating in the Netherlands that criticized Scientology.[4]

Each of these recent examples reveals serious conflicts between the growth of the Internet as a forum for speech and the tremendous international diversity of laws regulating speech. Each of the speakers in these examples faced serious obstacles to freedom of speech in the form of legal costs and potential financial and criminal penalties even where, as in the case of Yahoo!, they were ultimately successful in using the law to avoid such penalties. Other speakers undoubtedly have felt the chilling effect of these kinds of cases and have limited their own speech in a variety of ways. There are no comprehensive international agreements governing Internet speech nor are there international organizations empowered to resolve conflicts between the speech laws of different states. Such conflicts are legally messy and involve protracted court proceedings in several countries at a time. While France may have the constitutional power to regulate racist speech within its own borders and Australia has the power to severely regulate libel of public figures, serious questions remain about the reach of state regulation beyond national boundaries. The First Amendment framework offers only an impoverished account of the significant adverse effects on freedom of speech emerging along with the opportunities for expression presented by new technology.

The question of speech crossing borders is certainly not in itself new (books have always been imported and exported), but the Internet makes such cross-border speech easier, more common, and less intentional. For little or no cost to the speaker, his or her words will be available simultaneously in every part of the world connected to the Internet, whether or not the speaker intends to make that speech available in any particular country. Articles intended for publication in one country are posted routinely on the Web sites of newspapers and magazines, thus reaching a much broader audience than ever before. Speakers, especially professional speakers such as those in the examples above, are generally well aware of the restrictions on speech allowed in their home countries and in the other states that constitute their primary audience. Barring an incredibly onerous level of legal research, however, no speaker can be expected to be familiar with the speech regulations of the 190 countries connected to the Internet. Even if a speaker did have that kind of encyclopedic knowledge, it would be nearly impossible to satisfy the requirements of each state's speech regulations and still be an effective speaker. The incidence of criminal and civil suits filed in many different states threatens to limit the speech available to audiences not just in the states where these suits originate but also in those with much less restrictive speech laws. The range of ideas available on the Internet could be limited to that which is acceptable to the most restrictive state, thus giving restrictive countries an effective veto over the speech available in the rest of the world.

Cross-border speech claims occur outside the First Amendment framework. This can be explained in part by the importance of physical barriers to the authority of law. According to Johnson and Post, "There has until now been a general correspondence between borders drawn in physical space (between nation states or other political entities) and borders in 'law space.'"[5] The Internet presents an entirely new situation because there are no meaningful physical boundaries to Internet space that also would serve as boundaries for the law space that governs actions that occur over the Internet. The connection between physical space and law space derives from the ways that geographic boundaries give notice that one has entered the domain of a national system of laws.[6] For instance, if I travel across the border into Canada, I know that I will now be bound by Canadian law. I lack this warning when I post to the Internet because I have no idea if anyone in Canada will look at my posting and thus have no way of knowing whether Canadian law is relevant to my decisions about the content of my posting. For Johnson and Post, this comparison is crucial, because my decision to cross a physical border carries with it a form of consent to be bound by the laws of that state that does not exist when an anonymous reader in a different state chooses to read my posting. In effect, the reader subjects me to the authority of his or her state without my knowledge or consent. Johnson and Post see two alternatives to the hodgepodge of legal regulations illustrated by the examples of Yahoo! and Google above. Either states must try to extend their territorial boundaries into cyberspace through filtering mechanisms that would block objectionable content at the point of entry, or else they must withdraw and accede to a regime of self-regulation by users in cyberspace. Johnson and Post favor the latter and suggest a system of Internet self-regulation. The decision to enter cyberspace would subject one to a "law of cyberspace" that the First Amendment would not structure. It is unlikely, however, that all 190 Internet-connected states would agree to forego regulation of speech under their own laws.

The current legal approach to the problem of restrictions on Internet speech centers on battles over legal jurisdiction and questions of whose speech laws should apply in each case. It pays little attention to the speech acts involved or justification of protection of those acts. For instance, in the Yahoo! case, two civil rights groups concerned with anti-Semitism succeeded in bringing suit in French court under Section R645-1 of the French criminal code, which prohibits the sale or exhibition of Nazi artifacts.[7] The Yahoo! auction site offered, at the time, more than a thousand Nazi-related artifacts, including copies of *Mein Kampf* and *Protocols of the Elders of Zion*, along with stamps, medals, and flags. There is some question as to whether the court decided this case properly according to French law, but few would question the legitimacy of French law being applied by a French court to events that take place in France.[8] However, because of the way that the Internet works, it is not so clear that Yahoo! had performed actions in France. Yahoo! runs its auction site in California and stores the information on servers there. If we think of Yahoo! as the speaker and the computer information stored on its servers as speech, then Yahoo! has not acted in France and does not appear to be subject to French authority. On the other hand, Internet users in France could easily look up the Yahoo! auction site to view or purchase the proscribed Nazi-related items. Yahoo! has a French subsidiary (Yahoo! France) and French revenue. As far as the French court was concerned, Yahoo!'s speech took place in France and was subject to French law because there were French viewers. That court ordered Yahoo! to make the proscribed items unavailable to Web surfers inside France and to remove links in its search database to Holocaust revisionism Web sites. Yahoo! partially complied with the French court order by removing most of the items for sale from its worldwide auction site.

Yahoo! then sought relief from the French judgment in U.S. federal district court, arguing that the French order violated its free speech rights under the First Amendment. According to the U.S. court, Yahoo!'s speech took place within the United States and therefore should be subject to the protections of the U.S. Constitution.[9] Since American law clearly protects speech related to the sale of Nazi memorabilia as well as Holocaust denials, the U.S. court ordered that the French court's order could not be enforced within the United States. To this extent, then, Yahoo! has "won" its legal battle over the speech content of its auction site. However, Yahoo! continues to partially comply with the French order by banning racist and hate-related items from its auction site. In addition, Yahoo! incurred a significant legal cost that could have a chilling effect on its speech in the future. Unlike winning a case in the Supreme Court that would set a protective precedent for future instances of similar speech, there is nothing about the U.S. court decision that precludes further court proceedings in France. Yahoo! may have to fight this same battle over and over again. Yahoo!'s speech problem has not be solved. In fact, the free speech claim at the heart of Yahoo!'s case has not even been fully described.

Another battle over jurisdiction is the Australian libel suit brought by Joseph Gutnick against the Dow Jones Corporation as publisher of *Barron's*. The Australian high court held that Dow Jones could be sued for libel in a Victoria court under some of the strictest libel laws in the world.[10] Dow Jones took the position that since its operations are based in the United States and the *Barron's* article resided on servers in New Jersey, the Australian courts did not have jurisdiction. Any libel case against it should be filed in New Jersey. Of course, if the case were in New Jersey, Dow Jones would be almost sure to win since Gutnick would be a public figure in the context of the allegations made in the article. Dow Jones could be fairly certain that no case would even be brought against it in the United States given the slim chance of success for Gutnick under U.S. law. On the other hand, for this case to go forward in Australia poses a significant chill on Dow Jones's speech given the potential costs of litigation and adverse judgments.[11] There is no international tribunal to govern multinational speech cases like Yahoo! or *Barron's*. An international convention to govern Internet libel cases might provide clear-cut legal answers, but it would be very difficult to gather international agreement on such a convention. It would require either weakening libel laws like Australia's or creating restrictions on speech in the United States.[12] Barring such a convention, we are left with the same kind of jurisdictional conflict that we saw in the Yahoo! case.

The legal approach to the problem of cross-border speech claims centers on conflicts over who has jurisdiction in each case. Unfortunately, these jurisdictional conflicts transform a case about speech into a case about the boundaries of international legal systems. The real conflict between Yahoo! and the French penal code is one between Yahoo! as a speaker and the speech regulations the French have chosen to enforce their understanding of civil rights and equality. The basis of the American court's decision to negate the French court's ruling pits the authority of French law against the authority of American law. Once the case ends up in the American courts, it is no longer about Yahoo! as a speaker or its speech acts but rather about the relative status of two national legal systems. It becomes a conflict between France and the United States, not between a speaker and a government regulator of speech. The Gutnick libel case presents the same sort of transformation since the legal resolution of that case will turn on which state will be able to enforce its claims to jurisdiction rather than on the speaker (Dow Jones) or the speech.

A third example of cross-border speech claims involves a Web site called Operation Clambake, which operates from servers located in the Netherlands and has been targeted by the Church of Scientology for its criticism of Scientology and its practices.[13] The Church of Scientology has succeeded in using complaints under the DMCA to convince Google to remove various pages of the Operation Clambake site from Google's American Web index.[14] The DMCA exposes search engines like Google to potential liability if they provide links to sites that contain copyright-infringing materials. There is a safe harbor provision in the DMCA that protects a search engine (or other linking site) if, upon notification by the copyright holder, it removes links to the sites in question. The result of this has not been to remove Operation Clambake from the Internet—it is still accessible—but to make it more difficult to find the site when doing a search for Scientology and related key words. To take advantage of the safe harbor and protect itself from costly litigation, Google has to remove pages about which it has been notified by copyright holders, regardless of the merits of the copyright holder's claims. That is, these claims may be falsified or exaggerated by claimants in order to target speech the claimant wants to limit or suppress. With the DMCA complaint, the Church of Scientology has limited the availability and accessibility of information about Scientology to Internet users.

There are two free speech claims present in this example. The first concerns speakers themselves. For example, why should a private actor (Church of Scientology) in the United States have the power to restrict the speech of a Dutch citizen publishing in the Netherlands whose speech is protected by Dutch law?[15] Additionally, where does the author of Operation Clambake make his free speech claim? He cannot claim against his own government, because it is not a party to the situation and has nothing to do with it. He cannot easily claim against Google, because Google has no legal responsibility to index every page on the Internet and has acted in its own self-interest to garner the protections of the safe harbor in the DMCA. It would be legally difficult to file a claim in the United States against the enforcement of the DMCA, and it would be difficult to sue the Church of Scientology in the United States as well. The second kind of claim involves listeners or audiences and is a "denial of information" claim. Google's response to the Church of Scientology threats of action under the DMCA prevent those individuals in the United States who wish to read criticisms of Scientology from finding information posted on the Operation Clambake site not indexed by Google. An American denied information by this use of the DMCA might (and it is a big "might") have a First Amendment claim that could be effective against the federal government and the DMCA. However, Google's database is not only used by Americans researching inside the United States. The de-listing of certain sites from the index would also affect a researcher in Britain or Cameroon who uses Google. U.S. copyright law has been used to restrict information available not only to Americans but also to everyone else, even when neither the speaker nor the audience is located in the United States. All of this happens without even placing the burden of proof on the copyright holder who wants to restrict speech.[16]

While these jurisdictional questions are important and will probably determine the final legal resolution of these types of cases, the battle over jurisdiction does not tell us very much about the nature of the free speech claims being made by these speakers. The focus on jurisdiction is understandable because it is the only way in which to bring the separate legal frameworks that govern freedom of speech in different states into play. For instance, the only way that Dow Jones can hope to get the protection of First Amendment libel doctrine is to argue successfully first that American courts are the appropriate forum to hear the case. Then, if it wins that case, it can proceed to make a free speech claim under American law. There is something about free speech on the Internet, however, that just does not seem to fit with the diversity of international regulations on speech. Something is missing from the jurisdictional approach that requires a different way of defining the free speech problems and threats faced by Internet speakers. None of the primary legal alternatives to the problems of Internet speech and regulation seem to be effective or desirable. Legal fights over which states will have jurisdiction in a given case submerge the speech issues involved in favor of questions of state authority and power to impose law. International agreements to govern the law of cyberspace are also too limited to resolve the problem of hate sites located in the United States spreading their message to European states that prohibit such speech or American copyright violations alleged against sites in the Netherlands. The problem with these alternatives is that they are efforts to extend established legal categories by analogy when the current situation really has no precedent. The better approach to the problems caused by Internet speech is to conceptualize the phenomenon freshly through the pluralist framework.

Publishing on the Internet is different than importing and exporting books, magazines, and newspapers. The Internet is a new forum, and there is something unprecedented in the idea of simultaneous, low-cost publication available to readers around the world. Speakers reach listeners in many places where they never could have been heard before. Listeners have access to the speech of individuals who may have a freedom to publish that is unknown in the listener's own country. Speakers and listeners will lose these new benefits if Internet speech regulation is left to the determination of the most restrictive states. We also lose these benefits if regulation is so unpredictable as to make Internet speech more risky than warranted by the potential rewards it offers.

It is difficult to apply directly the familiar justifications for freedom of speech to this new situation because the key relationship that animates those justifications is that between the individual speaker and the state. The format of rights claims against one's own government is relatively well worked out, but how does one make a rights claim where it is so difficult to know against whom to make the claim? The claims are also difficult to make where it is equally unclear what the basis for the relief would be. In the simple case of a claim made by a citizen for relief from a limit on speech created by the citizen's own country, he or she should be able to make that claim on the basis of domestic constitutional law. Failing that, the claimant might look to the guarantees of international human rights documents designed to promote civil rights within individual states. In the case of a speech claim by a speaker who is a citizen of, and physically present in, one state against the government of another country, the situation is more complicated. No clear authority to appeal to exists, nor is there a substantial international agreement or understanding that defines what a free speech right looks like in this context. The jurisdictional contest seen in the Yahoo! case works to transform Yahoo!'s free speech claim against the French government into a much more manageable claim against the U.S. government and its enforcement of the French court order. However, due to the chilling effect of the French court's action (that has, after all, resulted in a change in Yahoo!'s behavior, despite their court victory in the United States), there is still a speech claim to be made, and we need to use new tools to articulate this claim.

Any free speech claim under the pluralist framework starts with the conditions for a speech act. In each of these three cross-border speech claims, it is relatively easy to apply the criteria for a speech act. Yahoo!, Dow Jones, and Google each performed speech acts. Dow Jones, for instance, published articles in their online version of *Barron's*. The articles were written with the intent to communicate a message and were received as such by a large audience. The articles are identical to conventional print journalism in content, and there is little question that the printed words succeed as speech acts, even if Gutnick is correct that the speech is libelous. Similarly, Yahoo! performed speech acts through the publication of their auction site. Yahoo!'s intent to perform a speech act is clear, and it is equally clear that the Web site was received as speech. While the French government considered it to be illegitimate speech and actionable under French law, it did not argue that the site failed to be speech. Google's speech act is a little less easy. It is not as obvious that a Web index is a speech act rather than a commercial service. The index itself is created through the use of software that scans the Internet to build the Google database rather than through direct human performance. However, the intention behind Google's software is to communicate messages about the location of Web pages. Google's audience (users of its index) seeks out this information and can understand the speech acts performed by Google, even if there is a layer of automation between users and the "authors" of the Google database. The Church of Scientology seeks to limit Google's database but also implicitly recognizes the search site as a kind of speech act, otherwise copyright law would be inapplicable.

The pluralist framework requires an account of the context for a speech act. An important element of this context is where the speech act takes place. In these cross-border claims, location is one of the most problematic elements. Some argue that these speech acts do not occur in physical space.[17] Nonetheless, cyberspace is not an ethereal plane; these speech acts do exist in physical space, albeit in various electronic storage media, disk drives, and the like. Viewers may be located thousands of miles from the storage site, and while readers of a book may also be thousands of miles from the author, they are generally in close proximity to a physical object, the book, that had to be shipped across borders. Much of the conflict over cross-border speech claims stems from the relatively novel question of where, exactly, the speech act takes place. As far as the application of a national legal framework is concerned, whether the speech act occurs where the data is stored or where the viewer is located is the question that determines which country's laws apply. However, since the application of law does not really solve these cross-border claims, the location of the speech might be considered differently. For instance, the distant location of some of the viewers of a Web page tells us that it is unlikely that a speaker intends to speak to those viewers directly or to design the speech act for that audience. *Barron's* has very few online readers in Australia, and it is unlikely that a journalist writing a story for the magazine has given much thought to the ways in which the story will be received by Australian readers. On the other hand, an American writer contributing to an Australian magazine would be likely to consider the Australian readership and the conventions for Australian journalism.

A pluralist approach to the claims made by speakers such as Dow Jones, Yahoo!, and Google considers the relationship between these speakers and their audiences. None of these speakers explicitly sought out the audiences that led to the legal efforts to regulate their speech. These speakers did not specifically expose themselves to the risk of speech regulation or consent to be bound by the laws of the states that sought to limit their speech. In a sense, the French or Australian viewers of these Web pages were incidental to the primary speaker-audience relationships. It is unlikely that Yahoo! intended its auction site to promote the growth of neo-Nazi parties in the United States or in France or even to spread information about nazism. Nazi-era memorabilia takes on a different meaning in France than it does in the United States given the significant differences in their respective historical experience of the Second World War and Nazi occupation. The speech act of advertising such memorabilia for sale does not mean the same thing in the United States as it does in France. Beyond the likely agreement that a specific article could be purchased in a particular auction, the message will be received in two very different ways. What to the French audience would be a speech act of offensive racist hate, or tolerance of racist hate if spoken by a French speaker, is more likely seen as a commercial offering in the United States. At most, it will be received by a U.S. audience as a milder expression of tolerance for hate when spoken by a U.S. speaker. In this sense, the French misapprehend the speech act as it was intended by a speaker who designs his or her speech in the U.S. context of the meaning of Nazi-era symbols and objects.

The same problem of disjuncture between intention and reception occurs in the Dow Jones libel case. In that case, Dow Jones may be making a mistake in intention, at least as far as the Australian point of view is concerned. While the speech act in question was probably not intended as a libel, it was received as such by at least some Australians (including Gutnick). Since Dow Jones did not expect a significant Australian audience for its online version of *Barron's*, it designed its speech act in accordance with the American understanding of libel.

There is no universal meaning of a speech act independent of the context in which that act occurs. It is unlikely that a universal, worldwide definition of libel will develop to warn all potential speakers of the consequences of libelous speech. To understand what a speaker does, we must consider what the speaker's act means in the context in which it is performed. We must also look at which values would justify the protection of that speech act. The international legal power struggle to settle jurisdiction in these cases does not tell us anything about the important questions of a speaker's meaning or the phenomenon of the speech act itself. Under the pluralist framework, we have to keep these contexts in mind. The implication for these examples is that the speech be interpreted along the lines of the speaker's intent rather than as it is received by certain audiences. We can then ask whether what the speaker intends should be protected speech. The chilling effect on Internet speech of the Australian and French court decisions could be quite severe if speakers worry that they will be held accountable to the laws of the most restrictive states. That chilling effect has significant consequences on the range of ideas available within the speaker's own country as well. In effect, the regulation imposed by incidental audiences in France or Australia could narrow or constrain an American debate about Nazism or the mining industry.

The value most clearly implicated by these speech acts is the democratic debate value of the search for truth or the best public policy. Yahoo!, Google, and Dow Jones perform speech acts that contribute information to public debate on these issues. If, for example, Yahoo! withdraws all copies of *Mein Kampf* from its auction site and other online retailers do the same thing to avoid French lawsuits, American debates about the history of Nazism and anti-Semitism will be less full. International Web users who depend on Google's American search index will have less information about Scientology if American copyright law is used to remove anti-Scientology sites from the Google index, which would seriously affect important debates about this topic in many countries. In fact, following the libertarian justification of freedom of speech, we can see that all three of these speech acts are closely related to the objective of truth and good public policy and should be protected on that basis. Yahoo! and Dow Jones performed speech acts well within the boundaries of protected speech in the United States. On the other hand, Australia places a high value on freedom from libel and makes it much easier for individuals who believe that they have been libeled to seek legal redress. France has strong laws against the distribution of Nazi-related memorabilia and publications based on its own evaluation of the proper balance between the values of public deliberation and freedom from racial discrimination. The disputes at the heart of these cases are caused by incommensurable values as articulated in national legal systems.

Public debate in the search for truth and good policy is a common value defended by First Amendment theorists.[18] When they defend public debate in terms of its constitutional importance, however, it is difficult to translate that value to a broader, multinational speech context. The proper resolution of these conflicts is not to force the rest of the world to adopt First Amendment law. While that would eliminate the conflicts, it is hardly a legitimate solution. Pluralists faced with incommensurable values would instead try to resolve the conflict by reference to a background of other shared values. The United States, France, and Australia have different free speech values (or different interpretations of similar values), so we should make reference to values that they do share to make judgments about what to do in these cross-border speech conflicts. In these cases, the laws of one state interfere in the democratic deliberation between citizens of a second state. Assuming that France and Australia did not single out Yahoo! and Dow Jones, respectively, for punishment because they were American companies and that these countries hold domestic corporations to the same standards, these are not simple cases of naked power relations between states. There are shared values that suggest possible responses to the conflict. A widely shared value in democratic states is that one state should not interfere, acting out of its own interests, in the internal democratic deliberations of another state. This is not to say that this principle is always honored, but there is widespread agreement that it is an important value. Nonetheless, Australian libel law, French hate crimes law, and American copyright law have been used in these cases to do just that, to interfere in the democratic deliberations of other states.

There are several suggestions for what to do in these cases consistent with the pluralist framework. First, taking into consideration the relationships between speakers and audiences, it would be appropriate to judge the speech acts according to the context in which the speakers perform them. That is, we should judge speakers by the standards of their own national understanding of freedom of speech or by the standards for speech prevalent in the countries that they see as their primary audience.[19] Incidental foreign audiences ought not to have a veto over speech intended primarily as a contribution to domestic public debate. Whenever the incidental audience exercises such a veto, as the Australian court did in the Dow Jones case, the value of noninterference in the democratic deliberations of another state has been violated. In essence, such interference is an effort by the interfering state to elevate its own standards and regulations for free speech to the status of international norm. Speakers cannot be held accountable for the speech regulations of 190 or more countries simultaneously; to do so would be to so seriously chill speech that most of the increase in freedom of speech made in the last century in many states would be lost.

States act against speakers to prevent listeners from having access to the speech and to prevent other effects of the speech. They rarely block a speech act just to target the individual speaker. Speech restrictions are instruments of other policy. The French action against Yahoo! was not primarily a statement of French revulsion for the speech but rather an effort to prevent French citizens from being harmed by the speech or encouraged to engage in hate speech crimes of their own. It is far more efficient to target a single speaker for hate speech than it is to enforce a ban on listening to certain messages. To forbid listening would involve difficult problems of enforcement (such as onerous surveillance) against millions of Internet users. Attempts to place age restrictions on broadcast programs offer many examples of how difficult it is to restrict speech at the audience's ear rather than at the speaker's mouth. Nonetheless, the best solution that remains sensitive to speech values may be to regulate at the level of listeners or audiences. Okoniewski suggests that France could prosecute its own citizens for intentionally viewing proscribed material, which does not require a higher degree of surveillance than French citizens would allow their government to perform.[20] If the problem is French neo-Nazis outfitting themselves with Nazi artifacts shipped from the United States, standard French customs controls at its borders should be sufficient to deal with the problem. A government could ban the possession of certain proscribed speech or artifacts. The United States and other countries ban the possession of child pornography, even if it has been obtained from a jurisdiction where such material is legal (if there are any such jurisdictions).

The negative effects of the speech that Australia and France try to limit in these cases still exist, even if speakers do not intend these effects on Australian and French audiences. States have legitimate power to try to control the effects of speech within their territory. To deny this power is to attempt to elevate the speech standards and regulations of the speaker's state to the status of international norm. To elevate speakers in this way interferes just as much in the internal deliberations of the audience state as the chilling effect interferes in the speaker's state. The best way to accommodate the interests of the audience state is by maintaining the same sort of control over speech on the way across the border that states have always exercised over printed books, magazines, and newspapers. It may not be easy to control the Internet at a national boundary, but it can be done, and technology will probably develop to make this even easier. For instance, a state can impose Internet filtering on content at the point its national networks connect to the worldwide Internet. Filtering creates some problems of its own, but if states think that they need to control the materials to which their citizens have access, there should be substantial incentives to develop effective software. Filtering at the point of entry respects the value of noninterference in the internal deliberations of other states, while allowing a state to regulate its own speech environment. When filtering is used, speakers will not be burdened by concerns about the restrictions of states that are only incidental audiences for their speech acts. The burden is placed on the regulating state, thus freeing speakers to act according to the more familiar standards and regulations of their own states. If a speaker wants to reach an audience that filters his or her speech, for example, if Yahoo! decides it wants to enter the French online auctions market, then the speaker may modify his or her speech in ways that satisfy the regulations of the filtering state.

Religious Speech in the Workplace

Religious expression poses special problems for any theory of free speech. We often treat it as a separate phenomenon entirely rather than as part of a comprehensive justification of speech. The First Amendment framework, for instance, addresses religious expression with the free exercise and establishment clauses rather than with the speech clause. Statements about religious beliefs or a speaker's faith are speech acts, but they are also religious acts with special status under the Constitution. Religious speech raises complicated questions in many different contexts in the United States and abroad. In some cases, religious expression may warrant greater protection than other kinds of speech, while in others it may receive less protection than political or artistic speech. Religious speech in the workplace illustrates the intersection of several different problems with the First Amendment framework for speech and the difficulties presented by speech conflicts in private settings.

The state is not the only threat to individual religious belief and practice. Assuming for the sake of argument the strictest possible separation of church and state that removed the state entirely from the religious sphere, believers would still face many other threats to religious expression. In addition, nonbelievers would still be worried about those who might try to impose beliefs upon them. Many people spend the majority of their waking hours in private workplaces, where they routinely face religious conflicts. The workplace is hierarchical and provides many opportunities for those with power in that hierarchy to impose their religious beliefs on the less powerful.[21] For instance, promotion and other benefits may hinge on outward adherence to the religious beliefs of the company owner. Peers also face many conflicts over religion, as when a worker loudly denounces the immoral conduct of a co-worker or prominently displays potentially offensive religious symbols in a work cubicle or on his or her person.

The First Amendment framework deals very poorly with speech in the private sector workplace because such situations lack the clear involvement of the state that normally allows First Amendment analysis. Instead, workplace speech conflicts usually exist between two employees or between an employee and the corporate hierarchy. In most cases, the First Amendment framework tells us that speech is not free in a private organization and therefore that all speech claims arising in those organizations are faulty. This is unfortunate. The values that make speech important to individual speakers are just as much at issue in the private workplace context as they are in more public interactions or in cases where the state plays an important role. A host of factors specific to the workplace may limit the speech of employees. Sexual and racial harassment rules place restrictions on what managers can say to workers and what employees can say to each other. Labor law sets forth many restrictions on the speech of management and union members. Formal rules set by the employer may limit the content, amount, or tone of employee speech. Workers may be required to speak only in English or to refrain from speaking outside of work breaks, or they may be given specific instructions on what they are allowed to say to outsiders. Corporations can require new hires to sign confidentiality or nondisclosure agreements as conditions of employment. Each of these restrictions may be completely reasonable and easily justified by reference to the overriding values and interests of the corporation. However, not all cases are clear, and even where justifiable, such rules restrict speech and should be examined more closely than the First Amendment framework allows.

Some employee religious speech has an impact on other employees when it involves potentially offensive or upsetting expression or exposes other workers to speech or behavior that threatens their own religious beliefs and practices. Richard Peterson was fired by Hewlett-Packard when he refused to remove biblical passages that he had printed in large type and posted in his cubicle in clear view of other employees and customers.[22] Peterson posted these passages in opposition to a Hewlett-Packard diversity program that took the form of posters of Hewlett-Packard employees with captions "Black," "Blonde," "Old," "Gay," and "Hispanic," along with the slogan "Diversity Is Our Strength." He described himself as devoutly Christian and religiously opposed to homosexuality and believed that the passages he had posted in his cubicle expressed his religious views. Christine Wilson made a religious vow to wear an anti-abortion button everywhere that she went, including to her job.[23] The button included a six-and-a-half-inch-high representation of an aborted five-month-old fetus. When her employer restricted her wearing of the button, Wilson tried to claim a legal right to express her religious beliefs in this way. Similarly, Charita Chalmers went to court after she was fired for writing letters chastising a coworker and her own supervisor for immoral behavior.[24] These claimants lost both their jobs and their legal battles to protect freedom of religious expression in the workplace, despite claiming rights within the First Amendment framework (via civil rights law). It is likely that many more employees give in to employer restrictions on their religious speech by refraining from button wearing, letter writing, or proselytizing after warnings from employers.

I would hesitate to generalize from these three cases, and I suspect that many employees desist from religious displays and speech when required by their employers. I also suspect that many more employees never engage in such speech, even if they are inclined to do so, because they are inhibited by the chilling effect of employer rules and regulations on employee expression. Potential disputes are not really with the state but rather with private employers or with other employees. Employer rules preclude whatever kind of religious or political dialogue these speakers might have had with fellow employees. Clearly, these cases require us to articulate some balance between the expression of these claimants and the religious beliefs of co-workers. The legal approach compelled by the First Amendment framework is inadequate to establish this balance or even to describe fully the nature of the conflicts involved.

One of the most serious difficulties in these situations is that the speaker's intended message may be very different from the meaning received by the listener. A speaker motivated by religious faith relies upon a large set of beliefs, ideas, and textual referents unavailable to the nonbeliever. A listener literally may have no idea what a speaker means by words such as "sin" or "redemption" when speaker and listener follow different faiths. Many nominally religious people may lack the socialization, informational context, and long period of education in religious texts and ideas that more devout speakers have. Interfaith dialogue and discussion are difficult enough for professional theologians in environments that support such debate, let alone for nonspecialists. Religious speech acts often fail because speakers and listeners lack the common vocabulary and referents that allow for coherent intention and reception of the speech act. The gap between Richard Peterson, for instance, and gay co-workers at Hewlett-Packard radically complicates any speech acts between them. Unsurprisingly, employers usually lack the qualifications and skills necessary to navigate these conflicts. Hewlett-Packard knows a lot about computers; it probably does not know much about religion and religious speech.

Workplace speech presents complicated value conflicts as well. Employers, speaking employees, and listeners share some values but also have divergent interests, beliefs, and motivations. Current law unambiguously favors employers' values in any conflict. The First Amendment does not protect employee expression, even when that speech is religious in nature. Under current law, employers are required to accommodate employee religious expression, observances, or practices only when such accommodation presents an utterly minimal cost to the employer.[25] Employers legitimately value productivity and profits, and antidiscrimination law as applied to workplace speech preserves those values. For instance, employers do not have to accommodate Sabbatarian workers when doing so would impose costs related to changes to other workers' schedules or the hiring of additional workers. Even relatively costless accommodations for expression, such as relaxing nonsafety-related uniform or dress codes (to allow beards or turbans, for instance), are unlikely to be imposed on employers. An amendment to Title VII of the Civil Rights Act, the Workplace Religious Freedom Act (WRFA), has been proposed several times in Congress to add legal protection to employee religious speech. The WRFA is designed to resolve many potential conflicts between the religious expression and practices of workers and the demands of employers and other employees. Accommodations that have a "temporary or tangential impact on the ability to perform job functions" would be required.[26] The WRFA would shift the burden to employers to demonstrate that an accommodation will require "significant difficulty or expense" by, for instance, showing specific costs associated with negative effects on productivity.

Even if the WRFA becomes law, it would only lead to marginal accommodations of employee religious expression. Furthermore, it does nothing to resolve conflicts between employees such as Peterson, Chalmers, Wilson, and their co-workers. The WRFA is a legislative guide on how to resolve some conflicts between employers and employees, but it cannot resolve all interemployee conflicts that result from significant value differences. Peterson's antihomosexual speech may not bother other employees with similar religious beliefs, but it clearly conflicts with the values both of gay employees and those who value equal treatment on the basis of sexual orientation. Chalmers's and Wilson's proselytizing behavior presents similar conflicts with religious and nonreligious co-workers. In these hard cases, private employers acted to restrict religious expression by first threatening and then carrying out termination of the employment of individual workers who were actively expressing their religious beliefs. These fired workers each made legal claims (by filing suit to be reinstated in their jobs) under provisions of Title VII, which requires companies to provide reasonable accommodations of employee religious practices. However, accommodation can have financial costs for employers and create constitutional conflicts with other employees' religious beliefs. In these cases, other employees would be forced to tolerate Wilson's graphic anti-abortion button and potentially receive Chalmers's proselytizing and chastising letters. Despite Hewlett-Packard's efforts to promote workplace tolerance, gay employees could not easily avoid the scriptural passages that Peterson "intended to be hurtful" and that he hoped would lead gay employees to renounce homosexuality and adopt his religious views.[27] Accommodation in these cases is problematic because it leaves co-workers exposed to religious speech with which they may not be comfortable or which interferes in their own religious (or nonreligious) practices. Accommodation is a zero sum game in these kinds of cases. If a Sabbatarian is excused from working Saturday overtime shifts, another employee (presumably not a Sabbatarian) will have to work those shifts. If an employer allows proselytizing on the shop floor, both religious and nonreligious employees will be subject to religious expression that they might rather avoid. Successful religious freedom claims by Peterson, Chalmers, or Wilson that protect their speech actually would create new religious freedom claims by co-workers who may feel that their right either to practice or to be free from religion has been infringed by accommodation of the other employees.

The First Amendment framework leads Peterson, Chalmers, and Wilson to use an absolutist understanding of what rights are. This absolutism is a product of applying the terms of First Amendment cases against government infringement of rights to the much more complex context of private social relationships. The First Amendment says that "Congress shall make no law" abridging freedom of speech.[28] This language and First Amendment doctrine do not require individuals to compromise with the government, and the state has no legitimate power over religious expression except as a by-product of advancing other state interests. When confronting the state, it is not surprising to see people articulate their claims in absolutist terms, refuse to compromise, and engage in civil disobedience. The state and its agents are expected to be very thick skinned and tolerant of irritating or offensive speech. The state itself has no religious beliefs or practice that can be offended or infringed upon by an individual's proselytizing speech and behavior. An analogy to libel may help illustrate this point. Libel doctrine makes it extremely difficult for a public figure to win a libel suit. One can accuse public officials of all kinds of terrible things with near impunity.[29] However, we do not require private figures to tolerate the same sorts of libels because interpersonal relations are governed by different standards than relations with the state.[30]

The solution to the problems caused by religious speech in the workplace cannot be found inside the First Amendment framework. Instead, we need to highlight the important political debate that cases like Peterson's and Chalmers's represent. Part of this debate takes the form of conventional politics directed at legislative change via laws like the WRFA. The WRFA or some sim-

ilar law would address the relatively easy cases of workplace religious expression
and practice where there is little cost to the employer or impact on other employees. We can think of the WRFA as a civil rights protection for situations to
which the First Amendment does not apply directly. In essence, the WRFA
would be a legislative choice to create new free speech rights for religious expression beyond the First Amendment. It does this by instructing employers, or
courts, how to compare religious values to nonreligious values. The WRFA
would be authoritative for these speech questions insofar as the First Amendment does not apply. The WRFA or similar legislation would create a presumption that restrictions on employee religious expression or practice are
illegitimate, except where those practices impose unreasonable costs on employers or create conflicts with other employees' rights of similar significance.
In many work situations, religiously mandated dress such as symbols, head cov-
erings, or beards will have little impact on the ability of employees to perform
their job functions, and the inconvenience to employers of making exceptions to
dress codes does not create an unreasonable burden of accommodation. In other
cases, the burden may be unreasonable. For instance, safety-related dress codes
should trump the free speech rights created by the WRFA. If a beard interferes
with the wearing of a respirator or other safety equipment, an employer may still
require employees to be clean shaven. We have to determine on a case-by-case
basis whether an accommodation such as transferring a bearded employee to another job that does not require a respirator creates an unreasonable burden on
employers, but courts are good at evaluating such questions when given sufficient legislative direction, such as that offered in the WRFA, on the weight to
be attached to a right.

   There are many cases of workplace restrictions on religious speech that are
not necessarily zero sum games leading to inevitable conflict between the interests and rights of religious and nonreligious employees. For instance, observant
Muslims who are required to answer the call to prayer one or more times during the course of their shifts may find that their employers do not accommodate
that practice in the rules governing the number of work breaks employees will
be allowed, when these breaks may be taken, and the duration or place of those
breaks. Depending on the kind of work involved, accommodation of such practices may have little impact on the employer and other employees, assuming the
missed time is made up. Current employment law does not require this sort of
accommodation. The restriction on the prayer (speech) of the Muslim employees is one imposed by the employer rather than by the state, so the First Amend-

ment does not apply. To claim a "right" to religious freedom in this case looks very different than to claim a constitutional right as a limitation on state action. Legislation like the WRFA creates a statutory, as opposed to a constitutional, right to accommodation that brokers a reasonable compromise between religious expression and the needs of employers and co-workers. Groups hoping to create this kind of speech right will organize into political movements to support legislative change rather than go to court to argue First Amendment cases.

Such political movements can argue a variety of points consistent with the pluralist framework for free speech. Employee religious expression generally should be accommodated when the argument against that expression is merely that it is irritating or strange to other employees who do not feel like tolerating it. Workplaces are full of all kinds of irritating expression, and there is no sense in which we require workplaces to be fully harmonious spaces free from offense or annoyance that falls short of our standards for harassment. The right to religious expression can be weighed or compared with the value of being free from irritation, and it is not hard to see that religious freedom is the more important value. Title VII is now, and the WRFA would be, inadequate to deal with cases requiring a balance between the religious freedom of employees with conflicting religious claims, because while competing religious claims sometimes may be comparable, they may also be incommensurable. We have a hard case when one employee's religious expression offends the religious beliefs of a second employee. There often will be no way to resolve such a conflict that satisfies each party to the dispute. We also have hard cases when an employee's religious practices conflict with other substantial interests or values, such as freedom from racial or sexual harassment. When a male supervisor routinely lectures female employees that their proper place is at home and that they should quit their jobs, and bases this in his interpretation of Scripture, the women have a legitimate complaint. An employer should sanction the supervisor in such cases, even if such sanction violated the supervisor's understanding of religious freedom under legislation like the WRFA.

New legislation is not the only pluralist response to religious speech conflicts in the workplace. Chalmers and Wilson cannot be the only two people who have ever aggravated tensions with co-workers by proselytizing in the workplace, and Peterson is probably not the only one to be caught between his religious beliefs and a corporate antidiscrimination policy. They probably are not the only people to ever lose their jobs over religious speech in the workplace. However, most of these other cases do not end up in court, so many of them must be resolved in some other way. In most cases, under pressure from employers, individuals probably compromise on their religious expression in the workplace. Peterson, Chalmers, and Wilson treat their co-workers the way that they would treat the state and fail to recognize that they have applied a First Amendment logic to a situation that is not properly governed by the First Amendment. Their co-workers and employers do not automatically owe them freedom of speech, especially at the expense of their own religious freedoms. Their co-workers and employers do not have to agree to settle these cases under the terms of the First Amendment framework or agree to tolerate that which the state would not have to tolerate. Peterson, Chalmers, and Wilson have an absolute right to proselytize in public places and to criticize the government on religious grounds, but they have no analogous right against their co-workers.[31] This is not to say that Chalmers and Wilson necessarily deserved to lose their jobs or that it was the only possible outcome of their situations. Their co-workers do not have an absolute right to be free from religious expression in the workplace either. Compromise between religious expression and aversion to religious expression in the workplace is called for if people are going to get along in these settings and is probably quite common.

To deal with these kinds of hard cases, we need to move beyond the First Amendment framework to an alternative framework that works to develop compromises grounded in the specific context of the workplace. Pluralism takes into consideration the purposes of corporate organization and the values normally seen as appropriate to that context. It considers the kind of civility that workplace environments require for day-to-day functioning of the enterprise. A good deal of irritating behavior is usually tolerated in these environments, but there are limits beyond which work does not get done. There are also limits on behavior that reaches the threshold of sexual or racial harassment. In the workplace, no religious speaker has the kind of absolutist rights claim that the First Amendment framework mistakenly identifies. At the same time, the workplace is not entirely public space, and interactions between workers are not like political interactions in civil society. The environment calls for compromise, civility, and a willingness to separate work life from personal life. The workplace does not have to become a religion-free zone, but it cannot be a religious free-for-all either.

The Wilson and Chalmers cases may lead to different kinds of compromises. These cases can be distinguished by a key difference in the balance of values that each raises. Wilson's anti-abortion button is a religious expression required by her religious practice that offends co-workers not because of its religious content as much as by the graphic and disturbing representation of a fetus printed on the button. Her employer requested she remove the button because the disturbance of co-workers potentially disrupted office productivity. It is unlikely that the basis of offense taken was religious in nature, so the Wilson case does not involve a direct conflict between incommensurable religious values. Instead, it deals with a conflict between values that are not directly comparable but which we may be able to rank order. Wilson's button looks like religious expression that is annoying to co-workers but does not offend their religious views directly. Unless her button has had a substantial impact on office productivity, she should be allowed to wear it or at least to display similar materials inside her personal workspace. On the other hand, Chalmers's proselytizing letters involve conflicts with other employees' religious beliefs and practices (or their rejection of such beliefs). There is no simple way to reconcile Chalmers's freedom of religious expression with the religious freedom of the recipients of her letters. Under the pluralist framework, Chalmers's claim still fails, and she will have to desist from letter writing. Similarly, Peterson's antigay proselytizing conflicts with the important workplace value of diversity and a work environment free from harassment. To protect Peterson's speech at the expense of other employees is to elevate religious speech in the workplace to a special status above that of other workplace values, some of which are protected by law. Peterson's speech is unlikely to be protected by arguments made under the pluralist framework.

I began with the intuition that Americans have come to expect a great deal more from freedom of speech than the guarantee against state interference provided by First Amendment law. I was thinking about the "First Amendment" claims made in everyday circumstances in workplaces, families, schools, and social gatherings that have absolutely nothing to do with the First Amendment but represent a broader and more diffuse perception of the meaning of freedom of speech. I also suspected that there were many reasons that academics and lawyers are attracted to the First Amendment and that these reasons are not limited to those arguments that have proven effective in protecting speech in the courts. These things seem even more true now than they did when I started. The pluralist framework for debate over freedom of speech opens up questions about nonstate constraints on freedom of speech precluded by the First Amendment framework. It also makes room for values like self-realization that, once we stand back from the First Amendment, appear to ground more free speech arguments than is apparent today. By overrelying on the legal process of constitutional rights claims, we undermine the political organization and debate over the meaning of free speech that are necessary to fully account for the importance of free speech to liberal societies. If we want to understand submerged speech claims and to promote expression in a future of unknown innovations in communication technology, we need to move beyond the First Amendment and toward a pluralist framework for freedom of speech.

Notes

INTRODUCTION: Expression, Politics, and Pluralism

1. For instance, John Stuart Mill, John Rawls, or Jürgen Habermas.

2. See generally the essays in David S. Allen and Robert Jensen, eds., *Freeing the First Amendment: Critical Perspectives on Freedom of Expression* (New York: New York University Press, 1995).

3. Stanley Fish, "The Dance of Theory," in *Eternally Vigilant: Free Speech in the Modern Era*, ed. Lee C. Bollinger and Geoffrey R. Stone, 231 (Chicago: University of Chicago Press, 2002). Fish's argument is essentially a more developed version of his famous essay "There's No Such Thing as Free Speech, and It's a Good Thing, Too," in *There's No Such Thing as Free Speech* (New York: Oxford University Press, 1994), 103–19.

4. John Stuart Mill introduces the notion of a contest of ideas in *On Liberty*, an idea that Justice Holmes takes up in his dissent in *Abrams v. United States*, 250 U.S. 616 (1919). This "marketplace of ideas" has become the dominant metaphor for free speech questions.

5. Mergers and acquisitions in this business seek to bring together production and distribution of programming, including movies, television shows, and vast libraries of old materials and distribution channels such as the Internet, cable television, satellites, and telephone lines. These mergers cross media divisions as well to include publishing, newspapers, and web sites. The FCC has recently (June 2003) further reduced restrictions on cross-ownership in ways that will probably lead to further concentration of ownership, barring congressional action to overturn the new FCC rules.

6. Lawrence K. Grossman, *The Electronic Republic: Reshaping Democracy in the Information Age* (New York: 20th Century Fund/Viking, 1995); Robert W. McChesney, *The Problem of the Media: U.S. Communication Politics in the 21st Century* (New York: Monthly Review, 2004).

7. Lawrence Lessig, *The Future of Ideas: The Fate of the Commons in a Connected World* (New York: Random House, 2001); Lessig, *Free Culture: How Big Media Uses Technology and the Law to Lock Down Culture and Control Creativity* (New York: Penguin, 2004); Siva Vaidhyanathan, *The Anarchist in the Library: How the Clash between Freedom and Control Is Hacking the Real World and Crashing the System* (New York: Basic Books, 2004).

8. See Larry D. Eldridge, *A Distant Heritage: The Growth of Free Speech in Early America* (New York: New York University Press, 1994).

9. Frederick Schauer, "The First Amendment as Ideology," in Allen and Jensen, *Freeing the First Amendment*, 10–30.

10. See, for instance, John Rawls, *Political Liberalism* (New York: Columbia University Press, 1993), 340–55; and Stephen Holmes, *Passions and Constraint: On the Theory of Liberal Democracy* (Chicago: University of Chicago Press, 1995), 20–21.

11. Bork and Meiklejohn have very different arguments, but each limits the justification of freedom of speech to political speech and explicitly excludes other kinds of speech from protection. Meiklejohn later changed his view and moved toward a comprehensive justification of freedom of speech that did include artistic and other kinds of speech, although for their political value. Robert Bork, "Neutral Principles and Some First Amendment Problems," *Indiana Law Journal* 47 (1971): 1–35; Alexander Meiklejohn, *Free Speech and Its Relation to Self Government* (New York: Harper, 1948).

12. *Chaplinsky v. New Hampshire*, 315 U.S. 568 (1942).

13. Each school can be considered to have a project composed of goals, objectives, and values that adherents to the school seek to promote through freedom of speech.

14. *American Booksellers Association, Inc. v. Hudnut*, 771 F.2d 323 (7th Cir. 1985), affirmed by the Supreme Court in 1986. Judge Frank Easterbrook's decision focuses on the idea of "thought control" inherent in mandating approved viewpoints for different kinds of speech. Easterbrook also carefully argues for the status of pornography as speech, agreeing with the ordinance's premise that pornography perpetuates subordination while citing these effects as evidence of its power as speech.

Several versions of this ordinance were introduced in many other cities in the mid-1980s. A similar approach has become law in Canada, and the logic of the ordinance has been very influential in the movement for hate speech regulations on college campuses. Under *Miller v. California*, 413 U.S. 15 (1973), obscenity has a specific meaning in First Amendment jurisprudence, involving patent offensiveness, appeals to prurient interest, and lack of serious value. According to this doctrine, obscenity is speech but constitutes one of several categories of expression outside of First Amendment protection.

15. *Yahoo!, Inc. v. La Ligue Contre Le Racisme et L'Antisemitisme*, 169 F. Supp. 2d 1181 (U.S. District Court for the Northern District of California, San Jose Division, 2001).

16. See "A Jurisdictional Tangle," *Economist*, December 10, 2002, www.economist .com/research/articlesBySubject/displayStory.cfm?story_ID=1489053&subject= Australia (January 30, 2004).

O N E : The First Amendment Framework

1. See John Searle, *Speech Acts: An Essay in the Philosophy of Language* (Cambridge: Cambridge University Press, 1969); and J. L. Austin, *How to Do Things with Words* (Cambridge, Mass.: Harvard University Press, 1962).

2. Some American legal scholars even suggest that this framework, minus the institutional apparatus of the First Amendment, ought to be adopted internationally. Rodney Smolla, *Free Speech in an Open Society* (New York: Vintage, 1992), 343–67.

3. Schauer, "The First Amendment as Ideology"; Henry Louis Gates Jr., "War of Words: Critical Race Theory and the First Amendment," in *Speaking of Race, Speaking of Sex: Hate Speech, Civil Rights, and Civil Liberties*, ed. Henry Louis Gates Jr. et al., 17 (New York: New York University Press, 1994).

4. See Leonard Levy, *Legacy of Suppression: Freedom of Speech and Press in Early America* (Cambridge, Mass.: Belknap Press of Harvard University Press, 1960).

5. Rawls, *Political Liberalism*, 340–55; Joshua Cohen, "Freedom of Expression," *Philosophy and Public Affairs* 22 (1993): 207–63.

6. Frederick Schauer, *Free Speech: A Philosophical Enquiry* (Cambridge: Cambridge University Press, 1982).

7. See Cass R. Sunstein, *Legal Reasoning and Political Conflict* (New York: Oxford University Press, 1996).

8. Some follow Owen Fiss in suggesting that state inaction is grounds for a First Amendment claim, but these claims are highly controversial. Owen Fiss, "Why the State?" *Harvard Law Review* 100 (1987): 781–94; Fiss, "State Activism and State Censorship," *Yale Law Journal* 100 (1991): 2087–106; Fiss, *Liberalism Divided: Freedom of Speech and the Many Uses of State Power* (Boulder, Colo.: Westview, 1996).

9. This threat has reemerged in both familiar and in new forms since 9/11/2001.

10. Examples of interpersonal relationships include the marriage contract, parent-child relationships, and many kinds of business relationships. The heckler's veto refers to the harassment, heckling, or intimidation of a speaker by a hostile audience such that the speaker is prevented from speaking. Police are required to protect speakers from hostile audiences in order to allow their speech to take place. *Edwards v. South Carolina*, 372 U.S. 229 (1963).

11. Group claims have been considered in First Amendment jurisprudence but appear to be a dead end; see *Beauharnais v. Illinois*, 343 U.S. 250 (1952).

12. The actions of a private university do not meet the condition of state action in spite of partial federal funding of their activities. Frank Michelman, "Universities, Racist Speech and Democracy in America: An Essay for the ACLU," *Harvard Civil Rights—Civil Liberties Law Review* 27 (1992): 356. See also Samuel Walker, *Hate Speech: The History of an American Controversy* (Lincoln: University of Nebraska Press, 1994), 148–49; Alan Charles Kors and Harvey A. Silverglate, *The Shadow University* (New York: Free Press, 1998).

13. See Mari Matsuda et al., eds., *Words That Wound: Critical Race Theory, Assaultive Speech and the First Amendment* (Boulder, Colo.: Westview, 1993).

14. *R.A.V. v. St. Paul*, 505 U.S. 377 (1992); *UWM Post v. Board of Regents of the University of Wisconsin* 774 F. Supp. 1163 (E.D. Wis. 1991); *Doe v. University of Michigan* 721 F. Supp. 852 (E.D. Mich. 1989).

15. Andrew Altman, "Liberalism and Campus Hate Speech: A Philosophical Evaluation," *Ethics* 103 (1993): 312.

16. "Hate speech is antithetical to the underlying liberal democratic principles that inform the First Amendment and the Equal Protection clause." Mari Matsuda, introduction to Matsuda et al., *Words That Wound*, 9.

17. Mari Matsuda, "Public Response to Racist Speech: Considering the Victim's Story," in Matsuda et al., *Words That Wound*, 24; Howard J. Ehrlich, Barbara E. K. Larcom, and Robert D. Purvis, "The Traumatic Impact of Ethnoviolence," in *The Price We Pay: The Case against Racist Speech, Hate Propaganda, and Pornography*, ed. Laura Lederer and Richard Delgado, 66–68 (New York: Hill and Wang, 1995).

18. Charles Lawrence, "If He Hollers Let Him Go: Regulating Racist Speech on Campus," in Matsuda et al., *Words That Wound*, 68; Richard Delgado, "Words That Wound: A Tort Action for Racial Insults, Epithets and Name Calling," in Matsuda et al., *Words That Wound*, 91; Matsuda, "Public Response to Racist Speech," 24–25; Ehrlich et al., "Impact of Ethnoviolence," 74–75; Raphael Cohen-Almagor, "Harm Principle, Offense Principle and the Skokie Affair," *Political Studies* 41 (1993): 454.

19. Gates, "War of Words," 17, 23–25. Gates goes on to include the name "First Amendment" for the same criticism.

20. Ibid., 26–27. This is the categorization approach consistent with *Chaplinsky* (315

U.S. 568). Defamation enters First Amendment doctrine in this context in *Beauharnais* (343 U.S. 250).

21. Gates, "War of Words," 26–27, 52.

22. Consider an example of the effects of the First Amendment framework that extend outside the institutional context of the First Amendment. Private universities took care to design hate speech rules for their campuses that would pass a hypothetical First Amendment challenge, even though as private institutions they were not subject to the same kinds of suits that overturned hate speech rules at public universities. This reflects both the intellectual and the cultural hold that the First Amendment framework has on American thought on freedom of speech.

23. Steven A. Holmes, "Broker Asserts Political Views Drew Pressure," *New York Times*, July 10, 1998. Many state employees also face various levels of restriction on outside advocacy.

24. Jeffrey Rosen, "In Defense of Gender Blindness," *New Republic*, June 29, 1998, 25–35.

25. Richard Abel, *Speaking Respect, Respecting Speech* (Chicago: University of Chicago Press, 1998).

26. Any of the proposed "more speech" remedies can have effects that constrain the original speaker without implicating provisions of First Amendment law. For example, picketing and boycotts, to the extent that they are effective, work by either drowning out the original speaker or making his or her continued speech very costly. "More speech" remedies can lead to intimidation or humiliation of speakers and can make the original speaker an object of harassment or derision. While "more speech" legitimately may be directed at the arguments made by a speaker, it can also be an illegitimate technique to undermine the speaker and his or her opportunity to reach an audience.

27. Or, commonly, a misperception of what the First Amendment actually covers that indicates that a free speech claim is being made, but not a valid First Amendment claim.

TWO: Public Debate and the Libertarian Justification

1. Schauer, *Free Speech*, 129.

2. 376 U.S. 255 (1964).

3. Schauer, *Free Speech*, 11.

4. From this point, I will use the terms "free speech libertarian" and "libertarian" (as well as "free speech libertarianism" and "libertarianism") interchangeably, but in each instance the terms are meant to refer to those whom I describe in this chapter as free speech libertarians.

5. Fiss, "State Activism and State Censorship," 2087–106.

6. For examples, see Black's dissent in *Konigsberg v. State Bar*, 366 U.S. 36 (1961); *American Communication Ass'n, CIO v. Douds*, 339 U.S. 382 (1950); and *Dennis v. United States*, 341 U.S. 494 (1951).

7. A version of free speech absolutism grounded in abstract human rights or natural law might not fall to this criticism but would have to be justified by independent arguments. However, that defense would not look very much like the American version of absolutism established by constitutional authority.

8. Tinsley E. Yarbrough, *Mr. Justice Black and His Critics* (Durham, N.C.: Duke University Press, 1988), 140; *Valentine v. Chrestensen*, 316 U.S. 52 (1942).

9. Yarbrough, *Mr. Justice Black*, 143–46; *Brown v. Louisiana*, 383 U.S. 131 (1966).

10. For an extended criticism of the speech/conduct distinction as a threat to free speech, see Franklyn S. Haiman, *"Speech Acts" and the First Amendment* (Carbondale: Southern Illinois University Press, 1993).

11. *Areopagitica*, in *Complete Prose Works of John Milton*, ed. Ernest Sirluck, (New Haven, Conn.: Yale University Press, 1959); Henry Robinson, "Liberty of Conscience: Or the Sole Means to Obtaine Peace and Truth," in *Tracts on Liberty in the Puritan Revolution 1638–47*, ed. William Haller, 3:105–78 (New York: Octagon, 1965); William Walwyn, "The Compassionate Samaritane," in Haller, *Tracts on Liberty*, 3:59–105; Milton, *Areopagitica*, 550–51.

12. Walwyn, "The Compassionate Samaritane," 249–51.

13. Milton, *Areopagitica*, 491–42; Walwyn, "The Compassionate Samaritane," 251.

14. Ernest Sirluck, "1643–1645: Reformation of the Church and Relgious Toleration," in Sirluck, *Complete Prose Works of John Milton*, 83–84.

15. Milton, *Areopagitica*, 561.

16. Ibid., 491–92.

17. Milton makes reference to John Selden (ibid., 513) and Robinson (ibid., 491).

18. Ibid., 515, 562.

19. Ibid., 531.

20. John Stuart Mill, *On Liberty* (1859; repr., Indianapolis: Hackett, 1978), 36–38.

21. "Both teachers and learners go to sleep at their post as soon as there is no enemy in the field." Ibid., 41.

22. Ibid., 43–44, 50.

23. Ibid., 32.

24. Mark Graber, *Transforming Free Speech: The Ambiguous Legacy of Civil Libertarianism* (Berkeley: University of California Press, 1991), 18–19, 20, 24, 34.

25. *Abrams*, 250 U.S. 616. The strong pro–free speech rhetoric of this dissent has to be taken with a grain of salt once modified by Holmes's clear and present danger test. Holmes sees Abrams's speech protected by the market in ideas, but it is no more than "the surreptitious publishing of a silly leaflet by an unknown man." Speech with a greater possibility of effect, for instance, Eugene Debs's antidraft speech, does not receive Holmes's protection. *Debs v. United States*, 249 U.S. 211 (1919).

26. Mill, *On Liberty*, 17.

27. Graber, *Transforming Free Speech*, 11.

28. *Schenck v. United States*, 249 U.S. 47 (1919); *Debs*, 249 U.S. 211; *Abrams*, 250 U.S. 616; *Gitlow v. New York*, 268 U.S. 652 (1925).

29. See Schauer's criticism of general liberty defenses of free speech in *Free Speech* (6–11).

30. Zechariah Chafee, *Free Speech in the United States* (1941; repr., Cambridge, Mass.: Harvard University Press, 1964), 34–35; Graber, *Transforming Free Speech*, 165; Fiss, "Why the State?" 785–86; Schauer *Free Speech*, 47, 159.

31. Schauer, *Free Speech*, 159.

32. See chapter 3 for an examination of expressivist justifications that treat speech as an end in itself.

33. See Brandeis's concurring opinion in *Whitney v. California*, 274 U.S. 357 (1927); Thomas Emerson, *The System of Freedom of Expression* (New York: Random House, 1970); Emerson, *Toward a General Theory of the First Amendment* (New York: Vintage, 1966);

Martin Redish, *Freedom of Expression: A Critical Analysis* (Charlottesville, Va.: Michie, 1984).

34. Schauer, *Free Speech*, 52, 55–56.

35. Cass R. Sunstein, *Democracy and the Problem of Free Speech* (New York: Free Press, 1993), 140–41.

36. See the discussion of the no-cost argument (free speech minimalism) and its failure in Cohen, "Freedom of Expression," 218–19.

37. Jonathan Rauch, *Kindly Inquisitors: The New Attacks on Free Thought* (Chicago: University of Chicago Press, 1993).

38. Lee Bollinger, *The Tolerant Society: Freedom of Speech and Extremist Speech in America* (New York: Oxford University Press, 1986).

39. The clear and present danger test is not so much a test or rule as it is a statement that judges will make case-by-case determinations based on the circumstances at hand. "The question in every case is whether the words used are used in such circumstances and are of such a nature as to create a clear and present danger that they will bring about the substantive evils that Congress has a right to prevent. It is a question of proximity and degree." *Schenck*, 249 U.S. 47.

40. Emerson, *Freedom of Expression*.

41. See *New York Times v. Sullivan*, 376 U.S. 255 (1964).

42. Expressivists are concerned to protect freedom of expression as an end in itself necessary to individuals, regardless of the social value of expression.

43. *Schenck*, 249 U.S. 47; *Debs*, 249 U.S. 211.

44. Chafee, *Free Speech*, 510.

45. Roscoe Pound, *Jurisprudence* (St. Paul, Minn.: West, 1959), 3:63–64.

46. Owen Fiss, for instance, is concerned with public debate itself without going into much detail as to the ultimate objectives of that debate. See Fiss, "Why the State?" 783; Fiss, "State Activism," 2087–106.

47. Mill, *On Liberty*, ch. 2.

48. Even free speech absolutists eventually give in to balancing interests, although it may take place under the guise of a speech/action dichotomy that identifies problematic speech as action and thus outside of the bounds of free speech protection.

49. *Chaplinsky*, 315 U.S. 568; *Brandenburg v. Ohio*, 395 U.S. 444 (1969).

50. Sunstein, *Democracy*, 139–41.

51. This understanding of good policy as the political truth is used by free speech libertarians in keeping with the consequentialism of their arguments. However, such a claim would be extremely contentious as a general theory of political truth. Deontological political theorists would not accept good policy outcomes as a measure of political truth. That said, I do not see this point as an objection to my description of free speech libertarian arguments.

52. Cohen, "Freedom of Expression," 228.

53. See C. Edwin Baker, *Human Liberty and Freedom of Speech* (New York: Oxford University Press, 1989), ch. 2.

54. Graber, *Transforming Free Speech*, 87–121.

55. 274 U.S. 357 (1927).

56. Graber, *Transforming Free Speech*, 87.

57. Ibid., 102.

58. T. M. Scanlon, "Freedom of Expression and Categories of Expression," *University of Pittsburgh Law Review* 40 (1979): 527.

59. Ibid., 521.

60. T. M. Scanlon, "A Theory of Freedom of Expression," *Philosophy and Public Affairs* 1 (1972): 203–26.

61. Graber traces the procedural view to jurists strongly influenced by the Progressives and argues that Chafee transformed free speech into a "procedural prerequisite for any democratic society." Graber, *Transforming Free Speech*, 124–25. This procedural view is the central argument of John Hart Ely, *Democracy and Distrust: A Theory of Judicial Review* (Cambridge, Mass.: Harvard University Press, 1980).

62. There are social benefits in this view of democracy for everyone, even those who do not vote or otherwise participate, because they will benefit from the best possible policy-making procedure. Joseph Raz, "Free Expression and Personal Identification," *Oxford Journal of Legal Studies* 11 (1991): 309.

63. Schauer maintains that the argument from democracy is a subset of the argument from truth (*Free Speech*, 45). Baker makes a similar argument in *Human Liberty* (28).

64. Schauer, *Free Speech*, 123–29.

65. For an extensive discussion of the legal system's special role in freedom of expression, see Emerson, *General Theory*, ch. 3. In *Free Speech in an Open Society*, Rodney Smolla goes so far as to suggest that the United States export its legal free speech tradition to other countries with lesser protection for speech (345–47).

66. See *Near v. Minnesota*, 283 U.S. 697 (1931), which invalidated court injunctions to prevent newspapers from "publishing scandalous and defamatory matter." See also *Lovell v. Griffin*, 303 U.S. 444 (1938), which invalidated the city of Griffin's ordinance requiring licenses for the distribution of handbooks, advertising, or literature.

67. See *Buckley v. Valeo*, 424 U.S. 1 (1976).

68. Sunstein, *Democracy*, 28–34. On the role of the state action doctrine in constitutional law, see Cass R. Sunstein, *The Partial Constitution* (Cambridge, Mass.: Harvard University Press, 1993); and Frederick Schauer, "Act, Omissions and Constitutionalism," *Ethics* 105 (1995): 916–26.

69. Schauer, *Free Speech*, 122.

70. *Miami Herald v. Tornillo*, 418 U.S. 241 (1974), unanimously overturned a Florida "right of reply" statute that required that space be provided for rebuttals.

71. Sunstein, *Democracy*, ch. 3.

72. See the case of Edward J. Blum, a Paine Webber employee fired for political activities on his own time, unrelated to his job or his employer. Steven A. Holmes, "Broker Asserts Political Views Drew Pressure," *New York Times*, July 10, 1998.

73. 341 U.S. 494 (1951).

74. Carl Auerbach, "The Communist Control Act of 1954: A Proposed Legal-Political Theory of Free Speech," *University of Chicago Law Review* 23 (1956): 173–220.

75. Ibid., 188.

76. Ibid., 189.

77. Emerson, *Freedom of Expression*, 48.

78. Mark Graber, "Old Wine in New Bottles: The Constitutional Status of Unconstitutional Speech," *Vanderbilt Law Review* 48 (1995): 371–72.

79. *Yates v. United States*, 354 U.S. 66 (1957); *Brandenburg*, 395 U.S. 444.

80. Graber, "Old Wine," 376–78.
81. See the discussion of Milton above for the origins of this belief.
82. Emerson, *Freedom of Expression*, 51; Schauer, "The First Amendment as Ideology," 10–13.
83. Schauer, "The First Amendment as Ideology," 13, 21.
84. Graber, "Old Wine," 389.
85. For a contemporary example of the way in which this orthodox view grounds libertarian arguments, see Rauch, *Kindly Inquisitors*.
86. Fiss, "Why the State?" 786–87.
87. Ibid., 783, 788, 789–94; Fiss, "State Activism," 2087–106.
88. Fiss, "State Activism," 2088. See also Joseph Tussman, *Government and the Mind* (New York: Oxford University Press, 1977), for a strong argument against (without the corresponding call for state intervention) the ways in which government is involved in the lives of citizens through funding speech in libraries, as patron of the arts and sciences, and other cultural activities.
89. Sunstein, *Democracy*.
90. 500 U.S. 173 (1991).
91. *Regan v. Taxation with Representation of Washington*, 461 U.S. 540 (1983); *The Arkansas Writer's Project v. Ragland*, 481 U.S. 221 (1987).
92. Graber, "Old Wine," 387.
93. Judge Richard Posner, *Swank v. Smart*, 898 F.2d 1247 (7th Cir. 1990), quoted in Kent Greenawalt, *Fighting Words: Individuals, Communities, and Liberties of Speech* (Princeton, N.J.: Princeton University Press, 1995), 83.
94. "Ballots serve primarily to elect candidates, not as fora for political expression." *Timmons v. Twin Cities Area New Party*, 520 U.S. 351 (1997). In one sense, his view makes sense since voting is private, and there is no opportunity for others to debate your vote as it is cast.
95. See Catharine MacKinnon, *Feminism Unmodified* (Cambridge, Mass.: Harvard University Press, 1987); Attorney General's Commission on Pornography, *Final Report* (Washington, D.C.: U.S. Department of Justice, 1986).
96. In other words, works that appeal to the "prurient interest" do not count as speech by definition. *Miller*, 413 U.S. 15.
97. "Yet this simply demonstrates the power of pornography as speech. All of these unhappy effects depend on mental intermediation. Pornography affects how people see the world, their fellows, and social relations. If pornography is what pornography does than so is other speech." *American Booksellers' Association, Inc.*, 771 F.2d 323.
98. Schauer, *Free Speech*, 95–98.
99. Bork, "Neutral Principles," 27–28.
100. "It [revolutionary speech] is not political speech because it violates constitutional truths about processes and because it is not aimed at a new definition of political truth by a legislative majority." Ibid., 31. Bork's definition of political speech is highly specific to the U.S. Constitution and its underlying Madisonian principles. It appears that a statement such as "the terrorists had legitimate grievances against U.S. policies in the Middle East" would not be protected by Bork's definition of political speech, even though it is clearly a political statement by virtually any other definition, regardless of its truth or falsity.
101. Sunstein, *Democracy*, 131.

102. I do not mean that Barrie's attorney should be faulted for using a legally effective argument, but when we discuss prominent cases such as this, we are not bound by the same imperatives as the lawyer arguing the case.

103. Meiklejohn, *Free Speech*, 25.

104. Graber offers Herbert Croly and Walter Lippmann as examples of those who believed that democracy required only the opinions of an elite, enlightened, bureaucratic minority, not the opinions of the masses. Graber, *Transforming Free Speech*, 82.

105. See James Fishkin, *Democracy and Deliberation* (New Haven, Conn.: Yale University Press, 1991). This well-intended argument is quite scary, from the perspective of one who values individual expression. In conjunction with the procedural view of democracy favored by free speech libertarians, Fishkin's polls could theoretically replace voting and other democratic procedures. Fishkin seeks to combine the strengths of face-to-face democratic deliberation with the methods of survey research. He proposes bringing together hundreds of Americans selected according to random sampling techniques to meet for several days and discuss contemporary political issues. This sample then reports its conclusions as representative of how all Americans would decide these issues, were it physically possible to bring hundreds of millions of people together in one place to deliberate.

THREE: Self-Realization and the Expressivist Justification

1. Baker, *Human Liberty*, 48–55; Redish, *Freedom of Expression*, 11–12.

2. Meiklejohn, *Free Speech*; Sunstein, *Democracy*; Smolla, *Free Speech*.

3. Rabban and Graber are particularly critical of the role played by Zechariah Chafee in the shift from an earlier civil libertarian account of free speech to the modern consequentialist account. See David M. Rabban, *Free Speech in Its Forgotten Years* (Cambridge: Cambridge University Press, 1997), 2, 344; Graber, *Transforming Free Speech*, 2.

4. See Scanlon, "Freedom of Expression," 524–27.

5. See, for example, Redish, *Freedom of Expression*, 19–21; and Baker, *Human Liberty*, 30–31.

6. John Stuart Mill's famous argument for freedom of speech rests on this point. For an extended contemporary argument on the value of wide open public debate, see Rauch, *Kindly Inquisitors*.

7. J. G. Herder, *Reflections on the History of Mankind*, ed. Frank E. Manuel, trans. T. O. Churchill (1784; repr., Chicago: University of Chicago Press, 1968); Wilhelm von Humboldt, *The Limits of State Action*, ed. with intro. and notes by J. W. Burrow (Cambridge: Cambridge University Press, 1969); Friedrich Schlegel, *Philosophical Fragments*, trans. Peter Firchow (Minneapolis: University of Minnesota Press, 1991). For engaging discussions of Emerson and Whitman, see Steven Shiffrin, *The First Amendment, Democracy, and Romance* (Cambridge, Mass.: Harvard University Press, 1990); and Nancy Rosenblum, *Another Liberalism: Romanticism and the Reconstruction of Liberal Thought* (Cambridge, Mass.: Harvard University Press, 1987).

8. *Whitney*, 274 U.S. 357. Brandeis's opinion is multifaceted and also introduces a "civic courage" model of the First Amendment as a procedural guarantee of political truth. Vincent Blasi, "The First Amendment and the Ideal of Civic Courage," *William and Mary Law Review* 29 (1988): 673–74.

9. Emerson, *Freedom of Expression*, 6. The four values served by freedom of speech as

listed by Emerson are: individual self-fulfillment, truth, participation in decision making, and a more stable and adaptable community. "Self-fulfillment" and "self-realization" are used interchangeably in literature that treats these as objectives for freedom of speech.

10. The informational interest in free speech involves the need for reliable information to pursue individual interests. Cohen, "Freedom of Expression," 228.

11. The importance of this cultural environment is most clear in Herder's understanding of the distinctiveness of national cultures and their importance to the artistic work of members. "The happiness of man is in all places an individual good; consequently it is everywhere climatic and organic, the offspring of practice, tradition and custom." Herder, *Reflections*, 71. Perhaps the best discussion of Herder's views is Isaiah Berlin, *Vico and Herder: Two Studies in the History of Ideas* (London: Hogarth Press, 1976), 143–216.

12. It is, of course, far easier to perceive these experiences in the hindsight of history, biography, or life's later years, since people then feel they have a sense of self that they lacked earlier. That is, we go on every day often unaware that the process of self-realization is moving forward or of the effects on us of the expression to which we are exposed.

13. Baker, *Human Liberty*, 30–31, 48, 49–50, 51, 55, 59–69.

14. Ibid., 61.

15. Ibid., 54.

16. Ibid., 53–54.

17. Ibid., 54, 56–59.

18. Redish, *Freedom of Expression*, 11, 12, 19, 22, 41.

19. Shiffrin acknowledges that romanticism is quite diverse but carefully chooses those elements that pertain to dissent and are most easily related back to First Amendment doctrine. He further pursues this more political (and less romantic) understanding of dissent in *Dissent, Injustice and the Meaning of America* (Princeton, N.J.: Princeton University Press, 1999), 141–48.

20. Shiffrin, *The First Amendment*, 5.

21. Smolla, *Free Speech*, 9, 10.

22. Sunstein, *Democracy*, 140–41; Schauer, *Free Speech*, 49–58.

23. The social harms that result from a ban on hate speech are also difficult to evaluate and balance against social benefits of such a ban. Those opposed to regulation of hate speech often focus on this difficulty, while those favoring such regulation focus on social harms of the speech in question.

24. Baker, *Human Liberty*, 47.

25. Redish declares that vagueness is intentional. *Freedom of Expression*, 11.

26. Ibid., 12, 19.

27. Ibid., 21. Redish ignores the fact that just as several values suggest self-realization, democracy serves several important ends other than self-realization, such as the protection of individual rights, collective self-determination, and effective public policy.

28. Ibid., 23, 30–31.

29. Shiffrin, *The First Amendment*, 91.

30. Ibid., 95–96.

31. Schauer, *Free Speech*, 55–56.

32. Frederick Schauer, "Must Speech Be Special?" *Northwestern University Law Review* 78 (1983): 1284, 1290, 1291.

33. Schauer, *Free Speech*, 58.

34. Ibid., 60–62 (discussing an argument for freedom of speech based on the dignity of the individual speaker).

35. Schauer, "Must Speech Be Special?" 1295.

36. Sunstein, *Democracy*, 129–30, 132–36, 140–41.

37. Redish, *Freedom of Expression*, 11, 12.

38. Such as blackmail, libel, or obscenity.

39. Taylor includes Rousseau, Herder, Goethe, and Hegel as the most prominent philosophers of nature as a moral source. Charles Taylor, *Sources of the Self: The Making of Modern Identity* (Cambridge, Mass.: Harvard University Press, 1989), 368.

40. Ibid., 368, 375–76. As Taylor puts it, "Nothing is more evident, or more banal"; and "This has been a tremendously influential idea. Expressive individuation has become one of the cornerstones of modern culture. So much so that we barely notice it, and we find it hard to accept that it is such a recent idea in human history and would have been incomprehensible in earlier times." While this idea of difference is taken for granted now, it bears repeating that originality is an important feature of the self because it implies that there is some element of the self that is preexisting rather than socially constructed. A justification of freedom of speech grounded by social interests does not have to ask the question of whether the self has preexisting elements or even if individual selves are distinct and original.

41. Ibid., 370, 373.

42. Taylor states that "the modern subject is no longer defined just by the power of disengaged rational control but by this new power of expressive self-articulation as well—the power which has been ascribed since the Romantic period to the creative imagination." Ibid., 390.

43. Ibid., 374.

44. Ibid.

45. Rosenblum, *Another Liberalism*, 41–46.

46. Ibid., 46, 72–73.

47. Ibid., 79.

48. Ibid., 21, 72, 84, 89.

49. Ibid., 111–18. Rosenblum finds this idea of heroic self-assertion as a counter to self-abnegation particularly in Thoreau and to a lesser extent in Whitman.

50. See Schlegel, *Philosophical Fragments*; and Humboldt, *Limits of State Action*.

51. Herder called this ideal *Humanität* and placed it at the center of his philosophy. Herder, *Reflections*, Book 8.

52. Humboldt, *Limits of State Action*, 16.

53. Ibid.; Schlegel, *Philosophical Fragments*. Self-determination in this sense is to act from one's own will free from the influence of the external forces that generally form or determine the will.

54. Freedom is the ultimate concern of German romanticism. German intellectuals in the period from 1790 to 1810 were faced with a substantial problem set by Kant's dichotomization of natural necessity and human freedom, namely, how do individuals attain freedom when, according to Kant, one can never know if one has acted freely rather than as a result of physical necessity? For discussions of this problem, see Bernard Yack, *The Longing for Total Revolution: Philosophic Sources of Social Discontent from Rousseau to Marx and Nietzsche* (Princeton, N.J.: Princeton University Press, 1986), 89–132; and Tay-

lor, *Sources of the Self*, 381–85. The answer favored by Schiller began with aesthetic development and continued for Schlegel and other young romantics as an inward turn toward self-development and self-realization.

55. This is a serious problem. For Kant, we can never know if we have acted according to moral law by a free, undetermined adherence to the law or because of the influence of social mores or our own base self-interest. Immanuel Kant, *Fundamental Principles of the Metaphysics of Morals*, trans. Thomas K. Abbott (Indianapolis: Bobbs-Merrill, 1949).

56. In contrast, many authors who would ground freedom of speech in individual autonomy treat autonomy as a general preexisting right that individuals lack only because state action has taken it from them. Nineteenth-century radical libertarianism was based on such a notion of autonomy (see Rabban, *Free Speech*), as was Scanlon's early defense of freedom of speech. Scanlon, "A Theory of Freedom of Expression," 203.

57. Also consider, "For all moral culture springs solely and immediately from the inner life of the soul, and can only be stimulated in human nature, and never produced by external and artificial contrivances." Humboldt, *Limits of State Action*, 16, 63.

58. Ibid., 135.

59. For instance, *Bildung* is crucial to Herder's understanding that the individual develops a unique form in the context of strong attachment to a social group. Herder, *Reflections*, 71–75; Berlin, *Vico and Herder*, 165–69, 153.

60. Charles Taylor, "The Importance of Herder," in *Isaiah Berlin: A Celebration*, ed. Edna Margalit and Avishai Margalit, 40–45, 54 (Chicago: University of Chicago Press, 1991).

61. Schlegel, *Philosophical Fragments*.

62. "Only by being cultivated does a human being, who is wholly that, become altogether human and permeated by humanity." Schlegel, *Ideas* no. 65, in *Philosophical Fragments*, 100.

63. Schlegel, *Athenäum* no. 116, in *Philosophical Fragments*, 31. No. 116 is a much analyzed fragment and forms the basis of Lovejoy's famous interpretation of the genesis of romanticism in Schlegel's thought. A. O. Lovejoy, *Essays in the History of Ideas* (New York: George Braziller, 1955), 190–206.

64. Fragments relevant to this interpretation of Schlegel include *Critical Fragments* no. 18, *Athenäum* no. 222, and *Ideas* no. 3, in *Philosophical Fragments*, 2, 48, 94.

65. Baker, *Human Liberty*, 59.

66. Schauer, *Free Speech*, 58–62.

67. Unless, of course, these activities are expressive. In legal practice, boundaries have to be placed on what counts as expressive activity and what actions are regulable. We still need to treat expressive murder as a punishable act. Ultimately, expressivism may not be any more able to delineate the boundary between speech and conduct than standard free speech arguments, thus leaving this question for practical determination.

68. It is possible to imbue the act of smoking with meanings beyond the simple act itself. Smoking can be an act of defiance both for the underage and for adults who work in nonsmoking buildings. But, in fact, these would be expressive uses of smoking and thus come under the expressivist argument I offer here, subject to practical determinations between speech and conduct.

69. Whereas the opposite is true in the free speech libertarian justification, restrictions on speech must be content neutral to pass constitutional muster, but the important content neutrality doctrine exists to protect content, not the activity of expression.

70. For example, J. G. Herder, *Against Pure Reason: Writings on Religion, Language and History*, trans. Marcia Bunge (Minneapolis: Fortress Press, 1993); Charles Larmore, *The Romantic Legacy* (New York: Columbia University Press, 1996), 33–61. Larmore provides a first-rate account of this communitarian aspect.

71. Taylor, *Sources of the Self*, 368–92.

72. Although in this specific case, the artist was no longer alive.

73. I have in mind the politicization of sexual expression/art, which is, of course, a manifestation of the broader movement to politicize the body. It appears to have corrosive effects on art and on criticism.

74. For example, *Central Hudson Gas and Electric Corp. v. Public Service Commission of New York*, 447 U.S. 557 (1980).

75. "The radio as it now operates is not free. Nor is it entitled to the protection of the First Amendment. It is not engaged in the task of enlarging and enriching human communication. It is engaged in making money. And the First Amendment does not intend to guarantee one freedom to say what some private interest pays them to say for its own advantage. It intends only to make men free to say what, as citizens, they think, what they believe, about the general welfare." Meiklejohn, *Free Speech*, 104.

76. Baker, *Human Liberty*, 60.

77. Graber, *Transforming Free Speech*, 222–26.

78. For example, *Virginia State Board of Pharmacy v. Virginia Citizens Consumer Council*, 425 U.S. 748 (1976) (commercial speech protected when it serves the public interest); *Ohralik v. Ohio State Bar Association*, 436 U.S. 447 (1978) (commercial speech has a subordinate position in First Amendment values).

79. Baker, *Human Liberty*, 59–60.

80. Sunstein, *Democracy*, 153; Alexander Meiklejohn, "The First Amendment Is an Absolute," *Supreme Court Review* (1961): 245–66.

FOUR: Equality and the Egalitarian Justification

1. Some writers criticize egalitarians for pitting the political project of social equality against freedom of speech. Robert C. Post, "Free Speech and Religious, Racial, and Sexual Harassment: Racist Speech, Democracy and the First Amendment," *William and Mary Law Review* 32 (1991): 270; Lawrence Douglas, "The Force of Words: Fish, Matsuda, MacKinnon, and the Theory of Discursive Violence," *Law and Society Review* 29 (1995): 170–71.

2. See *R.A.V.*, 505 U.S. 377, striking down the St. Paul, Minnesota, ordinance against racist fighting words, and *American Booksellers Association, Inc.*, 771 F.2d 323, striking down the Indianapolis, Indiana, version of MacKinnon's antipornography ordinance.

3. See the exchange between Matsuda et. al., *Words That Wound*, and Gates et. al., *Speaking of Race*.

4. Cass Sunstein, "Words, Conduct, Caste," *University of Chicago Law Review* 60 (1993): 796–97; Ronald Dworkin, "The Coming Battles Over Free Speech," *New York Review of Books*, June 11, 1992, 58.

5. Critical race theory is a movement within sociolegal studies that offers an "outsider jurisprudence" based on the historical experiences of people of color in the United States. It is concerned with the ways in which the legal system reflects and reinforces racism and has as its general goal the use of law and legal argument to expose and attack this racism.

Like legal realism, the focus of critical race theory is on the effects of law rather than upon formal analysis of law.

6. The Fourteenth Amendment declares that no state shall "deny to any person within its jurisdiction the equal protection of the laws."

7. *Brown v. Board of Education*, 347 U.S. 483 (1954); *Griswold v. Connecticut*, 381 U.S. 479 (1965); *Planned Parenthood v. Casey*, 505 U.S. 833 (1992).

8. Ronald Dworkin, *Taking Rights Seriously* (Cambridge, Mass.: Harvard University Press, 1977), 178–79, 182.

9. Ronald Dworkin, *Sovereign Virtue: The Theory and Practice of Equality* (Cambridge, Mass.: Harvard University Press, 2000).

10. Ibid., 366.

11. Ronald Dworkin, *Freedom's Law* (Cambridge, Mass.: Harvard University Press, 1996), 10, 17, 24. See also Dworkin, *Sovereign Virtue*, 357–58, where he criticizes the "populist" account of majoritarianism, the view that government should enact laws favored by a current majority of the population.

12. Ronald Dworkin, "Women and Pornography," *New York Review of Books*, October 21, 1993, 41.

13. In Canada, the Supreme Court has taken the opposite position on this empirical question. See the discussion of the *Keegstra* case below.

14. Dworkin, *Sovereign Virtue*, 366–67.

15. Kenneth L. Karst, *Law's Promise, Law's Expression: Visions of Power in the Politics of Race, Gender, and Religion* (New Haven, Conn.: Yale University Press, 1993), 174–75.

16. Kenneth L. Karst, *Belonging to America: Equal Citizenship and the Constitution* (New Haven, Conn.: Yale University Press, 1989), 1–2, ch. 3.

17. Karst, *Law's Promise*, 182.

18. Dworkin, "Women and Pornography," 41.

19. Dworkin, "The Coming Battles," 56.

20. Dworkin stated his opposition to the St. Paul ordinance in this article written before the actual decision was announced. Ibid., 58.

21. See, for instance, *Bradwell v. Illinois*, 83 U.S. 130 (1873), in which the Supreme Court maintained that women were unfit to practice law.

22. Dworkin, "The Coming Battles," 57.

23. Karst, *Law's Promise*, x.

24. Ibid., 184–86.

25. Kenneth L. Karst, "Boundaries and Reasons: Freedom of Expression and the Subordination of Groups," *University of Illinois Law Review* (1990): 125.

26. A point that Karst recognizes. Ibid., 148.

27. Ibid., 126, 148.

28. Ibid., 131.

29. Dworkin, "Women and Pornography," 42.

30. Ibid., 42.

31. Dworkin, "The Coming Battles," 62. Dworkin suggests that the *Sullivan* actual malice rule be extended to apply in all libel cases, whether they involve public or private figures.

32. Dworkin, *Sovereign Virtue*, 369, 370.

33. Or inhabitants, if we consider the related problem of treatment of resident aliens and nonnaturalized immigrants.

34. Dworkin, *Sovereign Virtue*, 94–95.

35. Karst, "Boundaries and Reasons," 111.

36. Ibid., 112.

37. Work in political psychology, such as Pamela Johnston Conover's "The Role of Social Groups in Political Thinking," *British Journal of Political Science* 18 (1988): 51–76, describes the role of "outgroup schema" (stereotypes) in group relations. People develop heuristic schemes to help process information about members of in-groups and out-groups, favoring in-group members in cases of intergroup conflict.

38. Delgado, "Words That Wound," 91.

39. Matsuda, "Public Response to Racist Speech," 17, 20. "Hate speech is antithetical to the underlying liberal democratic principles that inform the First Amendment and the Equal Protection clause." Matsuda, introduction to Matsuda et. al., *Words That Wound*, 9.

40. Matsuda, "Public Response to Racist Speech," 35.

41. Ibid., 25.

42. Lawrence, "If He Hollers," 57–58.

43. Delgado, "Words That Wound," 94.

44. Matsuda, "Public Response to Racist Speech," 36.

45. Ibid.

46. Lederer and Delgado, *The Price We Pay*, 9. For instance, gender relations are not marked by segregation (MacKinnon, *Feminism Unmodified*, 167). Arguments against pornography have also led to strange alliances between feminists and moral conservatives (Donald A. Downs, *The New Politics of Pornography* [Chicago: University of Chicago Press, 1989]) that are not often seen over the issue of hate speech.

47. Catharine MacKinnon, *Only Words* (Cambridge, Mass.: Harvard University Press, 1993); MacKinnon, *Feminism Unmodified*, especially chs. 13 and 14.

48. MacKinnon, *Feminism Unmodified*, 154, 158, 161, 166, 172.

49. Ibid., 148, 160, 171.

50. MacKinnon's claims in this area are less convincing, so the following argument applies more to criticism of hate speech than to criticism of MacKinnon.

51. One possible extension would be to prohibit all coercive speech, as Baker argues in *Human Liberty and Freedom of Speech*. He suggests that only noncoercive speech should be protected and that excluded categories like false commercial speech can be explained as efforts to coerce consumers into poor market decisions. This view of coercion goes far beyond the subordination on the basis of race or gender, or status more generally, that I deal with in this chapter (see chapter 3 for a more complete discussion of Baker's views). Unfortunately, Baker finds all speech with a profit motive to be coercive, and he fails to explain how vital, profit-oriented institutions such as a free press would be maintained.

52. See German Basic Law, art. 130.

53. *R.A.V.*, 505 U.S. 377; Supreme Court of Canada, *R. v. Keegstra*, 3 S.C.R. 697 (1990).

54. Richard Moon, *The Constitutional Protection of Freedom of Expression* (Toronto: University of Toronto Press, 2000), 32–33; Donald L. Beschle, "Clearly Canadian? Hill vs Colorado and Free Speech Balancing in the United States and Canada," *Hastings Constitutional Law Quarterly* (Winter 2001): 198–99.

55. Beschle, "Clearly Canadian?" 189; Moon, *Constitutional Protection*, 33–34.

56. *Keegstra*, 3 S.C.R. 697, 730.

57. Canada, Charter of Rights and Freedoms, sec. 1.
58. Beschle, "Clearly Canadian?" 198–99.
59. Canada, Human Rights Act, ch. H-6, sec. 2.
60. *Keegstra*, 3 S.C.R. 697, 746, 767.
61. Dworkin, *Sovereign Virtue*, 366.
62. Dworkin suggests that cases of sexual harassment or racial intimidation in the workplace qualify, for instance. Dworkin, "Women and Pornography," 41.

F I V E :   A Model of Free Speech Justifications

1. Charles Larmore, *The Morals of Modernity* (Cambridge: Cambridge University Press, 1996), 157.
2. John Kekes, *The Morality of Pluralism* (Princeton, N.J.: Princeton University Press, 1993), 34.
3. In chapter 2, I argue that for the purposes of free speech libertarianism, truth and democracy are really the same value. Appeals to democracy refer to a wide-open public debate that leads to the best, or "true," public policy. Truth and democracy, in this policy sense, are interchangeable in the classic marketplace of ideas favored by Milton, Mill, and Holmes. Theorists of free speech to promote democracy assume that, in the long run, democracy results in political truth.
4. First Amendment–style language has been used by constitution writers in other states, albeit with modifications meant to allow for exceptions to broad protection for things such as hate speech and membership in neo-Nazi parties. However, it is not clear that American writers always understand the extent to which the First Amendment is an American phenomenon.
5. The First Amendment has changed in meaning quite dramatically. Leonard Levy traces out an original understanding at the time of its ratification of a very different First Amendment. Levy, *Legacy of Suppression*.
6. *Schenck*, 249 U.S. 47; *Debs*, 249 U.S. 211; *Abrams*, 250 U.S. 616; *Gitlow*, 268 U.S. 652. None of these early cases resulted in protection for speech under the First Amendment; all of these speech-related convictions were upheld and the speakers imprisoned.
7. See Graber, *Transforming Free Speech*, especially ch. 1, for a fine intellectual history of nineteenth-century views on free speech.
8. I will use the terms "audience," "listener," and "hearer" more or less interchangeably, although there are different connotations to each of these. "Hearer" is the most general, encompassing term but also the most awkward. "Listener" implies a voluntariness that is not always appropriate to the context. "Audience" generally refers to a group of hearers.
9. This is not to say that the motives of speakers and audiences are always in agreement. I rarely watch television for the purpose of seeking information about laundry soap and toothpaste, for example, but am often exposed to such information.
10. Examples of captive speakers might include persons compelled to testify in court.
11. In fact, it is difficult to get away from the entanglement of state action as the state pervades almost all aspects of social life. See Sunstein, *Democracy*, 37–46.
12. The speech of both workers and management is regulated by labor law.
13. Direct content-based censorship would obviously mediate speaker-hearer relationships by more or less eliminating the relationships that otherwise would be created

by the censored speech. However, censorship is direct state action to affect content rather than the indirect state action that I discuss here.

14. Mutability represents another reason that there can be no essentialist definition of freedom of speech. Freedom of speech, in itself, suggests that there are no essential definitions or truths. Libertarians, expressivists, and egalitarians agree that individuals change and that the social understanding of truth changes over time. If one denies these changes, then freedom of speech is only useful until such truths are discovered; otherwise it is a superfluous but popular form of liberty.

15. These relationships may not be pleasant, desirable, or voluntary. My point here is simply that the relations exist even for the most ardent of antistatist libertarians.

16. See chapter 3.

17. This is very common. Matsuda and others claim to be civil libertarians and adopt the libertarian project of truth and good policy as a closely related project to their own. Authors of campus speech codes defend those codes as necessary to ensure an environment of free inquiry and academic freedom consistent with the traditional mission of the university in the search for truth. Critics who claim that such codes challenge traditional protection for academic freedom may or may not be correct, but the point is that the project claimed by code authors is to advance inquiry by the broadest possible spectrum of members of the academic community.

18. C. Edwin Baker bases his defense of free speech on what he calls the "ethical postulate" of individual liberty, although I place him within the expressivist school. Baker, *Human Liberty*.

19. Nineteenth-century interpreters of the Constitution based their First Amendment analyses on individual liberty at a time when the Supreme Court heard very few, if any, First Amendment cases. These libertarian analyses lost out to social justifications once the court did begin to hear First Amendment cases in the years before 1920. See Graber, *Transforming Free Speech*, ch. 1.

20. The distinction between audience and consumer may not be clear. By this I mean to indicate that individuals are sometimes considered as interactive members of an audience, as in the classical public debate model of citizens participating in public meetings or even casual discourse. Recently, a great deal of attention has been given to individuals as passive consumers of speech whose freedom of speech includes the freedom to choose which information products (movies, books, cable television) they wish to purchase. This is a new kind of individualism grounded in consumer culture that increasingly dominates free speech thought in the United States. Two quick points suggest this is so. First, the debate over telecommunications policy is now dominated by the notion of maximizing competition in order to minimize costs to consumers (rather than by any reference to public debate or other traditional concerns). Second, the recent beatification of Larry Flynt as a martyr to free speech suggests that the consumption of *Hustler* magazine is an exercise of freedom of speech. The individual consumer is very different from the interactive audience participant, although I do not disagree that it is relevant to include each of these categories as a part of freedom of speech. Sunstein also argues that freedom of expression is becoming increasingly identified with unregulated economic markets. "Indeed, the identification has become so strong that it is sometimes hard even to see that the identification is both new and controversial, or that the free speech guarantee might be understood quite differently." Sunstein, *Democracy*, 3, 17.

21. Although these rights all represent basic social progress over past eras when such

rights were not protected, they do not in and of themselves push further social development. Protections against unreasonable searches, self-incrimination, and the right to counsel establish boundaries on state power. In the libertarian view, such limits allow individuals to pursue their own projects, resulting in social development. However, for many nonlibertarians, the primary justifications for such limits on state power concern intrinsic individual rights and are indifferent to the libertarian understanding of social progress. In fact, some (the law and order crowd) might argue that due process rights, while important, are actually a barrier to social progress because they are barriers to effective law enforcement.

22. John Stuart Mill makes the most familiar version of this argument in chapter 2 of *On Liberty*.

23. This is a tougher version of the first Bush administration's "gag rule" regulation altering Title X of the Public Health Services Act concerning federal funding for family planning services. This rule was upheld by the Supreme Court in *Rust v. Sullivan*, 500 U.S. 173 (1991).

24. Taylor, *Sources of the Self*, especially chs. 20–21.

25. In fact, this is exactly what contemporary expressivists such as Shiffrin or Redish do as they attempt to reconcile the value of self-realization with the truth-oriented public debate promoted by free speech libertarians. See my criticism of their positions in chapter 3.

26. Emerson, *The System of Freedom of Expression*.

SIX: Speech Acts

1. This assumption seems reasonable given the lack of convincing foundationalist arguments or consensus in this area. In addition, see Don Herzog's argument that there are no successful foundationalist arguments in political theory. Herzog, *Without Foundations: Justification in Political Theory* (Ithaca, N.Y.: Cornell University Press, 1985), 20–28.

2. See Searle, *Speech Acts*; and Austin, *How to Do Things*.

3. Austin, *How to Do Things*; Searle, *Speech Acts*; Paul Grice, *Studies in the Way of Words* (Cambridge, Mass.: Harvard University Press, 1989).

4. 315 U.S. 568 (1942).

5. Lawrence, "If He Hollers," 68; Matsuda, "Public Response to Racist Speech," 24–25.

6. An excellent discussion of how MacKinnon's approach can be seen to be consistent with a normative interpretation of speech act theory is found in Rae Langton, "Speech Acts and Unspeakable Acts," *Philosophy and Public Affairs* 22 (1993): 293–330.

7. Fish, "The Dance of Theory," 198–230.

8. *United States v. O'Brien*, 391 U.S. 367 (1968), upheld O'Brien's conviction for burning his draft card. Chief Justice Earl Warren's majority opinion argued that the burning of the draft card was regulable conduct. Even though O'Brien's actions had communicative elements, the *O'Brien* test considers whether the state restriction on the conduct was related to the expression or to the nonexpressive components of the conduct. In *Texas v. Johnson*, 491 U.S. 397 (1989), the court maintained that flag burning was expressive conduct and that the act in question was outside the *O'Brien* test since Texas's regulation of flag burning was an effort to suppress expression.

9. The weight placed on this distinction is further indicated by the title of MacKin-

non's *Only Words*. MacKinnon criticizes the idea that speech should be protected because it is words, thus ignoring it as conduct. Speech act theory denies the entire distinction—speech is always seen as an act that meets certain specific conditions.

10. Schauer has noted that this type of argument has been misused in a number of areas. Traditional examples of regulable conduct such as commercial advertising, nude dancing, and campaign donations win political support when turned into First Amendment speech questions in what he calls "First Amendment Opportunism." Schauer's criticisms in these arguments are exactly the sort of thing that a pluralist framework for free speech grounded in a sound, independent definition of speech seeks to avoid. Frederick Schauer, "First Amendment Opportunism," in *Eternally Vigilant: Free Speech in the Modern Era*, ed. Lee Bollinger and Geoffrey Stone, (Chicago: University of Chicago Press, 2002).

11. Searle, *Speech Acts*, 22.

12. Austin includes more in his use of "utterance." I use "utterance" to refer to what he calls the "phonetic act," the making of certain noises. Austin, *How to Do Things*, 90–94.

13. Ibid., 95.

14. Ibid., 14.

15. Searle, *Speech Acts*, 24.

16. Austin, *How to Do Things*, 105.

17. Ibid., 115–16.

18. Searle, *Speech Acts*, 43.

19. Ibid., 44.

20. Think of Quentin Skinner's work on textual interpretation here. The text (speech) of a historical figure can best be understood in the context of what he or she could have been saying given a certain vocabulary and social location at the time of the writing (saying). See, for example, Quentin Skinner, "Meaning and Understanding in the History of Ideas," and "A Reply to my Critics," in *Meaning and Context*, ed. James Tully (Princeton, N.J.: Princeton University Press, 1988).

21. Those offended by obscenity provide an interesting example. Various things (bestiality, for instance) are terribly offensive to some people. Exposure to a depiction of bestiality goes beyond a simple case of tolerating that which one despises, because such exposure throws one into an involuntary relationship with the person who creates the depiction. The offensive thing here is that one might be a party to such a relationship, not necessarily the depiction itself. Having to relate to someone who creates bestiality material disgusts the inadvertent or involuntary viewers, as does the realization that they belong to the same community. The depiction of bestiality serves as a symbol of a deep-set fissure in the group, one to which the offended would rather not face up. The bestiality becomes a statement about who the viewer is, even if exposed to it involuntarily, because it makes a statement about the social world in which he or she is embedded.

22. Paul Grice's theory of utterer's meaning relies upon the intentions of the utterer to induce beliefs or emotions in hearers. In cases where there is no hearer, Grice establishes the meaning of the utterance via one of three possible situations: assuming a possible future audience, pretending to address a specific audience, or designing the utterance with some indefinite audience in mind. Grice, *Studies in the Way of Words*, 112–14.

23. Expressivists might take issue with the requirement of a presumed audience as a prerequisite for writing. It is possible that something we could describe as writing exists

that is not a speech act—perhaps doodling that takes the form of words or the stringing together of seemingly random words with no meaning. However, it is not clear that such an exception makes any difference to the argument that I make.

24. Not all political relations require speech acts. Monarchs are born with a relationship to subjects, and many citizens of democratic polities have relations with political leaders they have never seen, heard, or read about. These relations are less directly related to speech acts but also are conditioned by speech in its role in the formation of overall political frameworks, institutions, and social hierarchies. Political relations between citizens also may arise from speech acts that do not involve them directly as parties. For instance, group relations partly created by speech acts of some members of society will affect every member of those groups. The racist speech of some may affect race relations for all.

25. Martin Luther King Jr. defended moral and constitutional principles shared by his opposition, even though they were regularly violated by that opposition.

26. According to Austin, no illocutionary act has been performed unless uptake is achieved. Austin, *How to Do Things*, 115–16. Workers might use the same vocal utterances, but the speech acts they perform are different from those performed by a manager with the same words. The meaning of the sentences will be different due to the different conditions of the statements. Managers "hear" the speech of workers in a different way than workers "hear" the same words from managers.

27. Of course, workers may sexually harass other workers, and this is a part of hierarchical gender relations more generally. Worker-worker harassment poses a somewhat different problem than manager-worker harassment, although it also has many implications for freedom of speech.

28. Austin, *How to Do Things*, 28.

29. Ibid., 14–15, 28–30.

30. Cass Sunstein sets a similar condition in his definition of political speech "when it [speech] is both intended and received as a contribution to public deliberation about some issue." This means, according to Sunstein, that any speech with political ramifications, even for a few people and even absent intent by the speaker, will count as political. Sunstein, *Democracy*, 130–31.

31. Karst argues that dominant groups brand the speech of various minority groups as "unreason," thus allowing it to be ignored or suppressed. Karst, "Boundaries and Reasons," 95–149.

32. Austin's example is "the slithy toves did gyre." This nonsense is an utterance but not a speech act because it does not meet the conditions of shared vocabulary and grammar. To say "the slithy toves did gyre" is to do no more than say it; there is no communication or other effect produced.

33. Though certainly they may not mean the same thing. What is for Astrid a polite request may be for the bartender another in a long string of tiresome demands by bar patrons. What is important is that the request makes sense in the context of their relationship and leads to mutually expected conclusions.

34. John R. Searle, *The Construction of Social Reality*, (New York: Free Press, 1995), 2; Searle, *Speech Acts*, 50.

35. Speech act theory differentiates between locutionary, illocutionary, and perlocutionary speech acts, but what I propose here is a different kind of categorization that is more closely related to the kinds of ad hoc categories favored by current free speech prac-

tice. While the distinction between illocution and locution can carry real normative force (Langton, "Speech Acts and Unspeakable Acts"), categories such as political speech, artistic speech, and scientific speech are more helpful to relate speech act theory to values such as equality or self-realization used to justify freedom of speech.

36. Alexander Meiklejohn, *Political Freedom* (New York: Harper, 1960). Cass Sunstein adapts the two-tier analysis in *Democracy*.

37. Meiklejohn, *Political Freedom*.

38. Meiklejohn, "The First Amendment," 245–66.

39. Sunstein, *Democracy*, 131.

40. In fact, in *Texas* (491 U.S. 397), the Supreme Court did ask the first and third of these questions. The second question was not raised explicitly, but the facts of this case, and a preceding case, *Spence v. Washington* (418 U.S. 405 [1974]), implicate political speech acts. Johnson was convicted for burning a flag at a political rally outside the Dallas city hall; Spence was convicted for taping a peace sign on his own flag to protest the Kent State shootings.

41. The flag-burning example highlights several potential problems in the definition of speech acts, depending upon one's perspective. It is easy to imagine a time, place, or context where flag burning would not meet the conditions of intention and reception. If one is looking for an essentialist or acontextual definition of speech that will always protect the widest range of speech acts from suppression, the notion that conditions might exist where flag burning is not received as political speech, and therefore fails one of the criteria of a speech act, has to be troubling. The second difficulty is almost traditional in the debate over the speech/conduct distinction and might be raised here as well: Where do you draw the line? Could murder be a speech act as long as the criteria of intention, condition, and reception are met? My answer to the second question is yes but that the whole point of treating all speech acts as acts and doing away with the speech/conduct distinction is that just because something is a speech act does not mean that it should be a protected speech act. The criteria for a speech act are obviously met in the scene in the *Godfather* where Don Corleone sends a message to an associate with the head of the man's prize racehorse. However, I would not suggest that such a speech act falls under the rubric of free speech.

42. If he ignites the flag flying in my front yard, I (or anyone else) will have no way of knowing what he means, and the act fails as a speech act, probably reverting to petty arson.

43. Thus a blanket proscription on flag burning runs into two difficulties. First, it curtails political speech. Second, it limits valid scientific speech about the combustibility of flags.

SEVEN: The Pluralist Framework for Freedom of Speech

1. Larmore, *The Morals of Modernity*, 154.

2. Ibid., 155–56.

3. William Galston, *Liberal Pluralism: The Implications of Value Pluralism for Political Theory and Practice* (Cambridge: Cambridge University Press, 2002), 6.

4. Larmore, *The Morals of Modernity*, 157.

5. Kekes, *The Morality of Pluralism*, 21.

6. Ibid., 35.

7. Bernard Williams, "Conflicts of Values," in *The Idea of Freedom: Essays in Honour of Isaiah Berlin*, ed. Alan Ryan, 221 (Oxford: Oxford University Press, 1979).

8. John Gray, *Isaiah Berlin* (Princeton, N.J.: Princeton University Press, 1996), 53.

9. Kekes, *The Morality of Pluralism*, 21–22; Larmore, *The Morals of Modernity*, 158.

10. Williams, "Conflicts of Values," 225.

11. Kekes, *The Morality of Pluralism*, 21.

12. Larmore, *The Morals of Modernity*, 158.

13. Galston, *Liberal Pluralism*, 47.

14. Kekes, *The Morality of Pluralism*, 31.

15. Gray, *Isaiah Berlin*, 67; Galston, *Liberal Pluralism*, 48, 57–58.

16. Charles Larmore, *Patterns of Moral Complexity* (Cambridge: Cambridge University Press, 1987).

17. Those advocating regulation of hate speech call for the exclusion of speakers' racist speech but not for the political exclusion of racists as a class of persons.

18. Kenneth Karst argues persuasively that the "civic deliberation" model of freedom of speech protects cognitive speech, the speech of reason, but places low value on, and provides little protection for, the speech of unreason. He argues that clashes between culturally dominant groups and subordinate groups have relegated forms of expression common in subordinate cultures to the category of low-value, unprotected speech. He offers as an example the contrast between a standard political speech favoring gay rights and the acting out of sexual identities by advocates of gay liberation. The first is well protected by standard accounts of free speech; the second is rarely recognized as a speech act. Karst, "Boundaries and Reasons," 95–149.

19. The definition of speech act is described in greater detail in chapter 6.

20. For instance, says Austin, the question "Is the king of France bald?" fails as a performative (speech act) because the conditions that would allow this to be a speech act, namely an extant French monarchy, do not exist. Austin, *How to Do Things*, 136. I can utter the words "Is the king of France bald?" and a listener can recognize this as a grammatically correct question but one that has no meaning, because the state of affairs that would give meaning to the question does not exist. However, Austin does not mention the possibility that this question could qualify as a speech act if the words are uttered in the performance of a play about seventeenth-century France. In that case, dramatic conventions transport parties to the utterance to a time when there was a king of France who may or may not have been bald.

21. Austin, *How to Do Things*, 95.

22. 403 U.S. 15 (1971). The Supreme Court overturned Cohen's conviction, thus affirming the principle that offensiveness alone is insufficient to warrant prohibition. This case also introduces what has become a popular slogan, "one man's vulgarity is another's lyric."

23. This is not to say that Cohen's conviction should have been upheld just because he had not performed a speech act. He had not performed an intentional act of any kind since, from his perspective, it was merely an accident that the jacket he picked up to put on had offensive words written on it. In spite of this, we can move forward with a speech analysis of Cohen's case if we believe that the event in question would have been a speech act had Cohen intended it as such. If such a speech act qualifies as protected speech, then we cannot convict Cohen for something that, had he intended to say it, would have been protected.

24. If state action that reduces the diversity of points of view in the marketplace of ideas is an obstacle to the realization of truth and good policy, then other actors with the power and influence to reduce the diversity of the marketplace must also be obstacles to truth and good policy.

25. Contemporary controversies over NEA and NEH funding embroil expressivists in arguments about the state that they are ill-prepared to wage. None of the major players in these debates, that I am aware of, argues that the state should fund its own political opposition. Instead, consistent with the nonpolitical character of expressivism, defenders of state funding minimize the extent of such "political art" as exceptions to the general rule of funding local arts councils, folk dancing, community theater, or important museum exhibitions.

26. Flag burning is protected under First Amendment law (*Texas*, 491 U.S. 397), but that hardly settles the argument about whether flag burning ought to be protected or whether it gives rise to claims and counterclaims. Robert Justin Goldstein finds that public acts of flag burning are extremely rare occurrences in the United States. Goldstein, *Flag Burning and Free Speech: The Case of Texas v. Johnson* (Lawrence: University Press of Kansas, 2000).

27. Somewhere between 70 and 80 percent of respondents in a number of public opinion polls think that flag burning is inappropriate or should be illegal. This result is fairly stable over time. Roper Center, *Public Perspective* (June–July 1999): 36.

28. This is not to say that such acts are not a part of some kind of freedom, they just do not fit under freedom of speech.

29. Somewhat like a reasonable person standard in law, we can look to see whether at least some people would secure uptake of the meaning of the speech act in question, even if the actual audience involved fails to secure uptake. In cases such as *Cohen* where intention to perform a speech act is doubtful, we can ask whether a speech act would have occurred if the speaker had intended to perform a speech act.

30. Schauer, "First Amendment Opportunism."

31. "The constitutional guarantees of free speech and free press do not permit a State to forbid or proscribe advocacy of the use of force or of law violation except where such advocacy is directed to inciting or producing imminent lawless action and is likely to incite or produce such action." *Brandenburg*, 395 U.S. 444.

32. I am thinking of the contemporary American context, where the legitimacy of violent revolution appears untenable.

33. Of course, they can also point to the direct harm of such incitement-revolutionary violence. However, it is not the violence itself that is the illegitimate harm (the American Revolutionary War was violent, after all) but the subversion of the peaceful process of public debate established by the same Constitution that protects freedom of speech. The libertarian distinction between advocacy and incitement ultimately depends upon the possibility of debate allowed by advocacy of revolution and the impossibility of debate in cases of incitement.

EIGHT: Free Speech Claims under the Pluralist Framework

1. A number of casebooks collecting the precedents of nascent Internet law have already been published, but these miss, of course, the kinds of new claims that are obscured by the structure of First Amendment law.

2. See "A Jurisdictional Tangle."

3. *Yahoo!, Inc.*, 169 F. Supp. 2d 1181.

4. Jonathan Zittrain and Benjamin Edelman, "Localized Google Search Result Exclusions," http://cyber.law.harvard.edu/filtering/google/ (February 10, 2004).

5. David R. Johnson and David G. Post, "Law and Borders—The Rise of Law in Cyberspace," *Stanford Law Review* 48 (1996): 1367.

6. Ibid.

7. *Yahoo!, Inc.*, 169 F. Supp. 2d 1181.

8. Elissa A. Okoniewski, "*Yahoo!, Inc. v. LICRA*: The French Challenge to Free Expression on the Internet," *American University International Law Review* 18 (2003): 321.

9. *Yahoo!, Inc.*, 169 F. Supp. 2d 1186–87.

10. "A Jurisdictional Tangle."

11. We can think about the chilling effects on Dow Jones by analogy to the state of American libel law before *New York Times v. Sullivan* (376 U.S. 254). When libel law was left to the states and different standards for libel cases existed in each state, national publications like the *New York Times* faced the potential for debilitating libel suits even in states, such as Alabama in the *Sullivan* case, where they did very little business. The Supreme Court resolved the problem of diversity of libel law in the states by establishing a single national standard in *Sullivan* to govern libel cases brought by public figures. However, the protections of American libel law under *Sullivan* are not worth very much to the press if they are subject to the more restrictive libel laws in various countries in which their Web sites are available. The chilling effect of foreign libel restrictions works in the same way that the chilling effect of state libel laws worked prior to *Sullivan*.

12. Many international agreements on civil rights and civil liberties list freedom of speech as a key individual right. The United Nations Covenant on Civil and Political Rights, for instance, protects freedom of speech. In fact, the *Barron's* case is being brought before the Human Rights Committee of the U.N. by Bill Alpert, the author of the article in question. However, these conventions tend to conceptualize the protected right as one against one's own state rather than an overarching right to protect one's speech against all states. In a sense, the U.N. Covenant stresses the importance of each state developing its own framework for the protection of freedom of speech while leaving a great deal of room for states to balance free speech and other values, such as equal dignity or national security. Thus, there is no international agreement on what constitutes libel. The restrictive libel law of Australia or the United Kingdom meets the requirements of the U.N. Covenant, as does the much less restrictive U.S. libel law. The same flexibility allows France and Germany to condition freedom of speech on the equal dignity of persons, thus allowing these states to restrict racist and anti-Semitic speech consistent with their own constitutional frameworks.

13. Operation Clambake, www.xenu.net/ (February 10, 2004).

14. Zittrain and Edelman, "Localized Google Search Results Exclusions." Google is one of the most popular of all search engines, and the company claims to have indexed over three billion pages.

15. It is a kind of indirect interference in the sense that Operation Clambake itself remains in place, but the DMCA claim against Google restricts Operation Clambake's access to its audience in a way somewhat analogous to the "heckler's veto."

16. There are, of course, international agreements on the enforcement of copyright that allow U.S. firms to pursue copyright claims in Europe or Asia. However, the DMCA

appears to go beyond these international agreements by, for instance, empowering copyright holders to use technological means that prevent the limited fair use of copyrighted works that these international copyright agreements currently protect.

17. Johnson and Post, "Law Beyond Borders."

18. Sunstein, *Democracy*.

19. Okoniewski, "*Yahoo!, Inc. v. LICRA*," 334.

20. Ibid., 329.

21. This hierarchy also allows for the suppression of religious expression and the potential to "turn workplaces of America into something like religion-free zones." Michael McConnell, "Symposium: Religion in the Workplace: Proceedings of the 2000 Annual Meeting of the Association of American Law Schools Section on Law and Religion," *Employee Rights and Employment Policy Journal* 4 (1999): 99. Douglas Laycock argues in the same symposium that employees who merely affirm their own faiths rather than attacking another's should be protected by the First Amendment. Laycock, "Symposium: Religion in the Workplace," 126–28.

22. *Peterson v. Hewlett-Packard Co.*, 358 F.3d 599 (9th Cir. 2004).

23. *Wilson v. U.S. West Communications*, 58 F.3d 1337 (8th Cir. 1995).

24. *Chalmers v. Tulon Co. of Richmond*, 101 F.3d 1012 (4th Cir. 1996).

25. Civil Rights Act of 1964, Title VII.

26. Workplace Religious Freedom Act of 2003, S 893, 108th Cong., 1st sess., *Congressional Record* 149 (April 11, 2003): S 5342.

27. *Peterson*, 358 F.3d 602.

28. This goes back to where I started in chapter 1 with Justice Hugo Black, who held that "no law means no law" to defend an absolutist position on First Amendment issues. Over the course of this book, we have seen many examples where First Amendment law allows for balancing of interests and values, but absolutism is still the form of First Amendment claims.

29. *Sullivan*, 376 U.S. 255.

30. *Gertz v. Welch*, 418 U.S. 323 (1974).

31. Peterson's outside activities appear, on the court record, to have had no effect on his termination. He had a bumper sticker on his car that read "Sodomy Is Not a Family Value" and had written a letter to the *Idaho Statesman* criticizing Hewlett-Packard's diversity program. Managers neither complained about this letter nor prohibited him from parking his car in the company parking lot. *Peterson*, 358 F.3d 604.

Selected Bibliography

Abel, Richard. *Speaking Respect, Respecting Speech*. Chicago: University of Chicago Press, 1998.

Abrams, M. H. *The Mirror and the Lamp: Romantic Theory and the Critical Tradition*. London: Oxford University Press, 1971.

Allen, David S., and Robert Jensen, eds. *Freeing the First Amendment: Critical Perspectives on Freedom of Expression*. New York: New York University Press, 1995.

Altman, Andrew. "Liberalism and Campus Hate Speech: A Philosophical Evaluation." *Ethics* 103 (1993): 302–17.

Aris, Reinhold. *A History of Political Thought in Germany, 1789–1815*. London: G. Allen and Unwin, 1936.

Attorney General's Commission on Pornography. *Final Report*. Washington, D.C.: U.S. Department of Justice, 1986.

Auerbach, Carl. "The Communist Control Act of 1954: A Proposed Legal-Political Theory of Free Speech." *University of Chicago Law Review* 23 (1956): 173–220.

Austin, J. L. *How to Do Things with Words*. Cambridge, Mass.: Harvard University Press, 1962.

Bagdikian, Ben H. *The Media Monopoly*. Boston: Beacon, 2000.

Baker, C. Edwin. *Human Liberty and Freedom of Speech*. New York: Oxford University Press, 1989.

———. "Of Course, More Than Words." *University of Chicago Law Review* 61 (1994): 1181–211.

Beiser, Frederick C. *Enlightenment, Revolution and Romanticism: The Genesis of Modern German Political Thought, 1790–1800*. Cambridge, Mass.: Harvard University Press, 1992.

Benn, Stanley I. *A Theory of Freedom*. Cambridge: Cambridge University Press, 1988.

Berlin, Isaiah. *Four Essays on Liberty*. New York: Oxford University Press, 1969.

———. *Vico and Herder: Two Studies in the History of Ideas*. London: Hogarth Press, 1976.

———. *Against the Current: Essays in the History of Ideas*. New York: Viking, 1979.

———. *The Roots of Romanticism*. Ed. Henry Hardy. Princeton, N.J.: Princeton University Press, 1999.

Berns, Walter. *The First Amendment and the Future of American Democracy*. New York: Basic Books, 1976.

Beschle, Donald L. "Clearly Canadian? Hill vs Colorado and Free Speech Balancing in the United States and Canada." *Hastings Constitutional Law Quarterly* (Winter 2001): 187–233.

Bezanson, Randall P. "Institutional Speech." *Iowa Law Review* 80 (1995): 735–824.

Bickel, Alexander. *The Morality of Consent*. New Haven, Conn.: Yale University Press, 1975.

Blasi, Vincent. "The First Amendment and the Ideal of Civic Courage." *William and Mary Law Review* 29 (1988): 653–98.

———. "Reading Holmes through the Lens of Schauer: The *Abrams* Dissent." *Notre Dame Law Review* 72 (1997): 1343–60.

Bollinger, Lee. *The Tolerant Society: Freedom of Speech and Extremist Speech in America*. New York: Oxford University Press, 1986.

Bollinger, Lee, and Geoffrey Stone, eds. *Eternally Vigilant: Free Speech in the Modern Era*. Chicago: University of Chicago Press, 2002.

Bork, Robert. "Neutral Principles and Some First Amendment Problems." *Indiana Law Journal* 47 (1971): 1–35.

Borovoy, Alan, et al. "Language as Violence: Canadian and American Perspectives on Group Defamation." *Buffalo Law Review* 37 (1988/89): 337–73.

Bosmajian, Haig. *The Freedom Not to Speak*. New York: New York University Press, 1999.

Brest, Paul, and Ann Vandenberg. "Politics, Feminism, and the Constitution: The Anti-Pornography Movement in Minneapolis." *Stanford Law Review* 39 (1987): 607–61.

Brigham, John. *The Constitution of Interests: Beyond the Politics of Rights*. New York: New York University Press, 1996.

Brown, Steven P. *Trumping Religion: The New Christian Right, the Free Speech Clause, and the Courts*. Tuscaloosa: University of Alabama Press, 2002.

Brown, Wendy. *States of Injury: Power and Freedom in Late Modernity*. Princeton, N.J.: Princeton University Press, 1995.

Butler, Judith. *Excitable Speech: A Politics of the Performative*. New York: Routledge, 1997.

Carter, Stephen L. *The Culture of Disbelief*. New York: Basic Books, 1993.

———. "1997–98 Brennan Center Symposium Lecture: Religious Freedom as if Religion Matters: A Tribute to Justice Brennan." *California Law Review* 87 (1999): 1059–86.

Chafee, Zechariah. *Free Speech in the United States*. 1941. Reprint, Cambridge, Mass.: Harvard University Press, 1964.

Chambers, Simone. *Reasonable Democracy: Jürgen Habermas and the Politics of Discourse*. Ithaca, N.Y.: Cornell University Press, 1996.

Choper, Jesse H. *Securing Religious Liberty*. Chicago: University of Chicago Press, 1995.

Cohen, Joshua. "Freedom of Expression." *Philosophy and Public Affairs* 22 (1993): 207–63.

Cohen-Almagor, Raphael. "Harm Principle, Offence Principle and the Skokie Affair." *Political Studies* 41 (1993): 453–70.

Cole, David. "Faith and Funding: Toward an Expressivist Model of the Establishment Clause." *Southern California Law Review* 75 (2002): 559–603.

Collins, Ronald K. L., and David M. Skover. *The Death of Discourse*. Boulder, Colo.: Westview, 1996.

Conover, Pamela Johnston. "The Role of Social Groups in Political Thinking." *British Journal of Political Science* 18 (1988): 51–76.

Delgado, Richard. "Words That Wound: A Tort Action for Racial Insults, Epithets and Name Calling." In *Words That Wound: Critical Race Theory, Assaultive Speech and the First Amendment*, ed. Mari J. Matsuda, Charles R. Lawrence III, Richard Delgado, and Kimberlie Williams Crenshaw. Boulder, Colo.: Westview, 1993.

Delgado, Richard, and David Yun. "The Neoconservative Case against Hate-Speech Regulation—Lively, D'Souza, Gates, Carter, and the Toughlove Crowd." *Vanderbilt Law Review* 47 (1994): 1807–25.

Douglas, Lawrence. "The Force of Words: Fish, Matsuda, MacKinnon, and the Theory of Discursive Violence." *Law and Society Review* 29 (1995): 169–90.

Downs, Donald A. "Skokie Revisited: Hate Group Speech and the First Amendment." *Notre Dame Law Review* 67 (1985): 629–85.

———. *The New Politics of Pornography.* Chicago: University of Chicago Press, 1989.

Dworkin, Ronald. *Taking Rights Seriously.* Cambridge, Mass.: Harvard University Press, 1977.

———. "Two Concepts of Liberty." In *Isaiah Berlin: A Celebration,* ed. Edna Margalit and Avishai Margalit. Chicago: University of Chicago Press, 1991.

———. "The Coming Battles Over Free Speech." *New York Review of Books,* June 11, 1992, 55–64.

———. "Women and Pornography." *New York Review of Books,* October 21, 1993, 36–42.

———. *Freedom's Law.* Cambridge, Mass.: Harvard University Press, 1996.

———. *Sovereign Virtue: The Theory and Practice of Equality.* Cambridge, Mass.: Harvard University Press, 2000.

Ehrlich, Howard J., Barbara E. K. Larcom, and Robert D. Purvis. "The Traumatic Impact of Ethnoviolence." In *The Price We Pay: The Case against Racist Speech, Hate Propaganda, and Pornography,* ed. Laura Lederer and Richard Delgado. New York: Hill and Wang, 1995.

Eldridge, Larry D. *A Distant Heritage: The Growth of Free Speech in Early America.* New York: New York University Press, 1994.

Ely, John Hart. *Democracy and Distrust: A Theory of Judicial Review.* Cambridge, Mass.: Harvard University Press, 1980.

Emerson, Thomas. *Toward a General Theory of the First Amendment.* New York: Vintage, 1966.

———. *The System of Freedom of Expression.* New York: Random House, 1970.

Fichte, J. G. *The Science of Knowledge [Wissenshaftslehre].* Trans. Peter Heath and John Lachs. 1794–95. Reprint, Cambridge: Cambridge University Press, 1970.

———. *The Science of Rights.* Trans. A. E Kroeger. 1796. Reprint, London: Routledge and Kegan Paul, 1970.

Finley, M. I. *Politics in the Ancient World.* Cambridge: Cambridge University Press, 1983.

Fish, Stanley. *There's No Such Thing as Free Speech.* Oxford: Oxford University Press, 1992.

———. "Mission Impossible: Settling the Just Bounds between Church and State." *Columbia Law Review* 97 (1997): 2255–333.

———. "The Dance of Theory." In *Eternally Vigilant: Free Speech in the Modern Era,* ed. Lee Bollinger and Geoffrey Stone. Chicago: University of Chicago Press, 2002.

Fishkin, James. *Democracy and Deliberation: New Directions for Democratic Reform.* New Haven, Conn.: Yale University Press, 1991.

Fiss, Owen. "Groups and the Equal Protection Clause." *Philosophy and Public Affairs* 5 (1976): 107–47.

———. "Why the State?" *Harvard Law Review* 100 (1987): 781–94.

———. "State Activism and State Censorship." *Yale Law Journal* 100 (1991): 2087–106.

———. *Liberalism Divided: Freedom of Speech and the Many Uses of State Power*. Boulder, Colo.: Westview, 1996.

Frye, Northrop, ed. *Romanticism Reconsidered: Selected Papers from the English Institute*. New York: Columbia University Press, 1963.

Furst, Lilian R. *The Contours of European Romanticism*. Lincoln: University of Nebraska Press, 1979.

Galston, William A. *Liberal Pluralism: The Implications of Value Pluralism for Political Theory and Practice*. Cambridge: Cambridge University Press, 2002.

Garry, Patrick M. *Scrambling for Protection: The New Media and the First Amendment*. Pittsburgh: University of Pittsburgh Press, 1994.

Gates, Henry Louis, Jr. "War of Words: Critical Race Theory and The First Amendment." In *Speaking of Race, Speaking of Sex: Hate Speech, Civil Rights, and Civil Liberties*, ed. Henry Louis Gates Jr., Anthony P. Griffin, Donald E. Lively, Robert C. Post, William B. Rubenstein, and Nadine Strossen. New York: New York University Press, 1994.

Gibson, John L. "The Structure of Attitudinal Tolerance in the U.S." *British Journal of Political Science* 19 (1989): 562–72.

Goldstein, Robert Justin, *Flag Burning and Free Speech: The Case of Texas v. Johnson*. Lawrence: University Press of Kansas, 2000.

Graber, Mark. *Transforming Free Speech: The Ambiguous Legacy of Civil Libertarianism*. Berkeley: University of California Press, 1991.

———. "Old Wine in New Bottles: The Constitutional Status of Unconstitutional Speech." *Vanderbilt Law Review* 48 (1995): 349–89.

Gray, John N. "On Negative and Positive Liberty." *Political Studies* 28 (1980): 507–26.

———. *Isaiah Berlin*. Princeton, N.J.: Princeton University Press, 1996.

Green, T. H. "On the Different Senses of Freedom as Applied to Will and to the Moral Progress of Man." In *Lectures on the Principles of Obligation*, ed. Paul Harris and John Morrow. Cambridge: Cambridge University Press, 1985.

Greenawalt, Kent. "Free Speech Justifications." *Columbia Law Review* 89 (1989): 119–55.

———. *Speech, Crime and the Uses of Language*. New York: Oxford University Press, 1989.

———. *Fighting Words: Individuals, Communities, and Liberties of Speech*. Princeton, N.J.: Princeton University Press, 1995.

———. *Private Consciences and Public Reasons*. New York: Oxford University Press, 1995.

Greene, T. M. Introduction to *Religion within the Limits of Reason Alone*, by Immanuel Kant. New York: Harper Torchbooks, 1960.

Grice, Paul. *Studies in the Way of Words*. Cambridge, Mass.: Harvard University Press, 1989.

Griffith, G. T. "*Isegoria* in the Assembly at Athens." In *Ancient Society and Institutions: Studies Presented to Victor Ehrenberg on His 75th Birthday*, ed. E. Badian. Oxford: Basil Blackwell, 1966.

Grossman, Lawrence K. *The Electronic Republic: Reshaping Democracy in the Information Age*. New York: 20th Century Fund/Viking, 1995.

Haiman, Franklyn S. *"Speech Acts" and the First Amendment*. Carbondale: Southern Illinois University Press, 1993.

Heller, Erich. *The Artist's Journey into the Interior and Other Essays*. New York: Random House, 1965.

Hentoff, Nat. *Free Speech for Me—But Not for Thee*. New York: HarperCollins, 1992.

Herder, J. G. *Reflections on the History of Mankind*. Ed. Frank E. Manuel, trans. T. O. Churchill. 1784–91. Reprint, Chicago: University of Chicago Press, 1968.

———. *Against Pure Reason: Writings on Religion, Language and History*. Trans. Marcia Bunge. Minneapolis: Fortress Press, 1993.

Herzog, Don. *Without Foundations: Justification in Political Theory*. Ithaca, N.Y.: Cornell University Press, 1985.

Hinton, Timothy. "Must Egalitarians Choose between Fairness and Respect?" *Philosophy and Public Affairs* 30 (2001): 72–87.

Hobbes, Thomas. *Leviathan*. Ed. Edwin Curley. 1651. Reprint, Indianapolis, Ind.: Hackett, 1994.

Hollis, Martin, and Quentin Skinner. "Action and Context." In *Philosophy in History*, ed. Richard Rorty, J. B. Schneewind, and Quentin Skinner. Cambridge: Cambridge University Press, 1985.

Holmes, Stephen. *Benjamin Constant and the Making of Modern Liberalism*. New Haven, Conn.: Yale University Press, 1984.

———. *Passions and Constraint: On the Theory of Liberal Democracy*. Chicago: University of Chicago Press, 1995.

Humboldt, Wilhelm von. *The Limits of State Action*. Ed. with intro. and notes by J. W. Burrow. Cambridge: Cambridge University Press, 1969.

Itzin, Catherine, ed. *The Case against Pornography: Sex Discrimination, Sexual Violence and Civil Liberties*. Oxford: Oxford University Press, 1992.

Izenberg, G. *Impossible Individuality: Romanticism, Revolution and the Origins of Modern Selfhood, 1787–1802*. Princeton, N.J.: Princeton University Press, 1992.

Johnson, David R., and David G. Post. "Law and Borders—The Rise of Law in Cyberspace." *Stanford Law Review* 48 (1996): 1367–402.

"Jurisdictional Tangle, A." *Economist*, December 10, 2002, www.economist.com/research/articlesBySubject/displayStory.cfm?story_ID=1489053&subject=Australia (January 30, 2004).

Kant, Immanuel. *Fundamental Principles of the Metaphysics of Morals*. Trans. Thomas K. Abbott. Indianapolis, Ind.: Bobbs-Merrill, 1949.

———. *Religion within the Limits of Reason Alone*. Trans. with intro. and notes by T. H. Greene. New York: Harper Torchbooks, 1960.

Karst, Kenneth L. *Belonging to America: Equal Citizenship and the Constitution*. New Haven, Conn.: Yale University Press, 1989.

———. "Boundaries and Reasons: Freedom of Expression and the Subordination of Groups." *University of Illinois Law Review* (1990): 95–149.

———. *Law's Promise, Law's Expression: Visions of Power in the Politics of Race, Gender, and Religion*. New Haven, Conn.: Yale University Press, 1993.

Kekes, John. *The Morality of Pluralism*. Princeton, N.J.: Princeton University Press, 1993.

Kors, Alan Charles, and Harvey A. Silverglate. *The Shadow University*. New York: Free Press, 1998.

Kretzmer, David. "Freedom of Speech and Racism." *Cardozo Law Review* 8 (1987): 445–513.

Langton, Rae. "Whose Right? Ronald Dworkin, Women and Pornographers." *Philosophy and Public Affairs* 19 (1990): 311–59.

―――. "Speech Acts and Unspeakable Acts." *Philosophy and Public Affairs* 22 (1993): 293–330.

Larmore, Charles. *Patterns of Moral Complexity*. Cambridge: Cambridge University Press, 1987.

―――. *The Morals of Modernity*. Cambridge: Cambridge University Press, 1996.

―――. *The Romantic Legacy*. New York: Columbia University Press, 1996.

Lawrence, Charles R., III. "If He Hollers Let Him Go: Regulating Racist Speech on Campus." In *Words That Wound: Critical Race Theory, Assaultive Speech and the First Amendment*, ed. Mari J. Matsuda, Charles R. Lawrence III, Richard Delgado, and Kimberlie Williams Crenshaw. Boulder, Colo.: Westview, 1993.

Laycock, Douglas. "Symposium: Religion in the Workplace: Proceedings of the 2000 Annual Meeting of the Association of American Law Schools Section on Law and Religion." *Employee Rights and Employment Policy Journal* 4 (1999): 124–30.

Lederer, Laura, and Richard Delgado, eds. *The Price We Pay: The Case against Racist Speech, Hate Propaganda, and Pornography*. New York: Hill and Wang, 1995.

Lessig, Lawrence. *The Future of Ideas: The Fate of the Commons in a Connected World*. New York: Random House, 2001.

―――. *Free Culture: How Big Media Uses Technology and the Law to Lock Down Culture and Control Creativity*. New York: Penguin, 2004.

Levy, Leonard. *Legacy of Suppression: Freedom of Speech and Press in Early America*. Cambridge, Mass.: Belknap Press of Harvard University Press, 1960.

Lewis, Anthony. *Make No Law: The Sullivan Case and the First Amendment*. New York: Random House, 1991.

Lichtenberg, Judith. *Democracy and the Mass Media*. Cambridge: Cambridge University Press, 1990.

Lovejoy, A. O. *Essays in the History of Ideas*. New York: George Braziller, 1955.

MacCallum, Gerald. "Negative and Positive Freedom." *Philosophical Review* 17 (1967): 312–34.

Macedo, Stephen. *Liberal Virtues*. New York: Oxford University Press, 1990.

MacKinnon, Catharine. *Feminism Unmodified: Discourses on Life and Law*. Cambridge, Mass.: Harvard University Press, 1987.

―――. *Only Words*. Cambridge, Mass.: Harvard University Press, 1993.

Marcuse, Herbert. *One Dimensional Man*. Boston: Beacon Press, 1964.

―――. "Repressive Tolerance." In Robert Paul Wolff, Barrington Moore Jr., and Herbert Marcuse, *A Critique of Pure Tolerance*. Boston: Beacon Press, 1965.

Matsuda, Mari J. "Public Response to Racist Speech: Considering the Victim's Story." In *Words That Wound: Critical Race Theory, Assaultive Speech and the First Amendment*, ed. Mari J. Matsuda, Charles R. Lawrence III, Richard Delgado, and Kimberlie Williams Crenshaw. Boulder, Colo.: Westview, 1993.

Matsuda, Mari, Charles R. Lawrence III, Richard Delgado, and Kimberlie Williams Crenshaw, eds. *Words That Wound: Critical Race Theory, Assaultive Speech and the First Amendment*. Boulder, Colo.: Westview, 1993.

McChesney, Robert W. *The Problem of the Media: U.S. Communication Politics in the 21st Century*. New York: Monthly Review, 2004.

McCloskey, Herbert, and Alida Brill. *Dimensions of Tolerance: What Americans Believe About Civil Liberties*. New York: Russell Sage Foundation, 1983.

McConnell, Michael. "Accommodation of Religion." *Supreme Court Review* (1985): 1–59.

———. "Symposium: Religion in the Workplace: Proceedings of the 2000 Annual Meeting of the Association of American Law Schools Section on Law and Religion." *Employee Rights and Employment Policy Journal* 4 (1999): 98–109.

McGarry, Patrick. *Scrambling for Protection: The New Media and the First Amendment.* Pittsburgh: University of Pittsburgh Press, 1994.

Meiklejohn, Alexander. *Free Speech and Its Relation to Self Government.* New York: Harper, 1948.

———. *Political Freedom: The Constitutional Powers of the People.* New York: Harper, 1960.

———. "The First Amendment Is an Absolute." *Supreme Court Review* (1961): 245–66.

Meineke, Friedrich. *Cosmopolitanism and the National State.* Trans. Robert B. Kimber. 1907. Reprint, Princeton, N.J.: Princeton University Press, 1970.

Michelman, Frank. "Concepts of Democracy in American Constitutional Argument: The Case of Pornography Regulation." *Tennessee Law Review* 56 (1979): 291–319.

———. "Universities, Racist Speech and Democracy in America: An Essay for the ACLU." *Harvard Civil Rights—Civil Liberties Law Review* 27 (1992): 339–69.

Mill, John Stuart. *On Liberty.* 1859. Reprint, Indianapolis, Ind.: Hackett, 1978.

Milton, John. *Areopagitica.* In *Complete Prose Works of John Milton.* Ed. Ernest Sirluck. New Haven, Conn.: Yale University Press, 1959.

Molnár, Géza von. *Romantic Vision, Ethical Context: Novalis and Artistic Autonomy.* Minneapolis: University of Minnesota Press, 1987.

Monoson, S. Sara. "Was Plato an Enemy of Democracy?" Paper presented at the annual meeting of the American Political Science Association, Washington, D.C., August 1991.

Moon, Richard. *The Constitutional Protection of Freedom of Expression.* Toronto: University of Toronto Press, 2000.

Norman, W. J. "Taking 'Free Action' Too Seriously." *Ethics* 101 (1991): 505–20.

Okoniewski, Elissa A. "*Yahoo!, Inc. v. LICRA*: The French Challenge to Free Expression on the Internet." *American University International Law Review* 18 (2003): 295–338.

Palmer, R. R. *The World of the French Revolution.* New York: Harper and Row, 1971.

Patterson, Orlando. *Freedom in the Making of Western Civilization.* New York: Basic Books, 1991.

Pool, Ithiel de Sola. *Technologies of Freedom.* Cambridge, Mass.: Harvard University Press, 1983.

Posner, Richard. "Free Speech in an Economic Perspective." *Suffolk Law Review* 40 (1986): 2–54.

Post, Robert C. "Free Speech and Religious, Racial, and Sexual Harassment: Racist Speech, Democracy and the First Amendment." *William and Mary Law Review* 32 (1991): 267–328.

Pound, Roscoe. *Jurisprudence.* Vol. 3. St. Paul, Minn.: West, 1959.

Rabban, David M. *Free Speech in Its Forgotten Years.* Cambridge: Cambridge University Press, 1997.

Rauch, Jonathan. *Kindly Inquisitors: The New Attacks on Free Thought.* Chicago: University of Chicago Press, 1993.

Rawls, John. *A Theory of Justice*. Cambridge, Mass.: Belknap Press of Harvard University Press, 1971.

———. "Justice as Fairness, Political Not Metaphysical." *Philosophy and Public Affairs* 15 (1985): 223–51.

———. *Political Liberalism*. New York: Columbia University Press, 1993.

Raz, Joseph. *The Morality of Freedom*. Oxford: Clarendon Press, 1986.

———. "Free Expression and Personal Identification." *Oxford Journal of Legal Studies* 11 (1991): 303–24.

Redish, Martin H. *Freedom of Expression: A Critical Analysis*. Charlottesville, Va.: Michie, 1984.

Redish, Martin H., and Kirk J. Kaludis. "The Right of Expressive Access in First Amendment Theory: Redistributive Values and the Democratic Dilemma." *Northwestern University Law Review* 93 (1999): 1083–134.

Redish, Martin H., and Howard M. Wasserman. "What's Good for General Motors: Corporate Speech and the Theory of Free Expression." *George Washington Law Review* 66 (1998): 235–98.

Reiss, Hans Siegbert, ed. *The Political Thought of the German Romantics 1793–1815*. Oxford: Basil Blackwell, 1955.

Rheingold, Howard. *The Virtual Community*. New York: William Patrick/Addison Wesley, 1994.

Roper Center. *Public Perspective*. June–July 1999.

Rosen, Jeffrey. "The Limits of Limits." *New Republic*, February 7, 1994, 35.

———. "In Defense of Gender Blindness." *New Republic*, June 29, 1998, 25.

Rosenblum, Nancy. *Another Liberalism: Romanticism and the Reconstruction of Liberal Thought*. Cambridge, Mass.: Harvard University Press, 1987.

Rousseau, Jean-Jacques. *Politics and the Arts; Letters to M. D'Alembert on the Theatre*. Trans. Allan Bloom. Ithaca, N.Y.: Cornell University Press, 1968.

Ryan, Alan, ed. *The Idea of Freedom: Essays in Honour of Isaiah Berlin*. Oxford: Oxford University Press, 1979.

Scanlon, T. M. "A Theory of Freedom of Expression." *Philosophy and Public Affairs* 1 (1972): 203–26.

———. "Freedom of Expression and Categories of Expression." *University of Pittsburgh Law Review* 40 (1979): 519–50.

Schauer, Frederick. *Free Speech: A Philosophical Enquiry*. Cambridge: Cambridge University Press, 1982.

———. "Must Speech Be Special?" *Northwestern University Law Review* 78 (1983): 1284–1306.

———. "Uncoupling Free Speech." *Columbia Law Review* 92 (1992): 1321–57.

———. "The Phenomenology of Speech and Harm." *Ethics* 103 (1993): 635–53.

———. "Act, Omissions and Constitutionalism." *Ethics* 105 (1995): 916–26.

———. "The First Amendment as Ideology." In *Freeing the First Amendment*, ed. David S. Allen and Robert Jensen. New York: New York University Press, 1995.

———. "The Ontology of Censorship." In *Censorship and Silencing*, ed. Robert Post. Los Angeles: Getty Research Institute for the History of Art and the Humanities, 1998.

———. "First Amendment Opportunism." In *Eternally Vigilant: Free Speech in the Mod-*

ern Era, ed. Lee Bollinger and Geoffrey Stone. Chicago: University of Chicago Press, 2002.

Schiller, Friedrich. *Naive and Sentimental Poetry*. Trans. Julias A. Elias. 1795. Reprint, New York: Frederick Unger, 1966.

———. *On the Aesthetic Education of Man*. Ed. Elizabeth Wilkinson and L. A. Willoughby. Oxford: Oxford University Press, 1967.

Schlegel, Friedrich. *Philosophical Fragments*. Trans. Peter Firchow. Minneapolis: University of Minnesota Press, 1991.

Schleiermacher, Friedrich. *On Religion*. Trans. Richard Crouter. 1799. Reprint, Cambridge: Cambridge University Press, 1988.

Schmitt, Carl. *Political Romanticism*. Trans. Guy Oakes. 1919. Reprint, Cambridge, Mass.: MIT Press, 1986.

Searle, John R. *Speech Acts: An Essay in the Philosophy of Language*. Cambridge: Cambridge University Press, 1969.

———. *The Construction of Social Reality*. New York: Free Press, 1995.

Shell, Susan. "'A Determined Stand': Freedom and Security in Fichte's *Science of Right*." *Polity* 25 (1992): 95–121.

Shiffrin, Steven H. *The First Amendment, Democracy, and Romance*. Cambridge, Mass.: Harvard University Press, 1990.

———. *Dissent, Injustice and the Meaning of America*. Princeton, N.J.: Princeton University Press, 1999.

Skinner, Quentin. "Meaning and Understanding in the History of Ideas." In *Meaning and Context: Quentin Skinner and His Critics*, ed. James Tully. Princeton, N.J.: Princeton University Press, 1988.

———. "A Reply to my Critics." In *Meaning and Context: Quentin Skinner and His Critics*, ed. James Tully. Princeton, N.J.: Princeton University Press, 1988.

———. "The Paradoxes of Political Liberty." In *Equal Freedom: Selected Tanner Lectures on Human Values*, ed. Stephen Darwall. Ann Arbor: University of Michigan Press: 1995.

Smart, Carol. *Feminism and the Power of Law*. London: Routledge. 1989.

Smith, Rogers M. *Liberalism and American Constitutional Law*. Cambridge, Mass.: Harvard University Press, 1985.

Smith, Steven D. *Getting Over Equality: A Critical Diagnosis of Religious Freedom in America*. New York: New York University Press, 2001.

Smolla, Rodney. *Free Speech in an Open Society*. New York: Vintage, 1992.

Sorkin, David. "Wilhelm von Humboldt: The Theory and Practice of Self-Formation (*Bildung*), 1791–1810." *Journal of the History of Ideas* 44 (1983): 55–73.

Stein, Eric. "History against Free Speech: The New German Law against the 'Auschwitz' and Other 'Lies.'" *Michigan Law Review* 85 (1986): 277–324.

Strum, Philippa. *When the Nazis Came to Skokie: Freedom for Speech We Hate*. Lawrence: University Press of Kansas, 1999.

Sullivan, John L., James Pierson, and George E. Marcus. *Political Tolerance and American Democracy*. Chicago: University of Chicago Press, 1982.

Sunstein, Cass R. *Democracy and the Problem of Free Speech*. New York: Free Press, 1993.

———. *The Partial Constitution*. Cambridge, Mass.: Harvard University Press, 1993.

———. "Words, Conduct, Caste." *University of Chicago Law Review* 60 (1993): 795–844.

————. "On Legal Theory and Legal Practice." *Nomos* 37 (1995): 267–87.

————. *Legal Reasoning and Political Conflict*. New York: Oxford University Press, 1996.

————. *Designing Democracy: What Constitutions Do*. New York: Oxford University Press, 2001.

————. *Republic.Com*. Princeton, N.J.: Princeton University Press, 2002.

Taylor, Charles. "What's Wrong with Negative Liberty." In *Philosophy and the Human Sciences*. Vol. 2. Cambridge: Cambridge University Press, 1985.

————. *Sources of the Self: The Making of Modern Identity*. Cambridge, Mass.: Harvard University Press, 1989.

————. "The Importance of Herder." In *Isaiah Berlin: A Celebration*, ed. Edna Margalit and Avishai Margalit. Chicago: University of Chicago Press, 1991.

Tribe, Laurence H. *American Constitutional Law*. Mineola, N.Y.: Foundation Press, 1978.

Tussman, Joseph. *Government and the Mind*. New York: Oxford University Press, 1977.

United Nations. "Additional Protocol to the Convention on Cybercrime, Concerning the Criminalisation of Acts of a Racist and Xenophobic Nature Committed Through Computer Systems." ETS No. 189. (January 28, 2003) http://conventions.coe.int/treaty/EN/WhatYouWant.asp?NT=189&CM=1 (May 30, 2003).

Vaidhyanathan, Siva. *The Anarchist in the Library: How the Clash between Freedom and Control Is Hacking the Real World and Crashing the System*. New York: Basic Books, 2004.

Waldron, Jeremy. *Law and Disagreement*. New York: Oxford University Press, 1999.

Walker, Samuel. *Hate Speech: The History of an American Controversy*. Lincoln: University of Nebraska Press, 1994.

Wallace, Jonathan, and Mark Mangan. *Sex, Laws and Cyberspace*. New York: Henry Holt, 1996.

Waluchow, W. J., ed. *Free Expression: Essays in Law and Philosophy*. Oxford: Clarendon Press, 1994.

Walwyn, William. "The Compassionate Samaritane." In *Tracts on Liberty in the Puritan Revolution, 1638–47*. Vol. 3. Ed. William Haller. New York: Octagon Books, 1965.

Wellek, René. *Concepts of Criticism*. New Haven, Conn.: Yale University Press, 1963.

Williams, Bernard. "Conflicts of Values." In *The Idea of Freedom: Essays in Honour of Isaiah Berlin*, ed. Alan Ryan. Oxford: Oxford University Press, 1979.

Wolff, Robert Paul. *The Poverty of Liberalism*. Boston: Beacon Press, 1968.

Wootton, David, ed. *Divine Right and Democracy: An Anthology of Political Writing in Stuart England*. New York: Penguin, 1986.

Yack, Bernard. *The Longing for Total Revolution: Philosophic Sources of Social Discontent from Rousseau to Marx and Nietzsche*. Princeton, N.J.: Princeton University Press, 1986.

Yarbrough, Tinsley E. *Mr. Justice Black and His Critics*. Durham, N.C.: Duke University Press, 1988.

Young, Iris Marion. *Inclusion and Democracy*. Oxford: Oxford University Press, 2000.

Zittrain, Jonathan, and Benjamin Edelman. "Documentation of Internet Filtering in Saudi Arabia." http://cyber.law.harvard.edu/filtering/saudiarabia/ (May 30, 2003).

————. "Localized Google Search Result Exclusions." http://cyber.law.harvard.edu/filtering/google/ (February 10, 2004).

Index

AARP, 59
Abel, Richard, 186n25
abortion, discussion ban on, 120
absolutism: free speech, 3, 6, 31–33,
    207n28; rights claims, 177, 180; speech
    definition, 123–24
accommodation of employee religious
    expression, 175–78
ACLU, 32
adversarial process, 35–36
advocacy of violence, 158
age restrictions, 171
Allen, David S., 183n2
Altman, Andrew, 185n15
*American Booksellers Association, Inc. v. Hud-
    nut*, 184n14, 190n97
Another Liberalism (Rosenblum), 76
anti-Semitism, 100–102, 162–63
Areopagitica (Milton), 34–35
art: as political speech, 83; censorship, 82;
    contribution to public debate, 55
artistic speech, 7, 55–58, 83
ascriptive approach to speech, 125
audiences: consumers, 199n20; denial of in-
    formation, 165; incidental, 169, 171; in-
    ternational, 161; libertarian focus on, 63;
    members, 117; political speeches, 130–31;
    presumed, 129; relation to speakers,
    109–10, 131, 147, 168; terminology,
    198n8; veto, 171
Auerbach, Carl, 47–48
Austin, J. L., 127–28, 132, 184n1, 202n26,
    204nn20&21
Australia, libel law in, 14, 160–64, 168–72
autonomy: expressivism and, 65–66, 69,
    194n56; individual, 43; romanticism and,
    78

Baker, C. Edwin: on coercive speech, 85–86,
    197n51; liberty theory, 65–66; on self-
    government, 42; and self-realization, 69
balance of interests, 40–41, 101–2, 116
Barrie, Dennis, 58
Barron's, 160, 163, 167–69, 206n12
Beauharnais v. Illinois, 185n11
Berlin, Isaiah, 141–42, 192n11
Beschle, Donald L., 197nn54–55
bildung, 78, 194n59. *See also* development
Bill of Rights, 22
Black, Hugo, 32–33, 207n28
blacklist, 4
Blum, Edward J., 27, 189n72
Bollinger, Lee, 188n38
Bork, Robert, 6, 56–57, 107, 120, 190n100
Brandeis, Louis, 37, 42–43, 63
Brandenburg v. Ohio, 205n31

campaigns: finance, 95, 150; speech,
    130–31
categorical approach, 125–26, 134–35
censorship: arts, 82; prior restraint, 44;
    state interest in, 109–11; and subordinate
    groups, 152
Chafee, Zechariah, 187n30, 188n44
Chalmers, Charita, 174–81
Chaplinsky v. New Hampshire, 7, 125, 134
Charter of Rights and Freedoms (Canada),
    100–102
chilling effect, 14, 160, 163–64, 167–72,
    175, 206n11
Cincinnati Arts Center, 58, 82
citizens: relations between, 112; rights
    claims by, 167
citizenship: equal, 92–93; participation, 12;
    stigmatization and, 90

civil liberties, 4
civil rights, 93
Civil Rights Act, Title VII, 176
clear and present danger, 39, 188n39
cognition, 54–55, 101, 107
Cohen v. California, 148–49
Cohen, Joshua, 21, 64, 188nn36&52
Collegiate Speech Protection Act (1991), 26
commercial service or offering, 167, 169
commercial speech, 44, 80, 83–84, 135
communication: art as, 56; cognitive aspects, 54–55, 97, 101; intention, 167; speech acts and, 127–29; utterances, 127
Communist Control Act (1954), 47, 50
communitarianism, romantic, 78
community, political, 90, 102
comprehensive justifications: art and, 55; defined, 6–7; egalitarianism, 91, 104; excluded speech, 103; failure, 122, 139; value monism and, 2–3
concentration of ownership, 183n5
conduct. *See* speech/conduct distinction
Congress (U.S.), 28
Conover, Pamela Johnston, 197n37
consent to national law, 162
consequentialism: egalitarianism, 99; libertarianism, 32, 37–39, 41; public debate and, 47–50
conservatives, political, 119
Constitution (U.S.), 28, 33, 89
consumers, 199n20
contest of ideas, 4, 35–36
context: speech acts, 124, 128, 134–35; values, 150–51; variables, 154
conventional act, speech, 128
conventions: for political speech, 130–31; social, 128–133; speech acts, 148; use in categorization, 137
copyright law, 164, 170. *See also* DMCA
Corporation for Public Broadcasting, 52
corporations: hate speech rules, 26; expressive interests, 83–84; organization, 180; speech restrictions, 174–75
Covenant on Civil and Political Rights (UN), 206n12

creation science framework, 17
creativity: experience, 113; imagination, 75; individual, 77
critical race theory, 25, 89, 95–99, 152
cross-border speech conflicts, 160–72
culture, 81, 113
customs controls, 172
cyberspace, 1, 162, 166

definitional approach to speech, 125
Delgado, Richard, 96
democracy: procedural, 43; speech restrictions, 110; truth, 198n3; value of, 39
democratic deliberation, interference in internal, 170–71
democratic system, 3
Dennis v. United States, 47
development: cultural, 113; self, 77–79
Digital Millennium Copyright Act (DMCA, 1998), 160, 164–66, 170, 206n16
dignity, human right to, 99. *See also under* equality
dissent as metaphor, 67, 70–71
DMCA, 160, 164–66, 170, 206n16
Douglas, Lawrence, 195n1
Dow Jones, 14, 160, 163–64, 166–71
Downs, Donald A., 197n46
due process, 1, 119
Dworkin, Ronald: comprehensiveness and, 104; egalitarian justification, 103–5; importance of state neutrality, 7, 94–95, 104; on individualism, 117–18; on status equality, 87–92, 102

economic inequality, 52
Edelman, Benjamin, 206nn4&14
egalitarianism: American culture, 91; individualism, 117; objectives, 121; social mutability, 111; social relations, 113–14, 149; threats, 151–52
Eldridge, Larry D, 183n8
elitism, expressivist, 113
Emerson, Ralph Waldo, 67
Emerson, Thomas: and categorization of values, 64, 200n26; on public debate 48, 189n65

employees, 173–81
environment, relational, 110
equality: dignity, 99–103; gender and race, 11, 119; outcomes, 90; political, 13; respect, 89, 95–99; status, 88–95; status and respect, 24, 99; substantive, 93, 119; treatment of employees, 176
equal protection clause, 11, 21, 89, 119
establishment clause, 173
evaluative criteria, 140, 156–58
expression: activity, 75, 79, 81; creative, 69; cultural context, 80–81, 192n11; exclusion, 95; infinite striving, 113; liberating, 93
expressivism: audiences, 111; balancing values, 86; benefits, 62–63, 86; common features, 63; individualism, 118; threats, 152–53; two strands, 64, 80–81
expressivist justification, appropriateness of, 83
expressivists: commitments, 62–63; individualism, 113; speech definition, 123

fear, social relations affected by, 112
Federal Communications Commission (FCC), 68, 183n5
federal funding, 120
fighting words: category, 25; racist, 92
filtering mechanisms, Internet, 162, 172
First Amendment: applied to French court orders, 163; claims, 21, 116, 153; constitutional analysis, 22, 107; criticism, 16; doctrine, 109, 177; exceptions, 125; ideology, 20; institutional relevance, 23, 31–32, 140; narrow interpretation, 135; practice, 49; precedent, 160; rhetoric, 114
First Amendment framework: agenda setting, 23; ambiguous solutions to problems, 144; American legal debates, 20; categorization of speech, 134–35; civil rights law, 174; compared with pluralist framework, 153–54, 159; context, 151; cross-border claims, 161; dimensions, 16–17; flag-burning, 155; individualism, 114; institutional factors, 21; and monism, 147; philosophical debates, 21;

religion, 173–74; social relations, 108; speech definition, 125
Fishkin, James, 59, 191n105
Fish, Stanley, 2, 183n3, 200n7
Fiss, Owen, 32, 51–53, 185n8, 188n46
flag-burning, 18, 33, 131, 137–38, 153–56
Fourteenth Amendment, 89–90, 101
frameworks: alternative, 8–9, 23, 139; change, 20; for debate, 17, 140; weak, 19
France: ban on Nazi artifacts, 160–64, 167–72; criminal code, 162
freedom: individual, 114; moral, 113
free exercise clause, 173
free speech: absolutism, 3, 6, 30; barriers, 111, 160; confusion over, 5; efficiency, 50; exceptions, 88, 103, 126, fundamental liberty, 63; independence, 62; intrinsic good, 63; instrumental good, 48–49; objectives, 140; orthodoxy, 5, 50; overextension, 157; politics, 3, 140–41, 144; practice, 22, 109, 124, prerequisites, 125; principle, 30–31, 72; progressive, 118; social practice, 13; subordinate good, 115
free speech claims: benefits, 150; competing, 143; context, 151, criteria, 16, 20; emerging, 159–61; location, 165; parameters for, 139; pluralist framework, 154–56; recognition of, 14, 23, 140, 159; speech act condition for, 156
free speech justification: common elements, 121–22; speech definitions, 124
free speech libertarian justification: comprehensiveness, 32; definition of political speech, 83; egalitarianism and, 94, 98; First Amendment and, 40; Internet speech, 169; non-interference, 152; privileged by First Amendment, 145; social relations, 109, 111, 115, 149; threats, 152
free speech libertarians: conservative, 35–37; contrast with political libertarians, 31, 186n4; debate, 113; instrumental reason, 116; objectives, 151; self-realization, 120; speakers, 111
free will, 78

gag rule, 52
Galston, William, 141, 203n3, 204n13
Gates, Henry Louis, Jr., 25–26, 184n3
Godfather, The (film), 203n41
Goldstein, Robert Justin, 205n26
good life, 143
Google, 160, 162, 164–68, 170
Graber, Mark: on Brandeis, 188n54; on
    Chafee, 189n61; on conservative libertar-
    ians, 35–37; on speech for profit, 84;
    value of public debate, 48, 190n92,
    191n104, 199n19
Gray, John, 204n8, 204n15
Grice, Paul, 201n22
Grossman, Lawrence K., 183n6
group libel, 25, 185n11
Gutnick, Joseph, 160, 163–64, 169

Haiman, Franklyn S., 187n10
harassment, racial and sexual, 23, 131, 174,
    179–80
hate propaganda, 100
hate sites (Web), 166
hate speech: benefits, 69; in Canada,
    100–102; claims, 23; codes, 23; as criminal
    assault, 96–97; exception for, 98; flag-
    burning as, 154–56; opponents of regula-
    tion, 23–24, 114; physical consequences,
    24–25; private regulation, 26; psychologi-
    cal consequences, 25–26; social relations,
    117; state regulation, 24, 88
heckler's veto, 22, 185n10, 206n15
Herder, J. G., 192n11, 193n51, 194n59,
    195n70
Herzog, Don, 200n1
heuristics, frameworks as, 17
Hewlett-Packard, 174–81
hierarchy: employment and speech acts,
    131, 149, 173; social, 3, 117; within audi-
    ences, 110
Holmes, Oliver Wendell, 36, 187n25
Holmes, Stephen, 183n10
Holocaust revisionism Web sites, 163
How to Do Things with Words (Austin),
    127–28
human rights, 9, 167

Human Rights Act (Canada), 101–2
Humboldt, Wilhelm von, 77–78, 82,
    194nn57–58
Hyde, Henry, 26

ideas: communication, 97; content, 125;
    rational dialogue, 111
identity: expressivism, 68; group, 98
incitement, 24, 158
inclusiveness, 7, 9–10
incommensurability: frameworks, 19; goods,
    141; religious claims, 179; values, 121–22,
    142–44, 170, 179–80
incompatibility, 142
independence of speech definitions, 124
Indianapolis, 13
individualism: component of justification,
    114–18; development, 113;
infinite striving, 78, 80, 113, 120
information, access to, 2
informational interest, 64–65, 165
intellectual property, 4
intention, speech act theory and, 127–29,
    148
international agreements on speech, 160,
    164
international law, 14
Internet: medium, 1, 14, 129, 149; physical
    boundaries, 161–62; publishing, 166;
    speech claims, 160–72
interpersonal relations, effects of state
    power on, 22. *See also* social relations

Jensen, Robert, 183n2
Johnson, David R., 161–62, 207n17
journalists, 168
judgment: in frameworks, 19; of speech
    claims, 140, 143, 159; value, 107
judicial review, 22
jurisdiction, legal, 162–69
justification. *See* free speech justification

Kaczynski, Theodore, 24, 112
Kant, Immanuel, 193n54, 194n55
Karst, Kenneth, 90–93, 103–4, 202n31,
    204n18

Keegstra, Regina v. (Canada), 100–102
Kekes, John, 141, 198n2, 203nn5&6, 204nn9&11
King, Martin Luther Jr., 202n25
knowledge, shared, 133–34

Langton, Rae, 200n6, 203n35
language: philosophy of, 125, 127; shared, 133; speech acts and social construction, 128–29
Larmore, Charles, 141, 144, 195n70, 198n1, 203n4, 204n12
law: anti-discrimination, 175; as a discipline, 5; labor, 174; national systems of, 162
law space, 162
Lawrence, Charles, 96, 185n18, 200n5
lawyers, 21, 160
legal claims, 21–22
legal language, 9
legal practice: of First Amendment claims, 115–16; outcomes, 126; speech/conduct distinction, 126
legal procedure, 141
legal scholars, 5, 9, 11, 22
legislators, 12
Lessig, Lawrence, 183n7
Levy, Leonard, 184n4, 198n5
libel: analogy to workplace speech, 177; in Australia, 160–64, 168–72; First Amendment doctrine, 166; international agreement on, 164; law, 94, 206n12; seditious, 4
liberalism (theory), 14, 119–20, 141, 143
libertarianism, contrast with free speech libertarianism, 186n4
libertarians. *See* free speech libertarians
listeners: Internet, 166; potential, 148. *See also* audience

MacKinnon, Catharine: anti-pornography ordinance, 13; and cognition, 190n95; and Dworkin, 89; speech and conduct, 200n9; on subordination, 91, 95, 97–98
Mapplethorpe, Robert, 58, 82
marketplace of ideas: benefits, 150; competition, 34–36; efficiency, 121; metaphor,

62, 183n4; process, 4, 114; public discourse, 111
markets: correction, 53; failure, 51–53
mass media, 3–4
Matsuda, Mari J.: definition of racist speech, 8, 24–26, 200n5; on equality of respect, 95–99; and substantive equality, 93
McChesney, Robert W., 183n6
McConnell, Michael, 207n21
meaning: importance of convention to, 128–29; reception, 175; transmission of, 127
Meiklejohn, Alexander: on commercial speech, 84; limits on free speech, 6, 184n11; on priority of political speech, 58–59, 107–8, 135–36
methodological individualism, 116–18
Michelman, Frank, 185n12
Miller v. California, 55
Mill, John Stuart, 35–36, 183n4, 200n22
Milton, John, 34–35
modern science framework, 17
modus vivendi liberalism, 144
monism: theory, 141–43; value, 2–3, 106–8
Moon, Richard, 197n54
moral responsibility, 92
more speech response, 27

national boundaries, 161–62,
National Endowment for the Arts (NEA), 4, 28, 52–53
National Endowment for the Humanities (NEH), 4
National Science Foundation (NSF), 4
nazism and Nazi artifacts, 160–64, 167–72
negative liberty: free speech as, 21; role in pluralism, 143; social relations, 82, 108, 112
Netherlands, 160, 164–66
New York Times v. Sullivan, 31, 206n11
nondisclosure agreements, 174

obscenity, 201n21
offensive speech, 148–49, 174
Okoniewski, Elissa A., 172, 206n8, 207n19
On Liberty (Mill), 35–36

Operation Clambake (Web site), 164–65
opportunity: equal, 104; lack of, 3; to speak,
    88, 104
original intent, 21
orthodoxy, political, 47
overlapping justifications, 157

Paine Webber, 27
participation: equal, 113, 121; political,
    90–92; speech, 82–83
Patriot Act (2001), 1
Peterson, Richard, 174–81
physical barriers, authority of law and,
    161–62
pluralism: free speech, 124; interest group,
    141; liberal theory of, 141–47
pluralist framework: compared with First
    Amendment framework, 140–41, 145,
    153–55, 159; cross-border speech claims,
    160–72; excluded issues, 156–57; founda-
    tion, 127; Internet speech, 166; making
    claims, 153–55; and pluralism, 143–46;
    religious expression, 179; speech act
    theory, 125
political correctness, 23
political debate: democracy, 3; employee
    speech, 177–78; frameworks and, 18;
    over speech, 125, 159; social mutability,
    112
Political Liberalism (Rawls), 21
political movements, 141, 179
political speech, 41, 56–59, 117, 135–38
political theorists, 21
political theory, 2, 5–6, 9, 11
politics: candidates' speech, 130–31; civil
    society, 10; consequences, 19; expressive
    activity, 85; role in pluralist framework,
    140, 142–43, 146; speech definitions and,
    125
popular sovereignty, 135
pornography: as act, 125; child, 172; cogni-
    tion, 55; equality, 91; as hate speech, 88,
    97; regulation, 5, 13, 20
Posner, Richard, 190n93
Post, David G., 161–62, 207n17
Post, Robert C., 195n1

Pound, Roscoe, 40
power: political, 125; relation to speech acts,
    129; relations between states, 170–71
privacy: detachment, 76; personal, 77
private power: conflicts, 45; effects on op-
    portunity, 54, 104; institutions, 152; role
    in subordination, 95–98
progressivism, 118–21
projects, goals or objectives and, 6–10
proselytizing, 177, 179, 181
protest speech: conventions, 137; move-
    ments, 140; social relations and, 131
publication, site of, 161–62
public debate: contributions to, 148; diver-
    sity, 4; hate speech and, 26; libertarianism
    and, 38, 40; procedural criticism, 51; un-
    dermined by speech, 46–51; value, 7, 11,
    170
public figure, 163–64
public space, 179–80
public sphere, 10

R.A.V. v. St. Paul, 91–92, 101
racism and sexism, 152
racist insults, 26, 95–97
racist speakers, 92, 169
racist speech, 8, 24, 96, 151–52, 169
ranking: kinds of speech, 146–47; values,
    142–43, 181
rationality, 145–46
Rauch, Jonathan, 188n37, 190n85, 191n6
Rawls, John, 21, 89, 183n10
Raz, Joseph, 189n62
Redish, Martin, 66–70, 73, 143
Rehnquist, William, 54
relativism, 19, 124, 140–43
rights claims, 166–67, 179
Robinson, Henry, 34
romanticism: German, 77–79, 81, 118;
    literary, 67, 76; shared belief, 120
Rosen, Jeffrey, 186n24
Rosenblum, Nancy, 76
Rust v. Sullivan, 52

safe harbor in copyright law, 164
Scalia, Antonin, 92

Scanlon, Thomas, 43, 191n4, 194n56
Schauer, Frederick: on communication, 190n98; First Amendment rhetoric, 205n30; free speech principle, 30–31; ideology, 183n9; and private power, 44–45; on public debate, 49; on self-expression, 37–38, 71–72, 187n29; on speech/conduct distinction, 126, 201n10
Schlegel, Friedrich von, 77–79, 82
schools of justification, common characteristics of, 107
Scientology, Church of, 160, 164–65, 167–68, 170
search engine. *See* Google; Yahoo! Inc.
Searle, John, 127–28, 134, 184n1
Second Amendment, 80
self: conception of, 74, 193n40; as source of truth, 75
self-expression: self-realization, 67; valued highly, 56
self-fulfillment, 64
self-government, 42, 135
self-realization: as active process, 79–80; balancing, 73–74; democracy and, 66–67, 70; flag-burning, 155; infinite striving, 113; obstacles, 82; primary value, 7; rhetoric, 120; secondary value, 143–44; weakness, 74
separation of church and state, 173
sexual harassment, 27, 117. *See also* harassment, racial and sexual
Shiffrin, Steven, 67, 70
shunning, 27
silencing effect, 103
Sirluck, Ernest, 187n14
skepticism, element in free speech, 119
Skinner, Quentin, 201n20
Smolla, Rodney, 68
social construction: language, 128; personality, 111
social development, 118–19
social groups excluded from free speech, 145–46
social movements: free speech, 3, 15; response to hate speech, 27–28
social mutability, 111–12

social relations: authority in, 131–32; between groups, 90, 98; component of justification, 108–15; contracts, 129; hierarchical, 23, 117; listening, 109; speech acts, 9–10, 128–33, 149
Sources of the Self (Taylor), 75
speakers: claiming protection, 154, 159; diversity, 145; domestic conflict with foreign state, 160, 164–68; Dworkin's focus on, 104; employee, 173–81; individual, 63–64; intent, 169, 175; privileged, 82; relation to audiences, 109–10, 147, 168; relation to hearers, 128–33; relation to state, 166; state action and, 110–11
speech: artistic, 7, 55–56, 58, 83; balancing, 85; categories, 7, 57, 94, 126, 134–38; coercive, 66, 69, 197n51; costs, 38; definition, 9, 33, 123–26; environment, 64–65; exclusion of, 54–59; harms, 24, 74, 103; independence, 123; international restrictions, 161; lacking value, 41; practice, 12, 109, 124, private, 90, 95; religious, 173–81; scientific, 137; self-regarding, 109; situations, 140; social benefits, 31, 47; social consequences, 68; state funding, 52; values, 12; workplace, 28, 174–81. *See also specific speech categories*
speech acts: advertising, 169; computer information as, 162; context, 145–49, 169; external standards, 133; group, 117; illegitimate, 155, 167; intention, 127–29, 132, 169; international, 14; intrinsic value, 64, 68; linguistic conventions, 110; location, 168; misunderstood, 169; pluralist framework, 9, 125; political, 148; problem of dominance, 132–33; religious, 175; rule-governed, 128; social relations, 128–33, 149
speech act theory: framework, 18–19; independence, 124, 127; role in pluralist framework, 140, 147–48
speech codes, university, 23, 26, 186n22, 199n17
speech/conduct distinction: *Cohen v. California*, 148–49; complicated, 147; flag-burning, 33; hate speech, 24, 96; not

speech/conduct distinction (*continued*)
  recognized by speech act theory, 134;
  unworkable, 123, 126
state action: effects on public debate, 51;
  omission and, 22; opportunity to speak,
  110–11; speech claims, 140; threat, 5, 31,
  43–45
state interference: First Amendment framework, 40, 108, 125; in political speech,
  151; right against, 21; social relations,
  110, 116; threat, 5
state neutrality, 94, 104–5
state power, restrictions on, 91
state restriction: of Internet, 166; of religious expression, 177
stigmatization, 90, 93, 96
subordination: and censorship, 152; and
  hate speech, 24, 26; race and gender,
  95–98
subsidies, speech, 52–54
Sunstein, Cass: on conditions for reception
  and uptake, 136; on economic markets,
  199n20; exclusions from First Amendment, 188n50; and public debate, 143,
  207n18; role of political speech, 56–58,
  135–36; on self-fulfillment, 72, 192n22;
  understanding of state action 44, 52,
  185n7, 198n11
Supreme Court (U.S.): constitutional liberties and, 2, 51; precedent, 16, 163
surveillance, 172

Taking Rights Seriously (Dworkin), 89
Taylor, Charles, 75–77, 81, 194n60
telecommunications, 1, 4
terrorism, war on, 1, 4
Texas v. Johnson, 126
Thoreau, Henry David, 75, 77
threats: to Internet, 160; to speech, 3, 10,
  145, 151; state, 5, 22, 112
tolerance, 92
tragic choices, 141
truth: democracy as, 198n3; good policy as,
  41, 188n51; inner source for, 75–76, 81,
  85; interest or value, 34, 38–39, 111, 169;
  objective, 42; process, 119
two-tier theory, 107–8, 135

unitary justifications: defined, 6–7; privilege
  some speech, 145; and speech definitions,
  123; structure, 10–11; value monism and,
  3, 107
United States v. O'Brien, 126
Universal Declaration of Human Rights
  (UN), 6, 99
universalism, value, 107, 145
uptake, speech acts and, 128
utilitarianism, 107, 141
utterance, 18, 127, 147

Vaidhyanathan, Siva, 183n7
value pluralism, 3, 9, 144
values: comparing, 107, 115, 179–81; conflicts, 142, 175–76; evaluation, 157–58;
  incommensurable, 121–22, 170, 179–80;
  liberal, 2, 5, 21; misidentification, 143;
  of non-interference, 171; privileged,
  123; religious, 178; speech, 140, 159;
  unacceptable, 144; unitary, 106–7,
  123
veterans as speakers, 155–56
vocabulary: frameworks, 17–18, 20; legal,
  22, 159; speech acts, 110, 127

Walker, Samuel, 185n12
Walwyn, William, 34
Web index, 167. *See also* Google
Whitney v. California, 42–43, 63
Williams, Bernard, 204nn7&10
Wilson, Christine, 174–81
Workplace Religious Freedom Act
  (WFRA), 176–79
workplace, private, 173–81
World Wide Web, 1

Yack, Bernard, 193n54
Yahoo! France, 163
Yahoo!, Inc., 14, 160–64, 167–72
Yarbrough, Tinsley E., 186n8

Zittrain, Jonathan, 206nn4&14